Transatlantic Fictions of 9/11 and the War on Terror

New Horizons in Contemporary Writing

In the wake of unprecedented technological and social change, contemporary literature has evolved a dazzling array of new forms that traditional modes and terms of literary criticism have struggled to keep up with. *New Horizons in Contemporary Writing* presents cutting-edge scholarship that provides new insights into this unique period of creative and critical transformation.

Series Editors:
Peter Boxall and Bryan Cheyette

Volumes in the series:
Wanderwords: Language Migration in American Literature
by Maria Lauret

Transatlantic Fictions of 9/11 and the War on Terror
by Susana Araújo

Life Lines: Writing Transcultural Adoption
by John McLeod

South African Literature's Russian Soul: Narrative Forms of Global Isolation
by Jeanne-Marie Jackson

Transatlantic Fictions of 9/11 and the War on Terror

Images of Insecurity, Narratives of Captivity

Susana Araújo

Bloomsbury Academic
An imprint of Bloomsbury Publishing Plc

B L O O M S B U R Y
LONDON · OXFORD · NEW YORK · NEW DELHI · SYDNEY

Bloomsbury Academic

An imprint of Bloomsbury Publishing Plc

50 Bedford Square
London
WC1B 3DP
UK

1385 Broadway
New York
NY 10018
USA

www.bloomsbury.com

BLOOMSBURY and the Diana logo are trademarks of Bloomsbury Publishing Plc

First published 2015

British Library Cataloguing-in-Publication Data
A catalogue record for this book is available from the British Library.

ISBN: HB: 978-1-4725-0876-8
ePDF: 978-1-4725-0755-6
ePub: 978-1-4725-0604-7

Library of Congress Cataloging-in-Publication Data
A catalog record for this book is available from the Library of Congress.

Series: New Horizons in Contemporary Writing

Typeset by Integra Software Services Pvt. Ltd.

For Robert and Rafael Clowes
And in memory of Luísa Costa Araújo

Contents

Acknowledgments

This book owes much to colleagues on both sides of the Atlantic. I am most grateful to Amy Kaplan, who read sections of this work at an early stage and encouraged this project; her work has been a major reference to me. Maria Lauret, Pete Nichols, Sue Currell, and Laura Marcus read early versions of Chapter 3 while I was still at Sussex—they provided mentorship when I needed it the most. Sarah Florence Wood introduced me to narratives of captivity. Jacqueline Rose's approach to fantasy and Frank Furedi's work on fear provided two very different influences which greatly shaped my arguments. Christopher Bollas came to Portugal and elucidated difficult questions about trauma—I thank him for his openness and generosity. I met Donald Pease when I was writing the conclusion to this book; his work and our conversations added depth to my final thoughts.

The Centre for Comparative Studies (CEC) welcomed me back to Lisbon. The list of colleagues who have supported me at CEC is too long to include here—to them all I owe large debt. Manuela Ribeiro Sanches and Manuela Carvalho showed me that institutional management can emerge from collective (and yet not always nonconsensual) visions; they have been the best of colleagues and friends. Helena Buescu, Director of CEC during my first years at the University of Lisbon, and João Ferreira Duarte, Vice-Director, supported my work in this research center. Marta Pinto and Cate Miller proofread sections of this book and encouraged me at all times. Fundação José Saramago and Rita Paes promptly replied to my queries regarding an unidentified intertext in Saramago's *Seeing*, which was crucial to my reading of that novel. Cristina Ribeiro gave me precious advice on Mário Dionísio's work—I thank her for her rigor and generosity. The encouragement of Djelal Kadir, Paul Giles, Michael Boyden, and Pawel Jarzenko shattered my skepticism toward "international associations."

I am grateful to my colleagues at Project CILM (*City and (In)security in Literature and the Media*): Daniel Lourenço and Pedro Ferreira were there before the project was funded; Sandra Bettencourt and Ana Raquel Fernandes were fabulous teammates from the start; Marana Borges and Nuno Marques provided invaluable support. Fernanda Mota Alves, Isabel Fernandes, Catatina Frois, Igor Furão, Ana Romão, Susana Martins, Jacinta Matos, Francisco Serra-Lopes, Aliki Varvogli, and our advisers, Liam Kennedy, David Murakami Wood, Krisitaan Versluys, and Boaventura Sousa Santos, were also crucial to CILM's outputs. With them, I could, among other things, develop ideas contained in this book. I also owe a debt to my students for allowing me to test some of my arguments with them and providing me with significant insights of their own. My sincere thanks also go to my editors at Bloomsbury, David Avital and Mark Richardson, as well as project manager Rajakumari Ganessin for their patience.

By funding Project CILM (Ref. PTDC/CLE-LLI/110694/2009), *Fundação para a Ciência e Tecnologia* offered me the necessary tools to complete this book and pursue further research. In this book, I have drawn on essays I wrote previously and published in *Babilónia* 10/11. 2012; *Symbiosis* 11.2. 2007; *Postnationalism and the New Europe*, ed. by César Domínguez and Theodoor L. D'haen; *Trans/Oceanic, Trans-American, Trans/Lation*, ed. by Susana Araújo and Marta Pacheco Pinto e João Ferreira Duarte; *Filologia, Memória e Esquecimento*, ed. by Ricardo Soeiro and Daniela Di Pasquale e Sofia Tavares; and *Público/Privado: O Deslizar de uma Fronteira*, ed. by Francesca Negro. These represent earlier versions of what is argued here, but acknowledgments are due to these publications.

My last words of thanks go to my family. Without Luísa Nunes's constant support, this project would not have been possible. João Telmo Araújo has been an example of courage to me, and Maria da Graça Cabeçadas proved that one can be both a pragmatic grandmother and a defiant woman.

I owe my deepest debt to Rob. He has helped me to think and to live. Without him and Rafa, this would have been a very different book.

Introduction: Images of Terror, Narratives of (In)security

This book departs from three premises. First, that the outpouring of "9/11" novels can be understood beyond the expressions of trauma, mourning, or outrage generated by this event. Second, that 9/11 literature should not be read exclusively in relation to US literature but from international and transnational perspectives, and that its analysis should take into consideration geopolitical issues associated with the "War on Terror." Third, that since 9/11 and the War on Terror have been constructed as highly visual mass-media narratives, the study of their literary impact should be attentive to the relations between fictionality, visuality, and politicization. As the persistence of the label "9/11 literature" shows, the terrorist attacks on New York and Washington on September 11, 2001, have become recurrent motifs in literary works produced in the last decade. Discerning what to make of this vast corpus of works has not been an easy job for either critics or reviewers. This has partly to do with the heterogeneity of perspectives, themes, styles, and—not least—quality of the narratives produced in response to the attacks.

Most of the works devoted to 9/11 literature have tended to focus on this event through the lenses of trauma theory.[1] *Transatlantic Fictions of 9/11 and the War on Terror* interrogates the focus and supremacy of trauma studies in relation to 9/11 literature. This book will not take the predominant focus of trauma studies for granted. Instead, it will inquire if it is, in fact, accurate to speak about "trauma" when referring to the overall corpus of 9/11 novels. To be sure, the terrorist attacks of 9/11 provided shocking images which the western psyche is still trying to come to terms with. Anger, pain, and grief were justly aroused after 9/11. After all, the attacks resulted in the death of almost 3,000 innocent individuals and have had repercussions which have greatly shaken the sense of security of the United States and the Western world at large. However, one should consider the following questions: Was 9/11 internalized and actually relived as trauma by the majority of the authors who have re-created this episode into fiction? Was "trauma" not a term often simplistically—or automatically—adopted by western media, politicians, and cultural commentators to convey, in larger terms, the shock of an attack whose repercussions were, in fact, quite specific? In Freudian terms, trauma is not a straightforward process: it requires time and is the result of an internal development. It is the inner working of an event, not the immediate, direct, or simple response to a painful event. The painful experience of an event must be interiorized and revivified in order to become traumatic. As the author and psychoanalyst Christopher Bollas perceptively put it, "one (as patient or analyst) cannot go searching for it [trauma]. It shows up and finds the self" (Bollas 2011).[2] According to Bollas, "Many people never experience a trauma following a shock. Hence, the difference in people between those who are traumatized by a shocking event and those who are not" (2011). It can be argued that most people in the West were, naturally, overwhelmed by shock, disbelief, and perhaps, anger. All these feelings are worthy of analysis, but they are not necessarily associated with a traumatic process. As Christopher Bollas explains:

> For a shock to become traumatic requires two stages. First, the shock: a sexual transgression, a violent act against the self, or for that matter, any "intervention" from the Real that bypasses the imaginary and symbolic orders. Second, a seeming insignificant event years later that serves as an evocative object that congregates the shock of the first event. Only then, from Freud's point of view, is it possible to speak of a trauma because the self is overwhelmed with affect and ideation that is from the unconscious, delivered into the present as a type of tsunami. [...] One, as a patient or as an analyst, cannot go searching for it. It shows up and finds the self. Many people never experience a trauma following a shock. (Bollas 2011)

It is therefore debatable if the majority of 9/11 fiction has been, in fact, dominated by trauma, or if discourses about trauma, fueled by the media, have not been too readily applied to literary responses to this event. This tendency has certainly influenced academic circles, where trauma theory has often been straightforwardly applied to the myriad of responses created by 9/11. Even though literary responses to 9/11 range from shock, grief, rage to guilt, disbelief, or déjà-vu (caused by hyper-real configuration of the attacks), trauma remains the predominant *key word* in studies of 9/11 fiction. One of the main concerns of literary studies has, therefore, been the attention to the so-called challenges posed by the representation of the attacks (i.e., the impossibility of their representation). This is symptomatic of dominant trends in literary studies, where trauma studies have gained a prominent place, having been often misplaced and overused. In his book *The Trauma Question*, Roger Luckhurst, one of the major experts in trauma studies, explored the relations between cultural memory and trauma studies, drawing on psychiatric, legal, and cultural-political sources and mapping the routes through which notions of trauma came to dominate western thought. In his recent work, Luckhurst offers critical revisions to this paradigm, highlighting that "as Trauma theory becomes embedded in near conceptual formulations, standard historical moments and canonical literary and visual texts [...] rigidities and problematic occlusions inevitably creep in" (Luckhurst 2010, 11). The Holocaust is undoubtedly the main historical event around which trauma theory has been weaved, assuming a privileged site in memory studies. Experts have shown that trauma studies have seldom been applied to other historical realities or national contexts. Katherine Hodgkin and Susannah Radstone state that "other massacres and genocides, other experiences of violence, loss, suffering, displacement, are either little studied, or studied in other contexts than that of traumatic memory" (Hodgkin and Radstone 2006, 7). They maintain that "despite the association of memory with the capacity of minority or subordinated peoples to generate alternative narratives of their own pasts, academic papers dealing with the experiences of (for example) Rwandans, or Tamils, or East Timorese, or Kurds, or Armenians, or indeed Palestinians, seldom seem to address their sufferings in a framework of either trauma or memory" (7).

One immediate discursive tendency which contributed to the construction of 9/11 as a major "event"[3] has been the insistence on comparing this disaster with the Holocaust felt by the media and several cultural commentators. Even though there are obvious differences in terms of the magnitude and resonances of both tragedies, such comparisons certainly helped to amplify the horror of the terrorist attacks of 2001. This aggrandizement not only served both the practical purposes and ideological disposition of many journalists and writers in the West, but also symptomatized and reinforced the tendency to view the Holocaust as the dominant paradigm of memory studies, a model with patent politics attached. In what cultural and literary studies were concerned, theories of trauma and traumatic memory which had prevailed in the analysis of Holocaust fiction and cultural production were readily applied to the representation of the terrorist attacks on New York and Washington with predictable results in terms of the readings achieved. In Chapter 2, I will examine in more depth the impact of the trauma paradigm in relation to the main debates raised by early 9/11 fiction.

The purpose of this book is, therefore, not to bypass the debates on trauma raised by these events, but to examine the use of the trauma paradigm critically within the specific historical, social, and political contexts in which 9/11 and the War on Terror occurred. I will explore how trauma paradigms continue to play a role in western imagination and how they shape western narratives and to what extent have writers, themselves, effectively absorbed or challenged such tendencies. By interrogating these trends, I hope to suggest new ways to read 9/11 fictions, informed by the specific political contexts from which they emerge.

The very label "9/11 literature" corresponds to the denomination of a corpus that has become naturalized in literary studies. However, the majority of the so-called 9/11 novels were also written during the War on Terror and the military "interventions" in Afghanistan and Iraq. Even though critics have tended to read this corpus of novels mainly as commentaries or reflections on the terrorist attacks of September 2001, the majority of these novels also comment—more or less obliquely—on the events that immediately followed these attacks and the disproportionate amount of destruction, violence, and despair created by the War on Terror. Many of these novels hide images and narratives which are perhaps more uncomfortable and difficult for the western reader to face than the collapse of the Twin Towers. Indeed, if the collapse of the Twin Towers was the most photographed and televised event of all time, soon after the launching of the War on Terror, other images, such as the Abu Ghraib photographs, emerged, revealing the other side of "terror." Many of these "other" images found their way into the novels produced at the time. Yet, the pervasiveness of the label of "9/11 literature" continues to ignore these contents. In the first five years which followed the attacks, shock and pain fueled simplistic readings, blinding many western readers, reviewers, and critics to other sources of violence in these novels. As I will show, many of these novels comment upon the causes and consequences associated with the terrorist attacks of 2001, forcing us to confront violent realities promoted, not only by the US government at the time, but also by its political and military allies, particularly those in Europe. If, in some novels, references to the War on Terror remain implicit and merely suggested upon, in many others, they are quite overt, inviting readers to rethink and revise notions of terror and trauma. The juxtaposition of the notion of terror with the notion of security in the title of this book aims, thus, to emphasize how concepts such as terror and security, usually presented as conflicting, should be, in fact, seen as contiguous. The contiguity should be highlighted not due to the truism that advocates that certain instances of terror require measures of security, but because, paradoxically but significantly, much terror can often be created, generated, and promoted in the name of security practices and theories, themselves. Many of the novels examined in this book are not only aware of that irony but concerned with the paradoxical measures through which the United States and its allies have turned "security" into a source of "captivity."

Let me illustrate the above, by referring to the already canonical work of Don DeLillo. DeLillo has always been concerned with globalization and the junctures where economic power and forces of radical dissent are brought together. It is, therefore, no surprise that Don DeLillo's post-9/11 works should have attracted so much critical attention.[4] I will not go in-depth into Don Lillo's 9/11 fiction here, as there are already important books written on this matter, but I would like to suggest that novels such as *Falling Man* not only explore a number of the contradictions experienced by the western subject in late-capitalism, but also make specific use of the iconoclastic representation of 9/11 to examine an ongoing sense of entrapment, related to the supposed *death of history*, which, although exacerbated by 9/11, is far from new to western subjectivity. One of the main motifs of the novel is the iconic image of a performance artist that appears hanging from different buildings throughout New York. Wearing a business suit, the performing artist suspends himself upside down with rope and a harness—a pose that immediately evoked the famous photograph taken by Richard Drew of a man falling from the north tower of the World Trade Center which became known as the "Falling Man."[5] The body posture of the performance artist also evoked the idea of the Hanged Man in the tarot deck, a figure which conveys the idea of "suspension" and the need "for contemplation in the face of catastrophe" (Conte 2011, 580–581). The game also becomes an important motif in the novel: with his arms at his sides, one leg bent, he is a man set forever in free fall against the looming background of the column panels in the tower. The "falling body" in DeLillo's novel, concerned as it maybe with the role of the writer in an age of terror, is also a comment on a self-promoted fall engendered by the West. Indeed, one of the most striking—though often unnoticed elements in *Falling Man*—is the way DeLillo unashamedly dwells on trauma as a product of virtual reality. Like his previous novels convey (most notably *Mao II* written long before 9/11), terror is the result of a struggle, staged in a global net with highly visual weaponry.[6] Within this relation emerge conflicting self-portrayals of the United States—and West at large—which are alternatively and/or simultaneously depicted through the lenses of heroism and victimhood. Don DeLillo confirms, thus, how western culture paradoxically depends upon the dissemination of powerful narratives of insecurity.

Captivity narratives

Images such as that of the "falling man," like many other motifs present in 9/11 narratives, are linked to verbal and iconographic discourses which have survived in western culture throughout centuries. American Indian captivity narratives were stories of men and women of European descent who had been captured by Native Americans in the early days of the Atlantic coast. The famous memoir *A Narrative of the Captivity and Restoration of Mrs. Mary Rowlandson*, published in 1682, is a classic early example of the genre.[7] Captivity narratives have come to be mainly associated with settlers held captive by Native Americans and play a critical role in the foundation of US history and identity, justifying the spirit of the frontier. This has had a profound effect on US culture and survived in popular forms such as the western genre (in film, television, radio, literature, painting, and other media) and other popular genres such as science fiction and war films and novels which retained and transformed captivity motifs. However, captivity narratives were not an exclusively North American product. They were a founding motif for European identity as well: the name of the European continent comes, after all, from Greek mythology, where Europa (in Greek Εὐρώπη) was a Phoenician woman of high lineage abducted by Zeus, in the form of a white bull, and she, through this divine association (and the awkward suggestion of seduction, rape, and sex, typical of captivity narratives), later became queen. This myth gained several meanings and overtones throughout the centuries. It was, however, with the maritime exploration initiated by a number of European countries in the fifteenth century onward that captivity narratives flourished, forging ideological configurations that have been sustained on both sides of the Atlantic until today. Barbary Coast narratives, stories of Englishmen captured by pirates, popular in England since the sixteenth century, are the most well-known predecessors of the genre in the Anglo-Saxon world.[8] However, narratives of and by Europeans describing their imprisonment abroad were far from limited to English writings. As an international phenomenon, they became widespread with European exploration and the colonization of Africa and the Middle and Far East. Leading the maritime expansion, Portugal and Spain amplified the geographical range in which captivity narratives could be set. As Lisa Voigt notes, "accounts of captivity in a variety of official, learned, and popular genres both reflected and contributed to widespread anxiety in the Iberian peninsula about the possibility of capture and enslavement by Moors and Turks" (Voigt 2009, 8). From the Iberian Peninsula, the genre traveled— via Africa and Asia—toward the rest of Europe. This brief outline shows how captivity narratives have always been associated with territorial expansion and linked to either land-based or maritime frontiers. The links with territorial expansion also make clear why the genre tends to be associated with wartime narratives such as Cold War and Vietnam War fiction. Given that the post-9/11 period was also shaped by wars in Afghanistan and in Iraq, it is not surprising to see that new fictions of captivity proliferated in the past decade.

This book aims to show how captivity motifs are at work in these recent novels, sometimes in conflicting ways: the relation between captivity and insecurity can be used to justify military interventions such as the war in Iraq in some of these works (see, for example, the narrator's wavering feelings toward the war in McEwan's *Saturday*), while it is often used to undermine imperial enterprises in many other novels. National and international projections of fears and anxieties intersect, creating neo-captivity fictions which are in fact transnational, if not global. The links between rhetorical allusions to 9/11 and captivity narratives have been noticed, for instance, by Susan Faludi. Faludi addresses the idea of captivity in her book *The Terror Dream: Fear and Fantasy in Post-9/11 America* (2007), highlighting how political discourse has made use of the captivity motif. Although her emphasis is particularly focused on gender configurations—namely the "invention of a female rape and rescue drama" (216), which justifies old-style masculine narratives of necessary rescue and revenge—the author rightly shows how the captivity motif played an important role in US fantasies about its own vulnerability. According to Faludi, the terrorist instilled a sense of shame, reproducing a chiefly male burden about national vulnerability, which narratives of captivity attempted to resolve:

> American culture spent three hundred years rewriting such accounts. Faced with bloody attacks from a hostile antagonist, attacks in which women were not saved or refused to be saved or saved themselves, white America restored its sense of national security through the creation of a compensatory gender narrative. In the service of establishing a national story that would supplant intense humiliation with invincible invulnerability, the early captivity story would evolve through successive permutations, even into the twentieth century, where it would find expression in such iconic films as *The Searchers*. (214)

Related to the dynamics of gender and power mentioned above are a number of other motifs of early captivity narratives that had endured in twenty-first-century fiction worth referring to here. In her work *Hollywood's Frontier Captives*, Barbara Mortimer thoroughly conveyed how early captivity narratives continued to shape American popular culture of the twentieth century through Hollywood filming. Drawing on work of June Namias and Gary Ebersole, Mortimer highlights a number of anxieties that have continued to characterize later captivity narratives. Her list is worth mentioning here for the links it continues to establish with 9/11 fictions and some War on Terror novels.

The first anxiety highlighted by Mortimer is the primal fear of physical danger, since every captivity narrative naturally "dramatizes the possibility of becoming a victim of random violence" (Mortimer, 4). As we will see next, in what concerns 9/11 narratives, this anxiety was particularly noticeable in novels written in the first five years after the attacks, many of which depicted and reinvented the material destruction of the towers, or of other metropolitan sites, in great detail. Not unlike in early captivity narratives where women and children were privileged characters threatened by physical violence, in some 9/11 narratives such as those crafted by Frédéric Beigbeder and Ian McEwan, among others, the presence of children in the sites of danger—now, curiously, accompanied by their fathers rather than their mothers—continues to heighten the sense of physical vulnerability mentioned above in relation to an anxiety about future.

Fear of unrepressed sexuality, particularly female sexuality, was also very typical of early captivity narratives, and this motif persisted forcefully in nineteenth and twentieth-century popular culture. As Mortimer points out, "captivity narratives past and present address fear of white women's sexual relations outside the purview of male control" (4). In twenty-first-century narratives, it is therefore not surprising to acknowledge that in many 9/11 novels from Don DeLillo to Joseph O'Neill, power is presented as a narrative masculinity in crisis. As we will see, for some writers like Beigbeder, the collapse of the towers quite literally corresponds to the phallic symbol of male susceptibility and emasculation.

A third form of anxiety explored in early captivity narratives is cultural self-doubt or questioning. By forcing the encounter of people from different cultures, the time of imprisonment raised questions about the captive's cultural identity: "[B]eing captured by Indians is a 'multicultural moment'; the interactions which follow raise questions about American cultural identity and its presumed exceptionalism" (5). If, for the protagonists of early captivity narratives, this forced encounter could lead to the questioning of their cultural identity, for contemporary writers of different geopolitical backgrounds, however, questions or doubts are inevitably twofold. Indeed, for both US and European contemporary writers, as well as for writers from Asian and African backgrounds, it is not only, or not really, the encounter with the "other" (Muslim terrorist) that causes internal conflict. The unspecified desire for territorial expansion that has always characterized "frontier" narratives deeply concerns writers such as Mohsin Hamid and J.M. Coetzee, whose novels depict reshaping of borders imposed by the United States on the rest of the world in the name of international security.

Silences are, finally, also crucial elements of the early captivity narratives which deserve our attention. As Mortimer also recalls, the historian John Demos has notably demonstrated in his retelling of John William's narrative of 1707 ("The Redeemed Captive, Returning to Zion") how silences—what cannot be said—shape the narratives of accounts of captivity (Mortimer, 7). Voids, deletions, and gaps in the text structure most captivity narratives, as the narrator attempts to circumvent certain problematic events and themes. In most cases, silences convey "an unrecoverable missed opportunity for communication and connection." Indeed, as I have suggested above, images related to the hidden realities of the War on Terror in general, and specific incidents related to the wars in Afghanistan and Iraq in particular— exemplified by the horrendous images of torture and humiliation conveyed by that perverted spectacle of captivity, the Abu Ghraib photos—often haunt contemporary novels, even if the narratives that underlie these difficult images were not always clearly articulated, particularly in novels written in the first five years after 9/11. So damaging are these to western self-images that they are often erased and/or inverted in our cultural memory in order to reposition the white western subject as captive rather than captor.

Transatlantic and intermedial fictions of (in)security

Associated with the pervasiveness of the trauma paradigm mentioned above is the issue of the national perspective through which 9/11 fiction has been analyzed. Most of the studies concerned with these novels have focused on an exclusively US canon. However, as it is well known, the outpouring of fiction associated with 9/11 was far from a national phenomenon. As a highly televised incident, 9/11 was a historical event whose meanings and repercussions were discussed and debated all over the world. Habermas, for instance, points out that the presence of cameras transformed the local event into a global occasion: "Perhaps September 11 could be called the first historic world event in the strictest sense: the impact, the explosion, the slow collapse—everything that was not Hollywood anymore but, rather, a gruesome reality, literally took place in front of the 'universal eyewitness' of a global public" (Borradori 2003, 28). The meaning and projection of this event were examined and explored not only by philosophers but also by writers, directors, and artists on both sides of the Atlantic. It is only natural, then, to find a great number of European novels dedicated to this event.

What may be more striking is the fact that many European novels produced in the first decade after 9/11 seem to depart from an unquestioning identification with the United States. Kristian Versluys has pointed out that many of these novels demonstrate the extent to which September 11 has penetrated deep into the European psyche and thus has become "a European event" (Versluys 2007, 65–79). Versluys suggests that what "is surprising is that the gap between the continents seems smaller in fiction than in politics" (65). However, if examined carefully, this identification is far from straightforward. It is, on the contrary, replete with problems, engendered by Europe's divisive and conflict-ridden response toward US foreign policies after 9/11. Despite their strong sense of empathy toward the United States after 9/11, many of these early European novels also reveal discreet attempts at dissociation and demonstrate hesitations about the Euro-American political nexus which the Bush administration and some European governments (namely, the British, the Portuguese, and the Spanish governments) attempted to sustain. This uneasiness, fueled by the general climate of insecurity promoted by the media, begs our attention.

It should also be noted that later novels, particularly those written in the second half of the first decade of the new millennium, naturally benefit from greater critical detachment and more historical perspective. Less interested in the examination of the feelings of fear, anger, and shock which dominated the early days after 9/11, later novels are able to understand the wider and long-term repercussion of the War on Terror and to reflect on the disproportionate violence represented by the wars launched against Afghanistan and Iraq. More attentive to military and political issues, these novels reveal a growing skepticism toward international politics and politicians in general. Most of these novels attempt to situate 9/11 and the War on Terror within history, as a way to interrogate notions of globalization, democracy, and liberalism in the twenty-first century.

This book departs, thus, from a comparative approach which aims to examine how images and narratives travel via the mass media between the United States and Europe, and the ways writers respond to such transactions. By examining how this literary corpus relates to highly politicized images circulating in the media, this study will show how writers on both sides of the Atlantic absorb or resist ideological narratives which transcend national borders. The aim is to understand the connections as well as the disjunctions which constitute this transatlantic corpus of novels. I take the word "transatlantic" in the broader sense to refer to the North American and European literature in a manner that takes into consideration transatlantic influences, transactions, reactions, and projections. Although this book will examine US and British fiction, paying particular attention to the way novels portray the "special relationship" between the United Kingdom and the United States during the launching of the War on Terror, this study is not restricted to the study of Anglo-American literature. Within the European context, the book will also examine Spanish, Portuguese, and French novels which have been ignored by studies on this subject. This book will observe how Iberian writers, whose countries officially adhered to the "coalition of the willing," came to define "terror" in the face, for instance, of the rhetoric of deception promoted by Spanish politicians in the aftermath of the Madrid train bombings. It is equally important to consider fiction produced in nations such as France—a country that openly opposed the war against Iraq—in order to examine how writers find ways to convey the symbolic and material losses represented by 9/11 and the War on Terror at a time of fractious relations between France and the United States. Not unlike US writers, European writers, as a whole, offer surprising and diverging comments on the meanings of terror(ism). Overall, these works demonstrate how literature has a singular role in countering the rhetoric and fictional plots offered by official discourses both local and global. This book will, thus, not only explore and juxtapose novels by US, British, French, Spanish, and Portuguese authors, but it will also draw on the perspectives of novelists from countries such as Pakistan and India, like Mohsin Hamid and Salman Rushdie, who were not born in Europe or in the United States but made their careers in these countries. By examining the relationship between colonialism and contemporary global politics, their fiction offers us a privileged standpoint on the roles played by Europe and the

United States in several contexts of terror. Here is a significant body of novels whose comparative analysis sheds light on cultural and political trends, forcing the reader to review not only US and European self-images but also western values in the age of neoliberal capitalism. These are only some of the questions which the comparative transatlantic approach, initiated by this study, attempts to address.

The terrorist attacks of 2001 resurrected fears and anxieties that were dormant but not dead. Although it can be argued that these feelings are aroused in times of crisis, some authors believe that, in recent years, western societies have become more susceptible to fear. For Frank Furedi, for instance, risk-aversion is part of a culture of low expectations promoted by official discourse and cultural agents:

> In recent times, government officials have looked into the risk that killer asteroids pose to human survival. Some scientists have warned that a global influenza is around the corner. We are continually warned that, for the human race, "time is running out" unless we do something about global warming. "The end is nigh" is no longer a warning issued by religious fanatics. Scaremongering is increasingly represented as the act of a concerned and responsible citizen. (Furedi 2002, vii–viii)

For Furedi, the culture of fear is ultimately a question of political displacement: "[O]ur culture encourages us to fear the wrong things" (xvii). "Displacement" is an important word in Freudian terms and bears particular significance in the context of this study. Since his early works, the term *fear* was used by Freud, in contrast to *anxiety*, to refer to the reaction to some real danger. In 1916, in his *Introduction to Psychoanalysis*, Freud already referred to the use of these terms in popular speech, indicating that anxiety is related to a state which does not imply any direct allusion to an object, whereas in fear the subject's attention is specifically focused on an object (Freud 1966). In *Inhibitions, Symptoms, and Anxiety*, first published in 1926, Freud insisted on this difference:

> Anxiety has an unmistakable affinity with expectation: it is anxiety about something. It has a quality of indefiniteness and lack of object. In precise speech we use the word "fear" rather than "anxiety" if the feeling has found an object. (Freud 1936, 158)

For Freud, fear is used to represent the situation when "the feeling has found an object." What does that actually mean, though? Is it fear (the feeling itself) that finds its object? Or, is it up to the subject (via the psychoanalytic or cultural analyst?) to find an object for it? Freud's original definitions highlight, from the outset, the idea that fear is far from a simple, natural, or straightforward mechanism. Fearful objects are culturally and socially constructed, raising questions about the origins and sources of fear itself.

It is the feeling of extreme fear which underpins the concept of "terror" (a word that, now, threatens to dominate our everyday language). From the Latin "tremere" (i.e., to tremble), terror suggests "an involuntary shaking" associated with a specific source of dread. The concept was used in relation to specific political or military events such as "the Reign of Terror" in France in the eighteenth century, and it was often used, much later in time, in the English language to refer to the air raids of the Second World War. It could be argued that terrorism is far from a specific term. Its meaning depends on what type of order is being challenged. There is neither an academic nor a universally agreed, legally binding definition of terrorism: the term changes and shifts from culture to culture, from legal system to legal system, from government to government, from year to year, depending on the context which currently controls political discourse.[9] Since it is obviously a politically charged concept, no single definition of terrorism has been able to receive international approval. "Terrorist," one should remember, is a term which has been applied by governmental agencies to figures as different as Osama bin Laden and Nelson Mandela.

As an example of extreme fear, terror is the place where fiction and reality collapse. If policies of security can lead to new forms of (in)security, then political discourse becomes blurred: it becomes difficult to understand what is fictional and what is "real"; it is not easy to know who to trust; conspiracy theories proliferate. It is, therefore, not surprising to see that fiction—novels, short stories, films—is a privileged terrain where readers and writers display feelings of insecurity that are out of control. Most of the novels examined in this study reveal concerns about the impact of contemporary security measures on our lives and suggest that certain policies of security lead to further insecurity. This study will show how writers dwell, more or less explicitly, on issues such as the creation of the Department for Homeland

Security in the United States, the development of these policies in Europe and the undermining of human rights and civil liberties endorsed by the War on Terror all over the world.

The blur between fiction and reality in many of these novels can be examined from an intermedial perspective. Within the realm of theory, authors such as Slavoj Žižek and Jean Baudrillard have notably commented on the spectacular and cinematic elements which shaped the planning and staging of the attacks. A literary analysis of 9/11 and the War on Terror requires an understanding of how visual media shapes our collective imagination and changes the way we think and write about fiction. In this sense, it is significant to examine, for instance, the relation between the mass media and technology in the development of certain cultural themes, of certain literary tendencies as well as visual strategies used by both directors and novelists in their work. Fueled by the proliferation of digital technologies, visual media has had a vital role in shaping the political and social landscape which followed the 9/11 attacks. Since the attacks on the Twin Towers became the most "watched" event of all time, it is not surprising to see that this image was refigured and reconstructed and transformed by writers in their novels. This book will show how this reworking of visual texts suggests different sorts of historical links and ideological positions. As Žižek suggested, the destruction of the Twin Towers expanded the space left open to the great iconography of disaster which has always been associated with New York, that symbolic capital of modernity (Žižek 2002). It is therefore important to understand how popular culture (through photography, television, cinema, comic books, etc.) informs, competes, or undermines the work of novelists. More significant, however, will be to show how, during this same period, many writers rework other, perhaps more uncomfortable, images, such as those associated with the War on Terror. The Abu Ghraib photographs and the cinematic figurations of Guantanamo Bay are only some of the haunting images that, more or less reluctantly, penetrate both the novels examined here and our collective imagery, forcing the reader to acknowledge—if only momentarily—a painful compliance with the pornographic spectacle of war.

Hidden (in the original French *Caché*) is a critically acclaimed European film that came out in 2005, and whose narrative forcefully illustrates how anxieties about security travel both transatlantically and intermedially.

Directed by the Austrian director Michael Haneke, the film is a thriller set in France, starring Daniel Auteuil as George, a famous TV presenter. George has been receiving menacing, mysterious packages containing "surveillance videos." The videos show scenes from his private life, including images of his wife Anne and their 12-year-old son Pierrot. No one knows who has filmed or sent these videocassettes. These arrive on the family's doorstep and progressively disturb George's professional and personal life. They appear to be, at first, lifeless surveillance tapes (the first of these focuses on the family home's exterior from a stationary and unnoticed street camera), but they are later accompanied by disquieting childlike drawings. One of these tapes leads George to the small apartment of Majid, an Algerian man whose parents worked as farmhands for George's family before they were killed in the Paris massacre of 1961. George's parents had intended to adopt Majid but the viewer gets to know—via flashbacks—that due to a childish but violent game, ignited by George's sense of rivalry toward the other boy, his parents ultimately send the boy to an orphanage. As Majid later tells Georges, his life and his education were forever limited as a result of this eviction. George believes that Majid may be the author of the tapes, but the Algerian man always denies involvement, and disturbed by this reencounter, Majid ends up killing himself in front of George—in a scene that is also recorded. Haneke's film does not provide answers about the mysterious sender's tapes, but the film finishes with the encounter of Majid's son with George and Anne's son Pierrot, in front of the school. The relationship between the two boys is unexplained and the film finishes by dwelling on the uncertain future, embodied by the new generation. In terms of both themes and style, *Hidden* evokes many of the motifs explored by the 9/11 literary corpus we will examine in this book. This film interestingly reenacts themes that link security culture and surveillance, which we will explore in Chapter 2, while also dwelling on the possibility that twenty-first-century transnational terrorism may be a legacy of colonialism— concerns which we will explore in Chapter 7. By redirecting the visual imagery associated with CCTV cameras to a white middle-class Parisian family, the director inverts our expectations regarding the real foci and buried genealogy of violence. The film draws on the juxtaposition of different visual media— video, film, TV, and drawings—to explore hidden sources of transgenerational guilt. Through the painful evocation of France's colonial past and Algeria's painful fight for independence, it invites the viewer to reconsider the mechanisms of collective responsibility, hinting at the need to "rewind" historical instances of "(in)security," such as those associated with 9/11 and the War on Terror. Significantly, the film interrogates the relation between terror and security by unveiling the pressure of a circum-atlantic movement— from colonial Europe to the United States and vice-versa. By drawing on the context of the so-called War on Terror, the film explores how images and notions such as the "home(land)" travel, via the media, from the United States (where it has reemerged in the discourse of the Bush administration after the 9/11 attacks of 2001) to earlier colonial countries such as France.[10] Finally, the recurrent rewinding of videotapes in *Hidden* also serves as a metaphor for the way 9/11 novels will be examined in this book. Like George, I will be dealing with an awkward corpus of texts where highly politicized images are often hidden. Their analysis implies going back and forth, demanding that notions such as terror and security should be thoroughly reviewed and revised.

The New "New York Novel":
The Epicenter and Its Reverberations

Since the attacks on the World Trade Center on September 11, 2001, a great number of novels have been concerned with depicting, revising, and reimagining images of New York—a city which in popular culture and global imagination has often been on the verge of being destroyed.[1] In attempts to describe, chart out, preserve, and "secure" the image of this US metropolis, writers have been paving the way for an arguably new genre—the post-9/11 New York novel or what some reviewers have called "the new New York novel" ("The Year in Books" 2008).[2] This chapter explores some of the features of urban novels written about New York by US writers in the past decade, aiming to assess if such a representation can allow us to rethink the "eventfulness" of 9/11 and to examine the attacks and their aftermath in light of their political, social, and historical meanings.

Among the theorists who have written about the possibilities of navigating between urban and literary texts, it is worth evoking here the pioneering work of Michel de Certeau. As part of his attempt to develop a theory of the productive and consumptive activity inherent in everyday life, the French theorist Michel de Certeau has notably shown how different readings of the city provide us important insights about both relations of power and individual agency. Indeed, if the city can be captured by distanced and panoramic approaches, it can also be read through "close" readings, where the experience of the walking subject and its excursions are examined from below. Curiously, though not inadvertently, de Certeau's famous essay "Walking in the City" begins on the top of the World Trade Center:

> Seeing Manhattan from the 110th floor of the World Trade Centre. Beneath the haze stirred up by the winds, the urban island, a sea in the

middle of the sea, lifts up the skyscrapers over Wall Street, sinks down at
Greenwich, then rises again to the crests of Midtown, quietly passes over
Central Park and finally undulates off into the distance beyond Harlem.
A wave of verticals. [...] The gigantic mass is immobilized before the eyes.
(de Certeau, 91)

The World Trade Center is used by Michel de Certeau to illustrate the idea of
a synoptic, unified view which transforms the mass below "into a texturology
in which extremes coincide—extremes of ambition and degradation, brutal
oppositions of races and styles, contrasts between yesterday's buildings, already
transformed into trash cans, and today's urban irruptions that block out its
space" (91). According to Michel de Certeau, New York is "a city composed of
paroxysmal places in monumental reliefs. The spectator can read in it a universe
that is constantly exploding" (91). De Certeau's metaphorical attempt to depict
the bursting effect of New York's panoramic aesthetics sounds awkwardly
predictive when reread in the aftermath of the 2001 attacks, reminding us of
how the architectural presentation of the city always attracted an imagination
of disaster that could not be ignored by urban theorists. De Certeau's work
goes on to show how, in contrast to this towering vision, the more common
experience of the city is experienced from "down below," where the walking
subject navigates the streets moving in ways that, although meaningful, are not
fully determined by either architectural logic or urban discipline (93).

As we will see throughout this book, many 9/11 novels provide persistent,
and often obsessive, attempts to visually capture the city: from panoramic views
of the city experienced from other skyscrapers (Beigbeder), high windows,
and public observation points such as the London Eye (McEwan), via digital
maps (O'Neil), mobile visions of the city from carefully locked cars (McEwan,
DeLillo), door-to-door visits (Safran Foer) to dirty street corners in marginal
neighborhoods (McCann) and futuristic air chases within and beyond the
city (Cunningham). The ways writers approach and rewrite the city can offer
important insights about the anxieties and expectations which we project onto
urban spaces, as social and political sites. Since representations of the city
necessarily overlap with issues such as globalization, deterritorialization, and
the expansion of neoliberal capitalism, which, in turn, cannot be disconnected
from fictional renderings of 9/11 and the War on Terror, urban questions
have much to add to the ongoing debates about the literature of 9/11.

Domestication versus deterritorialization: Early debates on 9/11 fiction

As several literary critics have pointed out, a great number of 9/11 novels produced in the first five years after the attacks felt safer withdrawing into the domestic rather than directly addressing the public, political, and historical contours of the event. Richard Gray, for instance, saw a distinction between those authors that "simply assimilate the unfamiliar into familiar structures" (30) and those writers who were able to respond to the "bigger picture" (32). He insists that with 9/11 writers had "the chance, in short, of getting 'into' history, to participate in its processes and, in a perspectival sense at least, of getting 'out' of it too—and enabling us, the readers, to begin to understand just how those processes work" (19). Gray concludes that "many writers have seized that chance; others, apparently traumatized by accelerating social change and political crisis, have been unable or unwilling to do so." When referring to works such as *The Twilight of the Superheroes* by Deborah Eisenberg, *The Reluctant Fundamentalist* by Mohsin Hamid, *Netherland* by Joseph O'Neill, and the *Garden of the Last Days* by Andre Dubus III, Gray pointed out that they present a strategy of deterritorialization by presenting "post-9/11 America as transcultural space in which different cultures reflect and refract, confront and bleed into another" (55).

In his response to Richard Gray, Michael Rothberg commends the kind of deterritorialization of the novel that Gray would like to see thrive in the wake of 9/11 but finds limitations in an analysis that derives "mainly from recent immigrant fictions that open up and hybridize American culture" (153). Rothberg rightly calls for an additional form of deterritorialization: "In addition to Gray's model of critical multiculturalism, we need a fiction of international relations and extraterritorial citizenship" (153). Adding that "the most difficult thing for citizens of the US empire to grasp is not the internal difference of their motley multiculture, but the prosthetic reach of that empire into other world and its claims of 'the first universal nation'" "Rothberg therefore proposes a 'complementary centrifugal mapping that charts the outward movement of American power' (153) and sensibly defends a 'fiction of international relations and extraterritorial citizenship.' Rothberg is spot on in stating that we need 9/11 novels that work as 'cognitive maps that imagine how US citizenship looks and feels beyond the boundaries of the nation-state, both for Americans and for others' (158) and discerningly maintaining that such an imagination will necessarily be double and will be forced to balance two countervailing demands: to provincialize the claims of 'the first universal nation' and to mark its asymmetrical power to influence world events" (158).

It should be added, though, that the registered marks of US citizenship, however different ("how *US citizenship* looks and feels beyond the boundaries of the nation-state, both for Americans and for others;" italics mine), are only part of a larger map of insights offered by 9/11 fiction regarding international relations: other important cognitive positions could be acknowledged if we examine how *other forms of national citizenship* look and feel both in the United States and in abroad. It is in this wider literary corpus that we will fully understand the narratives of "international relations and extraterritorial citizenship" (153) which have emerged in the last decades.

Moreover, if we look for examples of "this extra-territorial literature of our new age of war and terror" in Rothberg's own work, we encounter further challenges to the "global aesthetic education" which the author defends (140), but which are fundamental for our understanding of post-9/11 and War on Terror literature. In Rotheberg's essay on 9/11 fiction "Seeing Terror, Feeling Art: Public and Private in Post 9/11 Literature," the author carefully selects a number of works by New York–based writers in order to present an "ethic for an age of terrorism, counter-terrorism and globalization" (140). In this article, the canonical US writer Don DeLillo is brought together with a number of other New York–based artists whose history of dislocations will inform their approach to 9/11: Anne Maríe Levine, born in Belgium (Germany) and raised in Southern California; Suheir Hammad, a US poet born in Jordan and descendent of Palestinian refugees; and D. Nurkse, a Brooklyn born poet whose Estonian parents escaped Nazi Europe during the Second World War. For Rothberg, these authors "seek to stimulate a movement out from writer's and reader's subjective experiences toward an encounter with global histories" (124). His essay ultimately highlights how the four of them explore a "slender bridge between intimacy and the wider world" (140) as a way to "recalibrate distance and proximity to match a world of asymmetrical power and experience" (140). This reading, although extremely valuable for the way it stresses the non-exceptional nature of 9/11's trauma, unintentionally dissolves distinctions between political histories which sustain the narratives of dislocation in these and other texts. Despite advocating a literature that "speaks in multiple tongues" (141), Rothberg's analysis is clearly monolingual (both in terms of the language provided by his corpus and in terms of the motifs through which his texts are brought together), conflating ideas and themes that characterize, beyond the recalibration mentioned above, diverse responses to 9/11. Structured as it is around trauma theory, it remains more interested in offering the "global history of wounding," as Richard Crownshaw called it (2011, 761), than to address specific social and political gestures which 9/11 fiction, willfully or not, necessarily embodies.

Ultimately, and to return to the concept of deterritorialization which initiated this debate, it may be worth adding that this is a word that needs to be used cautiously, as the viability of this concept in relation to wider notions of global literature depends not only on specific texts' canonic position and visibility (not least linguistic) within the wider charts of global literature but also on the ways they attempt to negotiate local and global demands.[3] It should be noted, thus, that for many US and non-US writers, 9/11 provided an opportunity not only to critique US hegemony, but also to explore different national and ideological positions assumed by specific governments. If 9/11 fiction is, indeed, read beyond the restrictive layer of the Anglo-Saxon canon, then it will reveal political nuances beyond those attached to mourning and trauma. As I will show, many non-US authors approach 9/11 fiction as a way to convey the lack of autonomy and overall weakness of their own nation-states, while others approach 9/11 to denounce, more specifically, how the political opportunism which brought together the "coalition of the willing" during the invasion of Iraq has shaped languages other than English. When considering the overall corpus of 9/11 literature, these different positions are worth taking into account since they also deal directly with transnational and deterritorializing pressures conveyed by the texts.

To critically assess the fiction of "international relations and extraterritorial citizenship" (as Rothberg cogently called it) or "deterritorialization" (with its stress on hybridism and otherness, according to Gray), one has to take into account a wider view of the 9/11 corpus and the manifold international pressures and political hierarchies that it encapsulates. If at least one part of what we need to do entails exploring "impact of America's global reach, and revealing the cracks in its necessarily incomplete hegemony," as Rothberg wisely suggested, then the emphasis placed on trauma by 9/11 criticism is still not sufficient. Although interrogating about the relation of 9/11 memorial culture and US exceptionalism (as Rothberg and Crownshaw, among others, have sensitively done), the overall dominance of trauma theory in relation to this field runs the risk of examining all 9/11 narratives through the paradigms of memory studies, neglecting how US and non-US novels directly engage with—and often attempt to rewrite—political language beyond that implicated in mourning. By political language, I also mean the *language of the polis*, as I will show next.

The "New" New York novel?

In this chapter, I will start by scrutinizing the "epicenter" of the tragedy, New York, before moving to the reverberations of this event in different points in the globe where national and local concerns are intersected with global pressures. Since the corpus of 9/11 or post-9/11 novels is a more dissonant body of work than critics have cared to show, I will use this initial chapter to convey how "new New York Novels," far from constituting a homogenous genre, reflect different trends and positions in relation to the urban memory of 9/11. In the second part of this chapter, I will, then, examine Amy Waldman's novel *The Submission*, a book which interrogates the culture of memorialization associated with 9/11 and revises dominant views of post-9/11 New York. In the chapters that follow and throughout the book, I will examine the impact of several global "events" associated with 9/11 and the War on Terror in the works of writers of different national contexts, by paying particular attention to the Euro-American nexus and the role it plays within current and historical configurations of power.

The tendency, registered by many 9/11 novels, to withdraw into the domestic, signaled by Richard Gray, has one obvious consequence in terms of the portrayal of urban experience. Many 9/11 novels set in New York offer very reductive visions of urban life, focused principally on the social dynamics of white middle- or upper-middle classes and thus unable to represent the city's heterogeneous spaces and diverse social configurations. Indeed, for many writers and artists, the city is a place best observed from within from the prism of private and exclusive spheres. Jay McInerney's highly popular novel *The Good Life* (2006) is emblematic of the way a traumatic imagination is associated with an inward vision predicted as symptomatic of the domestication of the crisis as Gray suggested. In this novel, a middle-class married couple observes, and reenacts, the wreckage of 9/11 from the windows of their Tribeca loft. The protagonists Corine and Russell Calloway have survived a separation and are parents of twins. Deceit and suspicion, arguably major traits of the rhetoric of the War on Terror, are here reduced to the manifold deceptions that plague this married couple, whose "good life" is more or less ironically quantified in terms of status, leisure activities, and properties (such as the house in the Hamptons). An extreme but parodic example of this domestication is Ken Kalfus's novel, a parodic, black comedy that shows how a bitter divorce works as a metaphor for United States' public calamities. Particularly interesting for the way it critiques and parodies how grief, victimhood, and revenge can be used to justify personal (or political) self-interests, this book interrogates, quite pertinently, the overall tendency toward the domestication of history, mentioned above. As Laura Miller pointed out, "Disorder Peculiar to the Country" is also "about the way a conflict takes on a logic and momentum of its own until the reasons for continuing it ('If we leave, my comrades will have died in vain,' and so on) become entirely self-perpetuating" (Miller 2006). In these novels, the city is either tamed into either idealized images of middle-class homeliness (McInerney) or parodic versions or homeland (Kalfus) which, more or less consciously, convey generalized anxieties about social change in a time of war.

In Don DeLillo's celebrated and widely discussed novel *Falling Man*, New York is both a stage of fearful anxieties and an icon of postmodern alienation. The private middle-class New York setting inhabited by the novel's protagonists is, nevertheless, juxtaposed with a number of "other places" which also structure the novel's fragmented plot (such as those inhabited by Hammad, one of the 9/11 hijackers, and Martin, an art dealer who, in his past, was involved with the Baader-Meinhof terrorist group in Germany). As Kristiaan Versluys suggests, the novel begins with a "familiar" structure only to depart from it through a number of strategies of defamiliarization: "[O]ne of the many estranged features of the novel is the fact that the narrative in the novel is not limited to Keith and Lianne and their immediate next of kin, interspersed with the interrupted family idyll and the account of the main characters' bouts of melancholia is the story of Hammad" (Versluys, 44). Although DeLillo is less interested in conveying New York as a historical site than a stage of virtual reality, his portrayal of New York's performatic modernity is subtly confronted with chronological allusions such as that of the Germany of 1970s which complicate, if only momentarily, prevailing notions of "terror." Ultimately, it is New York's pulverized self-image which haunts the author, a city engulfed by its hipper-reality.[4]

For other established writers such as Paul Auster and Phillip Roth whose novelistic work has been, to a great extent, connected to New York, the city becomes a mirror for the powerless writer, staging images of impotence and malaise regarding the role of fiction at the beginning of the twenty-first century. As Aliki Varvogli has shown, both Auster's *Travels in the Scriptorium* (2006) and Roth's *Exit Ghost* (2007) address the meaning and importance of authorship by exploring the lived world by means of the invented world, and both use the central trope of the ailing author to aid their investigations into contemporary authorship. If Auster and Roth have in the past associated the image of the author with that of the American terrorist, in these two recent novels, however, they offer a weaker image of the writer: in Auster the author suffers from weakness and amnesia, while in Roth the author is both impotent and incontinent. While Auster's character does not venture outside his room, Roth's character takes the subway to visit Ground Zero but, significantly, ends up in the Metropolitan Museum of Art. Writing in the aftermath of 9/11, Auster and Roth were, according to Varvogli, depicting the sense of marginalization of the writer during an inauspicious political climate. These works reveal important links with J.M. Coetzee's novel, which we will explore in Chapter 7, for whom the city also mirrors an authorial impasse at a time when the overall political environment shuns introspection and self-scrutiny.

Darker than this approach to city as a site of authorial ailment are some of the apocalyptic and highly dystopian images of New York which also emerge after 9/11. The city as an apocalyptic site emerges in a growing number of post-9/11 films as well as in many literary narratives associated not only with fears of global warfare and terrorism but with the sweeping outbreak of security measures In this context, the fractured family, also a recurrent motto of the 9/11 novels (as we will see in Chapter 3, the relation between fathers and their children is often—but not always— associated with feelings of powerlessness and damaged masculinity), is central to Cormac McCarthy's highly allusive novel, *The Road* (2006). In McCarthy's dystopian narrative, father and son traverse ruins of cities and pass by their outskirts, scavenging remains of food, recognizing in the debris what is left of old metropolitan icons and global aspirations. Cities are here deserted and haunted places, no longer able to provide solace to those who seek shelter. They are, above all, reminders of what was lost, places to scavenge for detritus of civilization, ruined emblems of a larger dystopia. Through the relation established between father and son, *The Road* interrogates the possibility of renewing trust in collective and communal dynamics in a historical path marked by fear and suspicion.

Dystopian cities are also imagined, in more clearly political lines, as a consequence of the boost of the society of control and the breakdown of higher social beliefs and ideals. Jonathan Raban's *Surveillance* (2008), set in Seattle in the near future, shows the impact of life under constant surveillance and uninterrupted security measures: identity cards are compulsory, terrorism alerts happen on a daily basis, and privacy has become a rare commodity. Not surprisingly, life in this highly controlled city is less rather than more secure. The city is stranded by emergency exercises or, as the narrator calls them, "dress rehearsals for terror" (Raban 2006, 5). These performances, called "TOPOFFs," were modeled in actual response exercises promoted by the Department of Homeland Security, which involved "top officials at every level of government, as well as representatives from the international community and private sector" (DHS 2008). In Raban's portrait of the near future, the Department of Homeland Security's main role is to maintain the public in a continuous state of insecurity. The novel concludes with the depiction of an earthquake— an ironic acknowledgment that not all disasters can be anticipated and an uncomfortable reminder of the government's ineffective response to hurricane Katrina in New Orleans.

The movement away from the private and the domestic and into a wider and socially heterogeneous reality, personified by the city at large, can be seen in novels as early as the narrative of *Extremely Loud and Incredibly Close* (2005) by Jonathan Safran Foer. Its protagonist, nine-year-old Oskar Schell, has lost his father in the terrorist attacks on the World Trade Center and sets off on an outlandish mission which impels him to venture alone into the streets of New York. In his search for a mysterious lock (for an unidentified key left by his father), Oskar devises the ambitious plan to contact every person living in New York City with the surname "Black." Oscar's peculiar behavior—his obsessive traits and other idiosyncrasies—has been considered to be linked by reviewers and critics to autism—a feature which was made more explicit in the film adaptation of the novel directed by Stephan Daldry and released in 2011.[5] This trait has often been analyzed in the light of trauma. Yet, one may ask if the much discussed autistic traits of the main character (which Oskar and his family attempt to challenge) are not themselves a reflection of the tendency toward inwardness which characterized initial reactions to the tragedy, not least from a number of writers. In this sense, Oskar's mission to face the city is a recognition and a challenge to such an insular tendency. Significantly in this *bildungsroman*, Oskar's eccentric narrative of mourning will be traversed with other histories of grief such as those of lives lost in Dresden and Hiroshima at the end of the Second World War. The bombings of these two cities remind readers of the role of the United States in a long history of wartime atrocities at a moment when the US government is proudly defending its leadership role in new military conflicts.

For many writers, New York after 9/11 became an ideal setting for a renewal of the novel of manners. The felt sense of exposure provoked by the attacks allowed writers to record customs, values, and mores of the middle classes, in particular. While most novels dwell on the social context of their characters, the self-conscious novel of manners observes post-9/11 urban and suburban settings from a documentary and critical point of view stance. Post-9/11 New York also becomes a stage where the white middle classes are observed in relation to their "others"—migrants, lower-class characters, or religious/ethnic "others." Claire Messud's *The Emperor's Children* (2006) is one of the first and most explicit post-9/11 comedies of manners. Mostly set in New York City, her novel depicts the lives of three friends in their early thirties, living in Manhattan in the months leading up to the attacks on the World Trade Center. It is a critique of the US chattering classes and their lifestyle, a society of appearances, dominated by the mass media, where even the lives of privileged and educated liberals lack real meanings and goals. It dwells on the relationship between perception and reality, the construction of personal myths, and the hypocrisy of the upper-middle classes. The 9/11 attacks are staged as both an impossible event that momentarily pierces through this reality of surfaces and an emblem of an inner and ongoing disintegration. Messud's characters struggle for personal intimacy and integrity in a city increasingly dominated by empty icons and shifty neoliberal values.

A very different type of urban geography is covered by John Updike's *The Terrorist* (2006), a novel that seeks to explore the worldview and motivations of religious fundamentalism by exploring the mind of a US-born Muslim teenager named Ahmad Ashmawy Mulloy, while at the same time scrutinizing the lives of the residents of the fictional Rust Belt suburb of "New Prospect." This fictional area which Updike has identified with Paterson, New Jersey, offers a vision of suburbs shaped by recent waves of immigrants, arriving mostly from outside of Europe. By creating different social needs (in terms of housing, healthcare, transport, and education), this new demography also tests suburbia's promise of upward mobility, reshaping white middle-class mentality. Interestingly, Kathy Knapp's study on suburban novels written after 9/11 shows that "writers now working in the suburban literary tradition do not offer the postwar suburb as a retreat from the larger world, but suggest instead that the world has come to the suburbs" (Knapp, 501). If critics of the suburban literary tradition prior to 9/11 have read the post-war suburb as static and monotonous, Knapp's work shows that post-9/11 suburban novels are now clearly attracted by the catastrophic and traumatic, participating "in nothing less than a dystopian orgy of mass destruction, depicting their middle-class male protagonists as crippled by panic, despair, and cowardice before sending their entire world up in flames—real and metaphorical" (501–502).

New York City has also been, significantly, portrayed from the perspective of its financial district. The protagonists of post-9/11 novels such as Joseph O'Neill's *Netherland*, Moshin Hamid's *Reluctant Terrorist*, Robert Harris's *The Fear Index*, and Ted Wayne's *Kapitoil* are either financial analysts or management consultants who become entangled in the knot that ties together 9/11, security culture, and neoliberal capitalism. O'Neill, Hamid, and Wayne allude to Fitzgerald's portrayal of New York in *the Great Gatsby*, but in Wayne's novel *Kapitoil*, this intertextual reference more explicitly shapes the narrative. If O'Neill and Hamid set their novels in the period immediately before and after the 9/11 attacks (as we will see in Chapter 5), Ted Wayne sets his novel only before 9/11, more specifically in 1999, at the end of the dot-com boom, at a time when US hegemony and excess were flagrantly conspicuous. *Kapitoil* revolves around the character of Karim Isaar, a computer programmer from Qatar who creates a program that uses news articles to predict oil prices. As Karim finds himself propelled to the top of the corporate ladder, a new version of New York opens up to him—one shaped by the lifestyle of the wealthy Manhattanites. Although the meaning of the valley of ashes that separated East Egg and West Egg has been updated in this novel, New York is still conveyed as a socially fragmented city whose world position both determines and manipulates the boundaries of East and West. Like other 9/11 novels, *Kapitoil* uses the city of New York to revise, through clear intertextual references, entrenched perceptions of the US dream in light of the tight relations between terrorism, oil, and neoliberal financial capitalism.

In an attempt to counter some of the superficial or nostalgically idealized images of the city which emerged immediately after 9/11, a number of writers wisely resort to history, inviting the reader to refocus on currently iconic urban spaces from unexpected chronological coordinates. Two novels that stand out in terms of this historical approach to the post-9/11 New York fiction, Cunningham's *Specimen Days* and Colum McCann's *Let the Great World Spin* (2009), which we will examine in more depth in Chapter 4, revisit New York with a combination of aesthetic intelligence and political sensitivity which was not common in early 9/11 fiction. In three different narratives, that function as alternative generic transfigurations of the city, Cunningham explores multiple temporalities: the past (New York City during the industrial revolution), the present (post-9/11 New York), and the future (a version of New York set 150 years in the future). Cunningham's work corrects and revises, thus, our ideas about urban terror. The workings of the polis are explored through an interconnected set of characters and their relations with the city, the way these have framed our past and may shape our future. Colum McCann's novel *Let the Great World Spin* (2009) winner of the national Book Award, also puts the idea of terror under historical perspective. The plot of the book revolves around two central events. The first, laid out clearly in the book's opening pages, is the sensational real-life feat of the Twin Towers tightrope walk of Philippe Petit 110 stories up, performed in 1974. This lays the groundwork for the author's description of the human ability to find meaning, even in the greatest of tragedies. The second central event, which is only revealed halfway through the book, is the fictional courtroom trial of a New York City prostitute. This serves as a sort of point of balance, bringing the book back down to its more earthly and, therefore, more real basic storylines. Like in Cunningham's novella "In the Machine," the Twin Towers are here read otherwise, inviting the texts to tell us other stories of violence in the city, revealing unexpected neighborhoods and forcing characters from contrasting backgrounds to meet at startling crossroads. Indeed, akin to Cunningham's narratives, McCann's powerful allegory allows the reader to focus on less obvious economical, social, and psychological points of injury in the urban fabric and insists on reading the city as an eminently social text.

There are, of course, many more 9/11 novels set in New York, or revolving around New York's iconic status, than I have been able to refer to here, and there is certainly more to say about the texts briefly mentioned in this outline. However, by outlining in rough strokes the ways in which the city has been depicted by US writers after 9/11, I hope to have put together a wide panoramic backdrop to the novels I will examine next. In light of this initial and nuclear corpus (the depiction of what I have called the "epicenter" of the tragedy which was 9/11), this book shows—in the following chapters—how some of the recurring motifs and images associated with urban insecurity, associated with post-9/11 New York, continue to shape the work of the writers from different parts of the world. While some of the writers straightforwardly incorporate or absorb iconic images into works which often erase or obfuscate "other" local and national realities, a significant number of novels written by both US and non-US writers are, nevertheless, able to offer challenging readings of urban spaces and their political (re)mapping, which diverge from and revise dominant notions of terror.

The Submission—Memorializing the polis

Waldman's novel, which was awarded an American Book Award among several other prizes and honorable mentions, was praised by critics for its reportorial realism and, more significantly, for its straightforward engagement with political issues emerging from 9/11. Pankaj Mishra, writing for *The Guardian*, points out that "Amy Waldman's *The Submission* makes you realise just how rare political intelligence, or even a shrewd worldliness, became in the prose fiction—as opposed to film—of this period" (Mishra 2014). Michiko Kakutani, writing for the *New York Times*, agreed that *The Submission* faces head-on the aftermath of the terrorist attack: "[T]he result reads as if the author had embraced Tom Wolfe's famous call for a new social realism—for fiction writers to use their reporting skills to depict 'this wild, bizarre, unpredictable, Hog-stomping baroque country of ours.'" In doing so, Kakutani suggests, Amy Waldman came up "with a story that has more verisimilitude, more political resonance and way more heart than Mr. Wolfe's own 1987 best seller, 'The Bonfire of the Vanities'" (Kakutani 2014).

The novel interrogates how urban memory is constructed by addressing the topical issue of monumental architecture. It explores an alternative version of history, by exploring a fictional turn of events following the announcement of an architectural design competition for the selection of a memorial for the World Trade Center. In this alternative version of events, all designs had been presented anonymously, and the Garden had been the project chosen by the jury, after a number of long meetings of the review panel constituted by famous architects, art critics, politicians, and representatives of the victims' families. It is only when the winning design is publicly announced that the jury finds out that the winning architect is of Muslim background. This creates a wave of anxiety about the project's potential hidden meanings and agenda. Backed by a number of politicians and academics, the media swiftly accuses the project's author of having conceived an Islamic garden designed as a martyr's paradise. A group of citizens, incited by the media, launches a crusade against the project and local politicians appropriate the climate of contention to increase their own popularity. Waldman's narrative dwells unflinchingly on the incestuous relation between media and political culture and the role of sensational images in the creation of urban memories.

Fuelled by the media, certain groups of people become particularly agitated. Defying the acceptance of Islamic laws in the United States, a group of white men start pulling headscarves worn by Islamic women, while Muslim communities form gangs of protectors to survey the streets. Gestures of suspicion and aggression eventually lead to the death of a Bangladeshi woman, Asma Asnwar. Asnwar, an illegal alien who had publicly spoken in favor of the Garden, is denounced as an illegal alien by the press and eventually killed—stabbed to death by someone in a crowd who had gathered to witness her departure. Following this episode, early supporters of the project start to retract their positions. Even Claire Burwell, a widow of 9/11—one of the early supporters of the project—demands that the architect, Mohammad Khan, should explain his project and slightly change his design. Mohammad (also known as Mo) refuses to appease islamophobic anxieties in order to justify his own patriotism. At this point, the multiple meanings of the noun "submission" in the novel's title become clear: the actual submission of an application to a competition will ultimately unveil a highly divided society which, despite New York's liberal façade, is only able to congregate its citizens through various forms of religious, social, and ideological obedience.

Architecture of memory and grief

Waldman explores and interrogates the construction of collective memory by drawing directly on architecture and its impact on the everyday life of the city. As the author revealed in a number of interviews, Maya Ying Lin and her project for the Vietnam Veterans Memorial served as an inspiration for the characterization of Mohammad Khan and his design (Book Review 2011). In 1981, while she was still an undergraduate at Yale, Maya Ying Lin won a blind competition for the design of Vietnam Veterans Memorial. Even though reactions to the chosen memorial design were at first quite positive, once the name and ethnicity of the author became known controversy sat in. Some criticized the project for its unconventional design—its black color and its lack of ornamentation—and many members of the public openly expressed the feeling that Lin's ethnicity would be a hindrance to the design of this "American" monument. The Vietnam Veterans Memorial remains, nevertheless, one of the most visited national parks today, and perhaps due to its minimalist style, it became a reference in terms of its architectural design. David Simpson explains the reason for its ongoing attraction: "Everything surrounding the coming into being of Lin's Vietnam Veterans Memorial was [...] congenial to ambiguity and uncertainty—about the rights and wrongs of the war itself, about the class distinctions governing who fought and died in it (the names of the dead are listed without military rank), about the treatment of the survivors" (77).

The design of the actual 9/11 memorial, "Reflecting Absence" by Michael Arad and Peter Walker, evokes the minimalism of the Vietnam Veterans Memorial. Not surprisingly, this project was supported Maya Lin herself—an aesthetic genealogy acknowledged by Waldman's text.[6] One should highlight, however, that Arad and Peter Walker's memorial is only a small part of the larger project proposed for the World Trade Center's site. It is in the larger context of the site that one should examine the questions of memory raised by the novel. The master plan for the site was created by Daniel Libeskind, incorporating six new skyscrapers, a memorial to those killed in the attacks and a transportation hub. The One World Trade Center—formerly known as Freedom Tower—was the lead building for the new complex, reaching more than 100 stories and at its completion was to be the tallest building in the United States. With its finger up to the sky, it was a loud interpellation of imperial triumphalism, as Simpson and others have suggested. Originally, the tower meant to accommodate a "Museum of Freedom" but—like its original name—the idea of the museum was eventually dropped.

While patriotism and imperialism became part of the official architecture of memory of 9/11 New York, different visions which attempted to engage with ideas of multiculturalism and alternative images of Islam were not completely absent from the overall debate about Manhattan's renewal. Emblematic of this was the uproar over the construction of Park51 Community Center, the Islamic facility proposed for contested land in Lower Manhattan near the World Trade Center site. In December 2009, the *New York Times* first reported plans for a Muslim Community Center, and this was followed by a number of protests organized by groups like the Freedom Defense Initiative and Stop Islamization of America. Fueled by the media, the controversy over the community center (designated by some as "ground zero mosque") reached its peak in 2010, and the project was finally changed (Otterman 2014). As the writer Claire Messud, the author of *Emperor's Children*, wrote "in the months that followed, other vociferous opponents of the project emerged, among them not only conservative politicians like Newt Gingrich and some of the families of victims of 9/11, but also a number of Muslim leaders, who felt that the choice of site was insensitive and would complicate Muslim relations with the broader community" (Messud 2011).

In light of this controversy, Messud admires the prescience of Waldman's novel: "One imagines that the former *New York Times* journalist Amy Waldman heard these arguments with a combination of recognition and, perhaps, faint dismay" since "the general topic of her as yet unpublished first novel [...] was proving disturbingly prescient." As she suggests, Waldman's "carefully imagined fiction was in the process of becoming fact" (Messud 2011).

Figure 2.1 9/11 Memorial in New York City. This file is made available under the Creative Commons CC0 via Pixabay.

The Garden—Heterotopia or common ground?

Staring at the site of the fallen towers, the protagonist, architect Mohammad Khan (Mo), reflects about the meanings embodied by the original towers and what they came to incorporate after their fall:

What was he trying to see? He had been indifferent to the buildings when they stood, preferring more fluid forms to their stark brutality, their self-conscious monumentalism. But he had never felt violent toward them, as he sometimes had toward that awful Verizon building on Pearl Street. Now he wanted to fix their image, their worth, their place. They were living rebukes to nostalgia, these Goliaths that had crushed small businesses, vibrant streetscapes, generational continuities, and other romantic notions beneath their giant feet. Yet it was nostalgia he felt for them. A skyline was a collaboration, if an inadvertent one, between generations, seeming no less natural than a mountain range that had shuddered up from the earth. This new gap in space reversed time. (36)

Baudrillard, who back in the 1980s had already prophetically used the Twin Towers to illustrate the logic of global capitalism, clearly showed that September 11 should be understood architecturally (Baudrillard 1983; Baudrillard 2002). What had been attacked was not only a prestigious building but a value system supported by the West. This world order was reinforced by the towers' emphasis on reduplication and symmetry. In the above passage, Mo recognizes that the future-oriented towers of commerce that "had crushed small businesses" had ironically acquired a nostalgic aura. Their logic had not been destroyed by the fall, it aimed to *return home* through further reduplications.

Mo's design, the Garden, contrasts greatly with this architecture of replication. Unlike the Void (and the actual 9/11 memorial by Arad and Walker) who echoed the towers directly, the Garden's allusion to the earlier buildings was secondary. Its aim was not to duplicate the towers, but to "reincarnate" them, transform them into something else:

The concept was simple: a walled, square garden guided by rigorous geometry. At the center would be a raised pavilion meant for contemplation. Two broad, perpendicular canals quartered the six-acre space. Pathways within each quadrant imposed a grid on the trees, both living and steel, that were studded in orchard-like rows. A white perimeter wall, eighteen feet high, enclosed the entire space. The victims would be listed on the wall's interior, their names patterned to mimic the geometric cladding of the destroyed buildings. The steel trees reincarnated the buildings even more literally: they would be made from their salvaged scraps. (4)

It is the possibility of a regenerative cycle, where death can be experienced as part of a vital chain, that partly attracts Claire Burwell to the Garden. She tells her son, William, that the Garden could be a place where "his father could be found" since "shards, less than shards, of Cal likely lay in the ground where the memorial would go" (43). The design had brought comfort to her son William: "The idea of the Garden seemed to console him and ever since, he had seen the design, he and his mother they had drawn trees and flowers, the pathways and canals" (43). For William and his mother, the Garden not only offered a more personal means to remember Cal but also provided a way to reconnect with a city still grief-stricken.

Since William had dreamt that his father "couldn't find his way home" (107), Claire and her children create a trail for Cal in the streets of Manhattan—a path that would allow him to retrace his steps. The trail evoked something profoundly personal, an unofficial guiding path: "There was something enjoyably illicit in making these tiny, easily missed interventions in the city" (107). Claire and her children personify de Certeau's vision of the walking subject moving in ways that, although meaningful, are not fully determined by either architectural logic or urban discipline (de Certeau, 93). Acknowledging the difficulty to mourn within the frame of official memorials, Claire and her children are able to register their own text into the streets of New York. Mo's design offered Claire a similar possibility: a space for personal contemplation at a time avert to introspection, a place where nightmares could be revised.

As the reactions against the Garden escalate, it is also through the language of dreams that Claire Burwell comes to terms with the intensity of her feelings toward Mo's design. Halfway into the novel, she dreams that Mo had come close to her to reveal a secret: "*in any garden, more is happening than you know, than you see. Something is always changing, being changed, outside out grasp*" (253). In the dream, she follows Mo into the Garden:

> *His meaning evaded her. She reached toward him in an effort to understand. His hands settled on her head, jolting her inside, and he guided her sight to fibbers rotting, leaves curling, aphids sucking sap, Japanese beetles gnawing petals, spider mites scorching leaves, oaks wilting [...] With microscopic vision, she saw it all.*
> *"Death, its all death," she said. "And no reason for it"*
> *"There is a reason." (253)*

In her reverie, both Mo and the Garden represent the realm of desire: "she leaned toward him, those green eyes, that soft mouth" (253). It is not surprising that this intense encounter should only be tested through the work of dreams. After all, according to Jacques Lacan, "the unconscious is the discourse of the Other" (1966, 16). Clare's desire is bound up with fear and staged as a perilous but sensual encounter where several elements of the Garden (fibbers rotting, leaves curling, aphids sucking sap, etc.) evoke vital processes of metamorphosis—transformation and change—which the Garden emblematizes but will never fully materialize.

Displacement, both psychological and physical dislocation, has a significant role in the narrative. It is not only an essential component of the mechanisms of dream-work and of our understanding of the character's fantasies, but also a central feature of Mo's design which, ultimately, gears the direction of the narrative into other geographical settings. By importing architectural elements from "other" cultures, and introducing them to New York, the Garden enacts a movement, producing an act of urban translation and opening up possibilities of political revision. The dislocation, promised by the Garden, would allow New Yorkers to reinscribe themselves in the symbols of others. In the middle of the United States' most iconic metropolis, Mo's Garden would summon the city to recognize itself elsewhere, not least through traces of its radical other (Kabul).

As counter-site for the present, Mo's design corresponds to a heterotopia. The heterotopic site is described by Foucault as "a kind of effectively enacted utopia in which the real sites, all the other real sites that can be found within the culture, are simultaneously represented, contested, and inverted" (Foucault 1986, 24). Moreover, gardens are used by Foucault as examples of some of the oldest examples of heterotopias, since they are capable of "juxtaposing in a single real place several spaces, several sites that are in themselves incompatible" (25). He explains:

> We must not forget that in the Orient the garden, an astonishing creation that is now a thousand years old, had very deep and seemingly superimposed meanings. The traditional garden of the Persians was a sacred space that was supposed to bring together inside its rectangle four parts representing the four parts of the world, with a space still more sacred than the others that were like an umbilicus, the navel of the world at its centre (the basin and water fountain were there); and all the vegetation of the garden was supposed to come together in this space, in this sort of microcosm. [...]

The garden is the smallest parcel of the world and then it is the totality of the world. The garden has been a sort of happy, universalizing heterotopia since the beginnings of antiquity (our modern zoological gardens spring from that source). (Foucault 1986, 25–26)

From this perspective, gardens can be said to accommodate counter-hegemonic qualities. In *The Submission* the counter-hegemonic potential of the Garden is more noticeably conveyed through the character of Asma Asnwar, an illegal immigrant—whose status highly contrasts with those of "official" 9/11 widows such as Claire Burwell. For Asma, the Garden signifies the possibility of social inclusion. Asma believes that the memory of her husband (a Muslim man, who worked as a janitor in the World Trade Center) should be remembered in a place where Muslim traditions are not equated with terror; a place of intertwining cultural influences, whose architecture would challenge the dichotomizing rhetoric of the War on Terror. Before her death, Asma argues that "a garden is right [...] because that is what America is—all the people Muslim and non-Muslim, who have come and grown together. How can you pretend we and our traditions are not part of this place?" (296). The answer to her question is bloody. Asma will be murdered by someone in a large crowd; her silencing forecasting the fate of the Garden in US territory.

Politicized common ground

As she succumbs to the general panic and media frenzy, Claire Burwell asks Mo to make certain changes to his design. She demands that the canals—potential reminders of a line in the Quran evoking paradise—should be removed from the design. This erasure would correspond to "a symbolic change, as much to show you are eager to find common ground, that you are flexible, as for any substantive reason" (345). The expression "common ground," employed by Claire, shows well how the memorial occupies, discursively as well as physically (we are talking after all about "ground zero") a highly politicized "terrain." Paul, the jury's pragmatic chairperson, laments the inconsistency of Claire's position but identifies its political pull: "He took umbrage not just at Claire's betrayal of her fellow jurors, their months of work, their willingness to argue through their differences, but at her lack of humility [...] she didn't understand her own country, he thought: it would take more than one memorial to unite it" (352). Claire's final stance unveils anxieties about difference and dissent at a time when the launching of the War on Terror depended on the iconology of a united and cohesive nation. Like the officially promoted images of a unified country (flags, words, and candles), Claire's demand for "common ground" conceals signs of dissonance, at a time when the US government was arguing for national and international unity to validate the invasion of Afghani and Iraqi grounds.

This language of unification is not new to theorists of urban space: the use of space in general, and of urban space and public monuments in particular, has always played an important political role in either endorsing or fabricating feelings of social cohesion. Henri Lefebvre famously argued that in addition to being a means of production "it [social space] is also a means of control, and hence of domination, of power; yet that, as such, it escapes in part from those who would make use of it" (1991, 26). Claire's final rejection of the Garden and endorsement of the more austere, more controlled design embodied by the Void reflects a politicized urge for control. In a final plea, attempting to humanize the language of fear, Claire asks Mo: "Can't you see that it's natural for people to be afraid?" To which Mo replies, in a line that evokes Lefebvre's critique of the naturalization of space: "As natural as a garden" (346). By refusing to have its Islamic influences washed away, Mo rejects contrived notions of unity and transparency demanded by official rhetoric and therefore removes his design from sanctioned approaches to memorialization.

Other narrative displacements

Significantly, the novel does not conclude in Manhattan but with images of the Garden built in Mumbai in India—images which are, then, filmed and viewed by Claire Burwell, back in New York City. Indeed, in the last section of the novel, the narrative travels with Mo, first to Kabul and then to Mumbai. As if in a *roman-a-clef*, a flashback takes the reader, firstly, to the garden of Mughal Emperor Babur that Mo had visited in Kabul and which had greatly influenced his design. To get to Babur's garden, we follow Mo through the streets of Kabul during his second day in city. The narrator describes the ruined, dirty, and smelly city and explains that its urban texture "spread like a grand carpet of indecipherable pattern, every house, every life a knot" (357). Boys trail behind him "dirty and scabrous, their hair matted, their clothes dust filmed, their eyes rich with curiosity and mirth" (358).

The scatological depiction of Mo's urban exploration is not innocent: the reader continues to follow Mo, as he searches for a toilet. An elderly man takes him to an alley where there was a "small outhouse." The old man wears the face of the city: "[H]is smile was riddled with stumps and holes, as if it had been mined" (359). Mo finds himself in an impossible place, best emblematized by the partitions of the outhouse which he cannot touch: "[I]nside Mo shut the door and squatted over the whole, gagging before he remembered to hold his breath, trying to keep his balance without touching the walls" (359). Mo's desire to sightsee concludes with his identification with a city out of control, a social body in agonizing spasms: "His bowels emptied in furious stinking squirts; he became pure animal. Standing up, rocking to get his balance, he looked down into a sea of islands of shit" (359). Kabul is a city turned into detritus, a body without autonomy, a feeble country shattered by war, and a nation unable to contain its own excretions. It is significantly in this squalid scenario that Mo finds himself in craving for the "fresh air clean breath" of a garden. It is here that he finds the genesis of his heterotopia:

> Before him a vast garden rose up to meet the slope of the mountain he had just descended. From his new vantage, the hillside slum's cantilevered houses looked like an Escher drawing, one that could be smeared—by an earthquake, a mudslide—as easily as wet ink on paper. The jumble on the hill broke abruptly at the garden's rear wall, which demarcated an entirely different landscape, one marked by symmetry, order, geometry. Straight paths climbed the garden's stepped terraces, a straight canal flowed down toward Mo. Trees—almond and cherry, walnut and pomegranate—marched off to the sides in neat orchard-like rows. (360)

The narrative confirms the Garden's Islamic influences, but it does more than that: it explains the appeal of Babur's garden by placing it in the specific historical and geographical context of the city in which Mo had found it. For the Afghani people who enter Babur's garden, the space offers something both simple and vital: a vision, a promise, of contemplation and order in a deprived city, now further degraded and destroyed by war. This vision will justify the appeal in Mo's own project of symmetrical and contemplative lines, whose logic had been subverted by the rhetoric of the War on Terror.

After this recollection, the narrative then moves to Mumbai—it is there that the reader will find Mo at the very end of the novel. After his design is rejected, Mo decides to leave New York: "Mo had found himself reinvented by others, so distorted he couldn't recognise himsel [...] so he had traced his parent's journey in reverse: back to India, which seemed a more promising land" (377). However, the narrator also reveals at this stage that—in a final ironic twist to the narrative—"The Garden" will be built in Mumbai as a pleasure garden of a wealthy Muslim client. Other narrative twists follow: when the reader reencounters Mo in Mumbai, he is being interviewed for a documentary "for the twentieth anniversary of the memorial competition" (368). The interview is led by a young US woman, named Molly, and her boyfriend, William—who will be revealed in the very end of the novel to be Claire's, now adult, son.

Aiming to explore the history of the design, Molly and William want to show Claire—who is now an older and ailing woman—how the design had actually turned out. Claire is able to see the Garden through video images. More significantly, William shows Claire that he had been able to leave his own mark in the Garden: he had placed a trail of cairns—like the one they had placed in the streets of New York when he was a child. William not only confirms, thus, his refusal of the spectacle of memorialization, but he also reminds the reader of that day when his mother had left a trail of stones for his father, Cal, to find his way home, "even as she [his mother, Claire] lost hers" (385).

This displacement to Mumbai, a very different megacity from New York, discloses further ironies at the core of the narrative. Mo introduces Mumbai to his interviewers as an illustration of how memorializing had spread and "metastasized" (368):

> As India continued to Westernize, it had become obsessed with naming its dead just as America did. The plaques were everywhere: at the train station, listing those who had fallen from overcrowded cars; at the airport, remembering those felled by ongoing terror attacks; in the slums, whose handwritten signs recorded those lost to sewage' *infections* or *police brutality*. (368–369)

Despite the memorializing impetus, remembering the dead seems to assume a very different function here, where it speaks about living conditions exacerbated by globalization. It denounces ongoing sources of bereavement: poor housing conditions, deficient transport systems, and recurrent crime and terrorism. In this *other* side of the spectrum, remembering the dead means bearing in mind the living.

In the context of the wider 9/11 corpus, this movement in terms of narrative setting—from the United States to India—is, therefore, highly significant. By guiding the reader into Mumbai and Kabul on the way back to New York, Waldman's text places the urban memory of New York in a wider map, intersected by specific political and economical coordinates. The novel chooses to engage with memory from a place where different urban histories, apparently distinct in their grief, are necessarily interwoven. Not unlike the protagonists of other 9/11 novels such as *The Reluctant Fundamentalist* and *Kapitoil*, Mo acknowledges his homelessness in the United States: "For nearly two decades now, he had been a global citizen, American only in name" (369). Mo's narrative rejects idealized images of New York but is far from embracing innocent portrayals of life outside the United States. Mo's own work as an architect confirms the weight of global pressures, as it depends on fluxes of capital which compete for global visibility: Mo's clients are described as "rich patrons; undemocratic governments; Gatsby nations in a hurry to buy identities with their newfound wealth—as his own talents" (368).

The Submission addresses the grief resulting from the 9/11 attacks, by approaching memory as a boldly public matter, a matter of the polis, rather than merely through the sphere of the private and domestic realm, as many early novels tend to do. It reflects upon transnational movements, without resorting to panoramic visions of the city (rejecting the "synoptic, unified view which transforms the mass below"). Instead, it opts from multiple views conveyed from below, from the perspective of the walking subject: paths shaped with tensions, contradictions, and pressures of different kinds, but which ultimately avoid the monumentality of guided paths to history. Through significant dislocations, the novel disrupts the narratives through which September 11 and New York have been remembered and portrayed. The city is experienced as an intricate net of relations, both local and global. *The Submission* leaves, thus, a very different trail in the urban landscape of 9/11 fiction.

Early Transatlantic Projections: Frédéric Beigbeder and Ian McEwan

This chapter will examine transatlantic projections resulting from 9/11 and the War on Terror by analyzing two European novels: *Windows on the World* by the French writer, critical commentator, and pop intellectual Frédéric Beigbeder and *Saturday* by the English writer Ian McEwan. First published in French in 2003, *Windows on the World* was translated into English in 2004 and won "The Independent Foreign Fiction Prize" in 2005. Like *Saturday* by Ian McEwan, Beigbeder's book was better received in the United States than it was in Europe, where the reviews were perceptibly mixed. The American critic Stephen Metcalf considered the novel "strangely moving."[1] Laura Miller pointed out critically, but not without praise, that the novel was "a discombobulated, contradictory work, but it rings true in a way that other stabs at the same topic haven't."[2] The author Jay McInerney provided the salable blurb for the novel: "an audacious and outrageous exercise, as well as a sober and erudite meditation on the meaning of the most painful chapter in our recent history."[3] This conveniently enthusiastic reception by American critics responded, in part, to Beigbeder's claimed motivation for writing this work: "I am writing this novel because I am sick of bigoted Anti-Americanism."[4]

Partly cultural commentary, partly fiction and autobiography, *Windows on the World* attempts to explore, and react against, dominant images of the United States in France in the aftermath of 9/11.[5] The structure depends upon two intercalated narratives. One of the narratives observes the last two hours of Carthew Yorston, a Texan real estate agent and his two young sons at the famous *Windows of the World* restaurant at the top of World Trade Center. A parallel narrative describes the life and ideas of the French narrator Frédéric.[6] Each chapter corresponds to one minute of that morning, two hours before the collapse of the first tower. The narration moves between provocation and self-loathing, not only incorporating the United States' shock but also attempting detachment from it through intellectual references, black humor, and parody.

Despite their different accents, the two male characters mirror each other: they are both divorced, middle-aged men, with dandyish fantasies of self-gratification and philandering. After his divorce, Carthew desperately yearns to be "the antithesis of George Babbitt, that dumb schmuck incapable of escaping his family and his town," a formula which equally applies to Frédéric.[7] Frédéric finds in Hugh Hefner and Warren Beatty in the United States, and in Sacha Disnel and Jean-Paul Belmondo in France examples of the vanishing figure of the "INTERNATIONAL PLAYBOY" (Beigbeder 2005, 143). This is an icon which Beigbeder feels has been under attack since the 1970s (ridiculed by Mike Myers in the United States and Jean Pierre Marnelle in France), and that he believes to have been symbolically wiped out with 9/11.

As the two narrators reflect each other, so do their cities. When the novel opens, Frédéric tells us he is writing his book at Le Ciel de Paris, the restaurant on the fifty-sixth floor of the Tour Montparnasse:

> I am in *Le Ciel de Paris* as I write these words. That's the name of the restaurant on the fifty-sixth floor of Tour Montparnasse, 33 Avenue du Maine, 75015 Paris. Telephone: + 33 1 40 64 77 64. Fax: + 33 1 43 22 58 43. Métro station: Montparnasse Bienvenue. They serve breakfast from 8:30 AM. For weeks now, I have been having my morning coffee here everyday. From here you can see the Eiffel tower eye to eye. The view is magnificent since it is the only place in Paris from which you can't see the Tour Montparnasse. (6–7)

By positioning himself up high, he can flaunt both his flirtation with the United States and an ideal of powerful maleness, no doubt as phallic as the towers. His plan is to shock the French chattering classes, where he feels a generalized anti-Americanism is rooted. To provoke his audience, he makes politically incorrect references to sex and race, but he finds in his infatuation with the United States the most efficient and disturbing device. The view from the tour Montparnasse is not, however, a sustaining ground for Beigbeder's provocations. It allows only for an ambivalent identification with the United States. From there, he can certainly see the Eiffel Tower "eye to eye" while standing *shoulder to shoulder* with the Twin Towers. This double vision highlights the political uneasiness of France's relation with the United States on the eve of the Iraq War. On the one hand, the Tour Montparnasse, the tallest skyscraper in France, gives a perfect panorama of what is called the classic view of the French capital and is facing, as Beigbeder notes, the Eiffel Tower, France's most powerful symbol. Placed in a line of buildings that extends from the center of Paris, the tower is located in the famous *quartier Montparnasse*, which at the beginning of the twentieth century was the heart of intellectual and artistic life in Paris. However, the Tour Montparnasse has other, very different, connotations. The tower can also be seen as a monument to globalization. Significantly located in "rue du Maine," and, as Beigbeder notes, reachable via the international phone and fax codes "+ 33," the tower smacks of transnationalism. In fact, the gigantic proportions and standardized appearance of this gigantic building lead to a great amount of criticism by French citizens, and as a result, two years after it was erected, the construction of skyscrapers in Paris was banned.

Vertigo arises, thus, from Beigbeder's towering position. The French narrator attempts to search for points of contact between France and the United States in order to close the schism opened between the two countries following the Iraq War: "Since war has been declared between France and the United States, you have to be careful when choosing sides if you don't want to wind up being fleeced later" (16). Beigbeder presents us not only with a Franco-American cartography, but with a new transatlantic historiography, suggesting, for instance, that American independence started in France, with the Treaty of Paris signed by John Adams and Benjamin Franklin. He also begins his narrative by presenting the reader with a list of his favorite US writers, directors, and musicians. The fact that not even one woman author is included in this three-paragraph-long list of US artists reinforces again of "America" as a dream-like land of opportunities where his fantasies of masculinity have been projected. Indeed, figures like Ernest Hemingway, Bret Easton Ellis, Chuck Palahniuk, and David Fincher seem to provide Beigbeder with a (fight) club, where his masculinity can be reaffirmed. Less fitting to this ideal of male art is, however, the figure of Walt Whitman, whose verses he quotes in the same chapter. These are the last two stanzas of the section from "Salut au Monde!" quoted by Beigbeder:

What cities the light or warmth penetrates I penetrate those cities myself,
All islands to which birds wing their way, I wing my way myself.

Toward you all, in America's name,
I raise high the perpendicular hand, I make the signal,
To remain after me in sight forever,
For all the haunts and homes of men.[8]

Beigbeder suggests that in "Salut au Monde" he finds "not the thrill of power but of pride" (16). There is, however, something more disturbing about this chosen excerpt than its supposed patriotic pride. Verses such as "What cities the light or warmth penetrates, I penetrate those cities myself" and "Toward you all in America's name" ring awkwardly since the invasion of Iraq. By quoting Whitman's "Salut au Monde" at a time when the Iraq War has been declared, Beigbeder's adopted song of pride reiterates disturbingly—and perhaps accidentally—recent neoconservative appropriations of Whitman.[9] Beigbeder, who advised the Communist party candidate Robert Hue for the French presidential elections of 2002, is moved less by the neoconservative agenda than by a desire to shock and shake liberal opinion. Like his other aimless jokes and provocations, the Whitman quotation is never explained, yet its differing message is unnervingly tangled up with Beigbeder's contradictory feelings toward the United States. Despite his stated aim to sing and celebrate the United States, there are several moments in the narrative when Beigbeder's complimentary remarks verge on insult. Carthew, for instance, describes New York as a city that "stretches out like a huge checkerboard, all the right angles, the perpendicular cubes, the adjoining squares, the intersecting rectangles, the parallel lines, the network of ridges, a whole artificial geometry in grey, black and white" (14). Images of incarceration proliferate in the description of the World Trade Center, whose destruction is described as "the collapse of a house of credit cards" (9). None of these ideas, which taint his otherwise flattering portrait of the United States, are ever fully developed, explained, or analyzed. Denial is indeed one of markers of his narrative as acknowledged by the narrator himself. Deviation and evasion create a shifting ground to the novel. When Beigbeder notices that "what we thought was fixed is still shifting" and "what we thought solid is liquid," (8). He is talking about the Twin Towers as emblems of our image of the United States after 9/11, but he is also denouncing the lack of firmness of his position.

The inevitable giddiness which starts hindering Beigbeder's vision is also conveyed by his numerous references to visual culture. A Baudriallardian concern with the media and the production of images fuels the narrative. In relation to the visual renditions of 9/11, Beigbeder asks, "Why did the dead go unseen? It was not some ethical code of practise, it was self-censorship, maybe just censorship period. [...] You could call it a spontaneous *omertà*, a media blackout unprecedented since the first Gulf War" (266). To respond to this media shutdown, he mines his narrative with multiple visions of aerial threats and exploded buildings. By referring to a wide list of catastrophic films from *Towering Inferno* (1974) to *Independence Day* (1996) via *Airplane!* (1979), Beigbeder plagues his text with visual allusions of disaster. More significantly, Beigbeder inserts three photographs into the main text which depict different monuments to the dead. Two of these photographs are taken in the Montparnasse cemetery. One of them is a monument in Baudelaire's honor, "the recumbent beribboned effigy of the artist, like an Egyptian mummy upon which the 'génie du mal' is perched sculpted in stone" (117). The statue, an alter ego of the author-made-terrorist (Beigbeder himself?), sits facing the Tour Montparnasse, "seeming to scorn it with its prominent chin" (117). The second photo shows an equally haunting image of the Tour Montparnasse. Also taken at the Montparnasse cemetery, this picture depicts a large cross emerging from one of the tombs, standing face to face with the Tour Montparnasse, which looms uncannily from behind the cemetery. The most interesting picture, however, is the last picture included in the book. Taken at the US sculpture garden, this photo displaces the idea of threat from Montparnasse to a more pressing location:

> I take a photo of a statue of St George slaying a dragon which looks uncannily like a fuselage of an airplane. Numerous TV outside-broadcast trucks make it difficult to see. Entitled *Good Defeats Evil*, this massive sculpture was a gift to the United Nations from the USSR in 1990. It is sculpted from the remains of two missiles, one Soviet, one American [...] In this square building, the members of the security council are gathered to vote on a resolution about the war in Iraq. (250)

The difficulty "to see" is a significant optical sign which speaks about the murkiness of our current political landscape and its hazy rhetoric. St. George's sword at the center of the image evokes Beigbeder's own description of terrorism as "a permanent sword of Damocles slaying buildings" (171). This specific "sword" was, nevertheless, plastically recreated from materials used in other weapons: "two missiles one Soviet, one American." The plasticity of western notions of terror is emphasized by the words "Good" and "Evil" in the title of the monument—expressions which are used to describe the Soviet Union during the Cold War and are now used in the rhetoric of the Bush administration to characterize the equally supple "axis" of countries accused of sponsoring terrorism.[10] Beigbeder acknowledges the irony evoked by this linguistic elasticity, even if he does not fully articulate it. Alongside the picture of the Tour Montparnasse facing a giant cross, the image of St. George slaying the Dragon is particularly poignant. The photograph of the statue becomes, in this context, a testimonial of an announced war, memorializing not the already dead, but the dead-to-be.

Despite the resonance of this image, the war on Iraq—the uncomfortable question haunting the relationship between France and the United States—is never fully verbalized or developed in the text. Instead, the narrative goes back to Beigbeder's private trauma. The narcissism which characterizes Beigbeder's personal remarks is reiterated in the public focus of the novel, where his double vision (Paris/New York) blurs the possibility of a "larger picture" (Bagdad or Kabul are conveniently absent from Beigbeder's cartography). Fear and powerlessness, and its felt emasculation, dominate the novel, justifying a new portrait of the western city under threat. Indeed, Beigbeder hits here on a motif which depicts only too well our current structure of feeling, an idea exacerbated by a culture of preemptive action:

> It would have been better all round to leave Manhattan to the Indians. The mistake dates from 1626, when Peter Minuit threw his twenty-four dollars down the drain. Should have been suspicious of someone with a name like Peter Midnight: midnight is the witching hour. Peter Minuit was proud as punch to have swindled the Algonquins, palming them off with a few glass beads in exchange for their island. But it was the Indians who swindled the Pale Faces. The glass beads were seeds which, planted in the earth, grew into a city of glass less substantial than a teepee. (248)

In this reworking of the old captivity narratives, the white middle-class western subject continues to portray itself as captive. The Indians, Beigbeder suggests, have "swindled the Pale Faces" who are hostages in cities of glass, forever threatened. Four centuries after Mrs. Rowlandson's account of her capture by the Indians, narratives of captivity continue to be copiously produced, rewritten, updated, and avidly consumed. Instead of the Indian capturer, we have a new source of barbaric, uncivilized "other" in the image of the "Islamic terrorist" that conveniently fits formulaic narratives of western popular culture.

As was mentioned in Chapter 1, captivity fictions are not, however, merely a staple of US culture. European culture has a long history of captivity narratives which goes back to the fifteenth century, with the so-called Age of Discoveries. Not surprisingly, thus, Europe has often been keen to recover, during different historical periods, captivity motifs, further developed in the US context, as a way to explore more recent anxieties of its own. Although no studies have yet been made on the transnational reworking of the captivity genre in the light of 9/11, some critics have, in fact, started to notice how references to "western" mythology have been recently recuperated by European novelists. Kristiaan Versluys, for instance, has found motifs of the "western" in two French novels written after September 11. In relation to *Windows on the World*, Versluys perceptively points out that the novel "depicts September 11 as a historical episode that re-establishes the category of the transatlantic west."[11] If the early captivity narratives were deeply tied up with issues of territorial conquest and cultural identity, similarly 9/11 fiction has had to come to terms with the projection of the US abroad, its economical, political, and cultural expansion. It is important to note that the protagonists of the early captivity narratives were not purely "Americans" but more accurately, then, Anglo-Americans or, more widely, Euro-Americans. This historical lineage is one which Beigbeder highlights in his novel, and which he relates to new forms of globalization: "[I]f we go back eight generations, all Americans are Europeans. We are the same: even if we are not all Americans, our problems are theirs, and theirs ours" (302). These links are emphasized by the autobiographical elements of Beigbeder's narrative, most notably his US genealogy, which he claims "goes back to the 'patriot' Amos Wheeler, hero of the American revolution" (302).

Another important link between early fictions of captivity and early 9/11 fiction is the way that concerns about territorial expansion become tied up with issues of gender and sexuality. As June Namias points out, "[T]he Frontier, and the captivity narrative thereof is a key to understanding American society, not because of the 'free land' or democracy but because of what it tells us about Anglo-Americans in contact with others and with their own notions of gender, sexuality and society."[12] Preoccupations with gender and sexuality play an extremely important role also in post-9/11 European narratives, where they speak of a different kind of international anxiety. In Beigbeder's narrative, for instance, it is not only the performance of white femininity but the very experience of white middle-class masculinity that is at stake. The emergence of new and potentially dangerous forms of femininity is emblematized by the regendering of the International Playboy. According to Beigbeder, the new International Playboy can now only be found in the figures of Bridget Jones and Carrie Bradshaw from *Sex and the City*. Reinforced by their consumer power, the liberated sexuality of these "sumptuous sluts" in their "devastating necklines" (189) is seen as a new form of terror: "They scare me shitless too, with their heavy artillery: mascara, lip gloss, oriental perfumes, silk lingerie" (189).[13] Female behavior is felt to be terrorizing because it exacerbates anxieties about masculinity itself: "The sons of 1968 are men with no instruction manual. Men with no solidity. Defective Men" (181).

As was mentioned in the introduction of this book, another significant form of anxiety raised in the early captivity narratives is "cultural self-doubt or questioning."[14] By forcing the encounter of people from different cultures, the time of imprisonment raised questions about the captive's cultural identity. For the protagonists of early captivity narratives, this meant the questioning of US cultural identity and its presumed exceptionalism. For the European writers, however, writing about their values in the aftermath of 9/11, the cultural conflict is double. As can be seen from Beigbeder's wavering narrative, the projection of the United States in Europe is both felt as unavoidable and excessive, both spontaneous and enforced. If in the early captivity narratives the sense of cultural conflict was also exacerbated by the captive's identification with the captors, this uncomfortable identification is also ironically reenacted in Beigbeder's politically incorrect remarks. Speaking about the influence of fundamentalist terror in our current way of life, Beigbeder suggests that "[t]heir terrorisation has produced precisely the reverse of what they had hoped. Hedonism is at its peak [...] Women aren't veiling their faces; on the contrary they're stripping off in restaurants, playing blindman's buff, making out with co-workers and kissing strange boys at 'speed-dating' evenings" (189). In this respect, Beigbeder announces mockingly, but not unrevealingly, the appeal of clichéd images of fundamentalist Islamic values: "Ok guys, you win, we'll all live like you: we will all be polygamous, and smoke dope" (189).

Silences, another crucial element of early captivity narratives, also deserve our attention in 9/11 European fiction.[15] As we have seen, silences and deviations not only plague Beigbeder's text but are well acknowledged by the author, leading to agonizing moments of self-loathing. Beigbeder's inability to face uncomfortable questions pestering his narrative: "I blame my parents for making me what I am: vague." Later in the novel, in a section entitled "Je m'accuse," Beigbeder accuses himself of, among other things, "complacency," "narcissism," "complete lack of courage" (209–211). He finishes that chapter by sentencing himself "to solitary [confinement] for life" (211). By positioning himself as a prisoner, Beigbeder reinforces the image of himself as the white western captive. Yet, Beigbeder's self-imposed captivity and his felt lack of agency results, more than anything else, from his inability to address an issue which continuously disturbs his narration (and which is crucial to any understanding of the relationship between the United States and France in the aftermath of 9/11): the declared war on Iraq. In fact, the Iraq War and, as I will show next, the *real* images of captivity enacted in the Abu Ghraib photographs are so damaging to western self-images that they are often transformed and reimagined by writers, in order to reposition the white western subject as captive rather than captor.

An English version of Anglo-American captivity: Ian McEwan's *Saturday*

Published in 2005, Ian McEwan's *Saturday* is set in London during the antiwar demonstration of February 2003. The primal scene that motivates the narrative is, nonetheless, of a prior date: September 11, 2001. The identification of London with New York is obvious from the beginning of the novel, if not from the very cover of the book.[16]

The novel opens when Henry Perowne, a neurosurgeon, awakes before dawn thinking that he has seen a plane on fire on its way to Heathrow, traveling, significantly, "east to west."[17] He finds out later in the day that the fire was

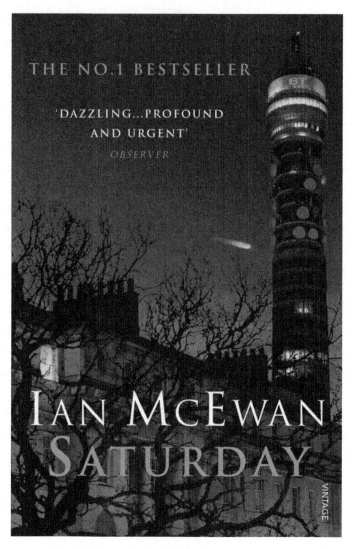

Figure 3.1 Artwork © Chris Frazer Smith. Reproduced by permission of The Random House Group Ltd.

caused by mechanical failure. Yet, the sense of threat never really dissipates. As he drives across London on his way to a squash game, his Mercedes clashes with a BMW. Baxter, the owner of the vehicle, physically threatens Perowne but the neurosurgeon manages to distract him, by claiming to find signs of a genetic disorder, Huntington's disease, in his "impaired ocular fixation" (McEwan 2005, 92). By momentarily alarming the ignorant man, Perowne manages to escape the brawl. He goes on with his weekend activities: he visits his elderly mother, listens to his son play in a band, and expects to spend the evening with his family celebrating the return of his daughter, Daisy, who had been living abroad. In his proud embrace of family life, he is the opposite of Beigbeder's philanderer. He emblematizes a rationalistic happiness, which McEwan wanted to juxtapose with our currently "anxious world."[18]

Perowne is not, however, impervious to anxiety. He has fleeting but recurrent glimpses of a red series five BMW, "a vehicle he associates for no very good reason with criminality, drug dealing" (83). Perowne's London is a society shaped by a culture of preemptive action and surveillance where personal and urban spaces are felt to be threatening. As an ambulatory one-day novel, *Saturday* evokes Virginia Woolf's *Mrs Dalloway*. As in Woolf's novel, there is an observing distance between the protagonist and the world, as they experience life in a city touched by war (in relation to which the social "othering" of Septimus Smith works, as we will see next, as a model to that of Baxter). The distancing effect gains other meanings here. The surgeon does not join the antiwar demonstration and remains throughout the novel ambivalent about the war. The novel opens with a discreet hymn to the city of London which nevertheless discloses inescapable fissures in the metropolitan nucleus: "Henry thinks the city is a success, a brilliant invention, a biological masterpiece—millions teeming around the accumulated and layered achievements of the centuries, as though around a coral reef, sleeping, working, entertaining themselves, harmonious for the most part, nearly everyone wanting it to work" (5). "Nearly" and for "the most part" mark the lingering presence of those ready to sabotage the harmony of the capital. Also not unlike *Mrs Dalloway*, Perowne is also cloistered by both material and social privilege. Perowne's thoughts about society and social behavior are very much shaped by his scientific beliefs and in particular by his uncomfortable penchant for sociobiology. Scientific reductionism is used as a way to understand and contain the excesses of the social and the haunting images of otherness propagated in the city. This is suggested by the way he describes the gardens of London, the "biological masterpiece," at lunch time:

> They loll on the grass in quiet groups, men and women of various races, mostly in their twenties and thirties, confident, cheerful, unoppressed, fit from private gym workouts, at home in their city. So much divides them

from the various broken figures that haunt the benches. Work is the outward sign. It can't just be class or opportunities. [...] No amount of social justice will cure or disperse this enfeebled army haunting the public spaces of every town. (272)

For Perowne, the professional reductionist, the city is shaped by irreducible differences: genetic inheritance is seen as the inward sign for the behavior of vagrants, drunks, and junkies which threaten the social community. Baxter embodies this mark of social otherness. Speaking in a working-class register, Baxter is immediately identified by Perowne as a "thug" whose behavior is literally degenerate: the product of a deteriorating sociobiological disorder. By diagnosing Baxter's behavior as a symptom of Huntington's disease, Perowne attempts to control the idea of violence through medical discourse. However, this medicalization is ultimately paradoxical as it perpetuates the image of violence as a transmissible disease: one which circulates from body to body indefinitely, posing a constant threat to the social order.

The narrative suggests a double infection threatening the social. Like violence, mediatized images are also seen to propagate and multiply themselves virulently, posing a constant threat to the social order and therefore justifying further security and control. Whereas in *Windows on the World*, Beigbeder reinforced the presence of media image by inviting them into the novel, here the relationship with the media seems more ambivalent. Perowne is aware of the way personal and public spaces are redefined by the mediatized culture of preemptive war. One of the various "invasions" referred to in the novel is the way television, and in particular the news broadcast, has come to reshape the rhythms of contemporary everyday life: "Perowne shifts position so the screen is no longer in view. Isn't it possible to enjoy an hour's recreation without this invasion? This infection from the public domain?" (108). The word "invasion" is meaningful given the current political context. Indeed, despite his complaints, Perowne soon surrenders to the various TV screens he encounters both outside and inside his home, assimilating their ongoing narratives of danger. Perowne's mediation between public and private awareness is safely achieved in his car, whose central locking allows for the more comforting textures of security culture. In his Mercedes, Perowne is well aware that control depends on a carefully edited gaze of the city's movements: "Shamelessly, he always enjoys the city from inside his car where the air is filtered and hi-fi music confers pathos on the humblest details" (76). Perowne has fully incorporated the mechanisms of security culture. Indeed, this is conveyed by the tracking narrative, with its power to control both Perowne's movements and his vision. Despite allowing for several digressions into Perowne's mind, the fleeting pace of the narrative heightens the sense of perpetual danger creating at times a generic register which is further away from the one-day narrative of *Mrs Dalloway* than from the "real time" narration of TV series such as *24*.[19]

Baxter, on the other hand, seems perplexingly unconcerned with the security gaze, a cognitive failure which refracts his own "impaired ocular fixation" (92). Armed and accompanied by a mate, Baxter invades Perowne's home and hijacks his family's civilized dinner. It is possible to see Baxter, with knife in hand, as personifying one of the 9/11 hijackers. He is after all described as "a man who believes he has no future and is therefore free of consequences" (210). But, Baxter's assault on Perowne's family brings home other more uncomfortable images. Baxter strikes Perowne's father-in-law in the face, threatens to kill Perowne's wife, and forces the whole family to watch as he attempts to rape and abuse Perowne's daughter Daisy. Baxter and his mate are described as "real fighters" (213) who know the logic of warfare, "when anything can happen" (207). By reenacting the juxtaposition between sexuality and torture and between sadism and voyeurism, the episode of Baxter's abuse toward the Perowne family revisits and reworks images from the infamous Abu Ghraib pictures.

The pictures of torture and abuse of Iraqi prisoners by American soldiers in Abu Ghraib, first broadcasted in the CBS's *60 Minutes* in April 2004, were widely reproduced by the British media at the time that McEwan was working on *Saturday*. Moreover, shortly after the Abu Ghraib pictures were exposed, images of British soldiers torturing and abusing Iraqi prisoners were also making the front pages of the British tabloids. These pictures, taken in Camp Bread Basket, a British-run aid-camp near Basra, became known, again in the shadow of the American images, as the "British Abu Ghraib pictures." Like their American counterparts, these pictures were above all products of a political discourse which divides the world in simplified binaries of "good versus evil," stating that you were "either with us or against us."[20]

While the photographs were endorsed by military hierarchies to produce "confessions" at all costs, what is also disclosed to the viewer is a doubly uncomfortable declaration of guilt. The pictures foreground the dehumanization of the Iraqi "other," while also disclosing the degradation and exploitation of the soldiers themselves. The pictures reveal this confessional excess in various ways.[21] Like Baxter, the soldiers in the Abu Ghraib and Camp Bread Basket pictures also suffer "from an impaired ocular fixation" (92). They are unable to articulate the image of the fixed binary between good and evil which they were, all too physically, supposed to embody. Similarly, Baxter's violence toward Perowne's family and his attempted rape of his daughter satisfy a sadistic impulse which cannot be dissociated from the voyeuristic gaze it invites. As Daisy is forced to strip naked before the assailants and her family, the reader is forced to acknowledge their involvement in a gaze not dissimilar from that which avidly fueled the circulation of the Abu Ghraib pictures. Daisy's naked body absorbs the tension created by the controlling eye of the tracking narrative. Images of sexuality and torture also gain further meanings when projected onto the body of Daisy. In the light of the Abu Ghraib pictures, Daisy's pregnant body works as a disturbing reminder of Lynndie England's pregnancy during her trial. The "dominatrix picture" where England is holding a kneeled Iraqi soldier on a leash became, no doubt because of its sexual and gendered overtones, one of the most reproduced pictures from the Abu Ghraib scandal.

England was the most demonized figure involved in the scandal, and therefore, it was no surprise to see that her pregnancy—which ensued from her time in Abu Ghraib—was also largely exploited by the media. Broadsheets, as well as tabloids, did not refrain from referring to the image of pregnant Lynndie England which was used as an evocative conclusion to a great number of articles.[22] Indeed, England's pregnancy was used by the media as a painful evidence of the way the Abu Ghraib pictures will be perpetuated in our cultural memories, possibly through various generations.

Daisy's womb becomes, thus, a space loaded with contradictory images about containment and reproduction, where images of idealized isolation and homeland security clash with visions of a war about to be "delivered" and anxieties about the breeding of further terrorism. Like England's pregnancy, Daisy's womb marks a moment of historical trauma, conveying anxieties not only about the exposure ("delivery/development") of pornography in the war,

Figure 3.2 Lynndie England, eight months pregnant, on her way to court. Reproduced by permission of Associated Press.

but more precisely, about their propagation, about the ways in which these dangerous images were being reproduced globally, spread and multiplied in the avid channels of the media and the fertile uterus of the internet. While McEwan shifts the image of pregnancy from a working-class to an upper-middle-class figure, assuring that the plot remains above all a story of white middle-class captivity, these visual palimpsests continue to haunt the narrative. If the demonization of Lynndie England reflects the need for a scapegoat onto which feelings of uneasiness about the war can be projected, the criminalization of Baxter also reflects the heightening of social discrepancies at a time of war. Incorporating multiple visual projections of violence, Baxter assimilates both the roles of Islamic terrorist prepared to invade and attack and the working-class soldiers ready to torture and abuse. This is best illustrated in the last chapters of the novel when the athletic Perowne and his healthy son capture their "captor." As they manage to get hold of Baxter, he falls down the stairs and is knocked unconscious as he lands. This moment is a literal performance of his final downfall:

[Baxter] falls backwards, with arms outstretched, still holding the knife in his right hand. There's a moment which seems to unfold and luxuriously expand, when all goes silent and still, when Baxter is entirely airborne, suspended in time, looking directly at Henry with an expression, not so much of terror, as dismay. And Henry thinks he sees in the wide brown eyes a sorrowful accusation of betrayal. (227)

For a brief moment, Henry Perowne seems to acknowledge the differences between Baxter's opportunities and his own. Airborne, Baxter becomes one to one with the image of the flaming plane ("arms outstretched, still holding the knife in his right hand"), but this swiftly gives way to another highly broadcasted image. Baxter also gives face—his wide brown eyes—to the image of "the falling man," as became known the sequence of photographs of a man falling from the Twin Towers taken by Richard Drew on the morning of the attacks.[23]

This image, which has fascinated the western media, as well as many writers, gains significant resonances in the context of McEwan's conclusion:[24] Baxter's falling body speaks about his position in society. Baxter's powerlessness is exceptionally acknowledged by Perowne at this moment in the narrative. The fracture in Baxter's head, which ensues from his fall, discloses a profound gap between himself and the surgeon. In order to assuage his guilt, Perowne decides to treat Baxter himself and perform on him a needed operation. This decision partly attempts to redeem Perowne, but ultimately, it works only to reinforce his controlling position. Perowne can, thus, get into Baxter's head and understand the mind of "the terrorist," while also committing "Baxter to his own torture" (278).

Despite Perowne's charitable act, the operating table stretches rather than closes the schism—in social power, position, and opportunities—which separates the two characters. Indeed, Perowne's regained sense of control is consolidated visually toward the end of the novel when Perowne "feels himself turning on a giant wheel, like the Eye on the south bank of the Thames, just about to arrive at its highest point—he's poised on a hinge of perception, before the drop, and he can see ahead calmly" (272). This image reveals how the anxieties which fuel the narrative of *Saturday* reenact within the text the very mechanisms of tracking, a form of the seeing that is always ahead of itself, an anticipatory vision which justifies preemptive action. In the end of

Figure 3.3 The Falling Man. Photograph by Richard Drew which accompanied the article with the same title by Tom Junod. Reproduced by permission of Associated Press.

the novel, the captivity narrative is resolved: captors are imprisoned and the captive family is avenged. Perowne can go back to his Regency house and his life of well-wrought and well-earned affluence. London escapes unharmed from another narrative of white western middle-class captivity.

* * *

Like in Beigbeder's novel, in McEwan's *Saturday*, we can see how anxieties about security, exacerbated by the War on Terror, rework and update the motifs of early captivity narratives. The issue of frontier and territorial conquest, central to early captivity accounts, offers the main background to McEwan's novel. This backdrop, however, suffers several displacements in the current political context. Although the novel is set during the antiwar demonstration, one month before troops are about to invade Iraq, it is still London and, symbolically the western metropolis, that is felt to be under threat. Physical danger is never felt to be "outside" but only "inside," and embodied by Perowne's family. We have here, like in most captivity fictions, an external threat invading and endangering the life and values of the "western" household.

Anxieties about security and physical threat are here also tangled up with concerns about gender and sexuality. Perowne embodies an ideal of masculinity which Beigbeder believes to be lost but that McEwan still wants to explore: he is highly rational, healthy, and fit and performs quite literally his role as rescuer within the conventional captivity plot. Both French and English novels convey, thus, nostalgia for solid old-fashioned forms of masculinity. This ideal is, of course, fashioned against anxieties about new patterns of female behavior. If for Beigbeder this is emblematized by female caricatures in the vein of Bridget Jones, in *Saturday*, it is the more complex figure of Daisy Perowne who incorporates these concerns. This embodiment takes place, as we have seen, in the multiple ideological messages (both private and public images) contained within her pregnant body.[25]

Like all captivity narratives, McEwan's novel is also besieged by cultural anxieties. Here, though, questions about ethnic and religious difference which surfaced in Beigbeder's text give place to concerns about social class and marginality. Baxter remains until the end of the novel a crucial social "other" to Perowne, through whom the surgeon's values and lifestyle can be measured and affirmed. The differences of status and possibilities between Perowne and Baxter evoke more than "domestic" problems. They also comment upon the disparities in power between the United States and its international enemies. These issues are, however, never fully examined in the text or resolved in the war/anti-war debate which arises between Perowne and the other characters in the novel. They emerge more powerfully than in language through visual memories. In *Saturday*, visual images also fill in the silences which shape most captivity narratives. Highly politicized and broadcasted photographs erupt in the text, coloring and refiguring what has not been said. This is best emblematized by the way Abu Ghraib pictures are reworked in McEwan's novel. These disquieting images challenge the dichotomies of good/evil, captive/ captor which sustain our culture of surveillance and preemptive action. By excavating the ideological layers of these visual texts, we can, thus, begin to understand why narratives of white western middle-class captivity continue to emerge in both the United States and Europe, circulating with more energy than ever across the Atlantic.

Democratic Vistas: Michael Cunningham and Walt Whitman

In the first part of Chapter 2, I demonstrated how in the aftermath of 9/11 several US writers attempted to depict, memorialize, or "secure" images of New York, often departing from idealized images of its urban history. Chapter 3 revealed how iconic images of New York influenced the work of two European novelists, as these obsessively attempt to depict their own cities after 9/11. In many of these early 9/11 fictions, the actual social and political history of New York is prone to be displaced or simplified in the face of a "foreign" threat. In this chapter, I will examine Michael Cunningham's *Specimen Days*, a book that stands out from the corpus of post-9/11 New York described above, by contesting historical idealizations of New York City.

Cunningham uses the history of New York as a mirror where the United States is forced to recognize itself and to see through its own forged narratives. The book is constituted by three interconnected novellas, which are set, or depart, from New York, in different periods in history. The three main characters—a man, an older woman, and a disabled child—reemerge, rotating places in each tale. Each novella corresponds to a distinct literary genre. The first narrative is a nineteenth-century ghost story set during the industrial revolution; the second is a post-9/11 detective story; the third is a science fiction narrative set 150 years into the future. This recycling of characters, a strategy already used in Cunningham's previous novel, *The Hours*, becomes particularly important here, as it corresponds to Walt Whitman's notion of renewed life or cyclic energy. It is, in fact, Whitman who haunts these three narratives, similarly to the way Virginia Woolf had inhabited *The Hours*. Critics were quick in pointing this out. Early reviewers were not, however, particularly convinced by Cunningham's portrayal of Whitman. Caleb Cain compares

Whitman here with Woolf in Cunningham's previous novel and finds that "although the relationship has the same near-death intensity, the chemistry is different. It isn't clear that Cunningham likes Whitman for one thing" (Cain 2005). Terrence Rafferty writing for the *New York Times* makes a similar point: "I did look and Walt Whitman isn't there in *Specimen Days*, not in the organic, dirt and grass way he believed in. Cunningham, try as he might, can't keep his attention on what's beneath his feet for long enough; he's a stargazer by nature" (Rafferty 2005). For Michiko Kakutani, "[Whitman] never feels like a natural fit for this novel: the poet's optimism and utopian yearnings stand in sharp contrast to Mr. Cunningham's dark view of American life" (Kakutani 2005).

There are good reasons, I will suggest, for this misreading or "misencounter." This rendering of Whitman as the bard of US democratic optimism, often dissociated from the more specific historical facts and political positions which shaped Whitman's career as a journalist, has dominated most critical approaches to the poet and to his role in US literary history. After all, Whitman, the "Poet of Strength and Hope," built much of his literary work around his faith in the democratic ideals, which he believed "America" could embody (Whitman 1984, 67). *Leaves of Grass*, first published in 1855, presented itself as a bold democratic project, both through subject matter and language. The poet aimed to surmount division and rivalry, containing contradictions, and his embrace for diversity was tied up with high national ideals. *Leaves of Grass* was meant as "a New Bible" that would bind a nation (Whitman 1984, 353). Although the Civil War would shake his belief in the Union, his later work continues to be read in the light of his optimism and democratic faith. His essay *Democratic Vistas*, written in 1871, has been considered by many as one of the great US pamphlets. Here, democracy is largely defined as the possibility of personal development for every individual. The "Vistas" in the title of this essay are the prophecy of the "seer," in Emerson's sense of the word, since "Democracy" is, for Whitman, as much a social as a spiritual concept. He believes that "America" holds a weather-like potential to embrace "an infinite number of currents and forces, and contributions, and temperatures, and cross purposes, whose ceaseless play of counterpart upon counterpart brings constant restoration and vitality" (Whitman 2004, 395). This essay envisioned a society unified by a "fervid and tremendous

Idea, melting everything else with resistless heat, and solving all lesser and definite distinctions in vast, indefinite, spiritual, emotional power" (2004, 402). The meanings and workings of Whitman's optimistic vision of history and democracy have been subject to a long and significant debate for some time now.[1] Betsy Erkkila's work, for instance, demonstrates how profound social anxieties concerning with the political struggles of the nineteenth century shape the poems of *Leaves of Grass* despite the poet's effort to erase or resolve them under a mystical belief in regenerative energies (Erkkila 1989). Indeed, as a poet that embraced multitudes and multiplicity, Whitman (and his optimism) necessarily contained contradictions. Whitman's optimism is, however, seen in cruder tones when appropriated for political purposes.

Ed Folsom noted that *Leaves of Grass* has been recently linked to George W. Bush's campaign for the war in Iraq. In January 2003, the First Lady, Laura Bush, sent out invitations to a group of scholars and poets for a White House Symposium on "Poetry and the American Voice" which was to be dedicated to an examination of Walt Whitman, Emily Dickinson, and Langston Hughes (Folsom 2005). This symposium, which aimed to explore the US voice in the work of these three authors, at this crucial historical moment, had to be later canceled due to the campaign organized by the antiwar protester and writer Sam Hamill.[2] Folsom also showed that this reading of Whitman was symptomatic of a larger interest in the poet by neoconservatives. In May 2003, at a time when Bush was famously announcing his end to combat operations in Iraq under the "Mission Accomplished" banner, David Brooks, a columnist for the *Atlantic Monthly*, published an article called "What Whitman Knew." Brooks quoted directly "Democratic Vistas," which he considers to be the "nation's most brilliant political sermon because it embodies the exuberant energy of American society—the energy that can make other peoples so nervous" (Brooks 2003). He goes on to show how Whitman not only had a unique sense of the US historical mission but also recognized the difficulty of that mission. Quoting directly from Whitman, Brooks discloses the bard's patriotic pride in its glorification of US exceptionalism: "It seems as if the Almighty had spread before this nation charts of imperial destinies, dazzling as the sun, yet with many a deep intestine difficulty, and human aggregate of cankerous imperfection

[...]." For Brooks Whitman's texts evoke the doctrine of Manifest Destiny that underlies American foreign policy:

> No one since Whitman has captured quite so well the motivating hopefulness that propels American policy and makes the nation a great and restless force in the world. No other essay communicates quite so well what it is like to live constantly in the shadow of the future, trusting that tomorrow's world will be better and will redeem the incompleteness of the present. Whitman's essay, with its nuanced understanding of the American national character, stands today as a powerful rebuttal to, for example, the parades of European anti-Americans. What these groups despise is a cliché—a flat and simpleminded image of American power. They do not see, as Whitman did, that despite its many imperfections, America is a force for democracy and progress. "Far, far indeed, stretch, in distance, our Vistas!" Whitman wrote. "How much is still to be disentangled, freed!" (Brooks 2003)

Several other authors, including novelists, have referred to Whitman in the post-9/11 period. Like we have seen in Chapter 3, Frédérick Beigbeder includes "Salut of Monde" as a token of patriotic American pride. Similarly, Joseph O'Neill's epigraph from *Leaves of Grass* (which reads "I DREAM'D in a dream, I saw a city invincible to the attacks of the whole of the rest of the earth/I dream'd that was the new City of Friends") also translates a generalized feeling that Whitman may help us think about the US current situation. The ways in which that reflective contribution can be achieved is left uncommented and unspecified in these novels. In Brooks's article, however, Whitman's contribution to our understanding of the political situation is clear: the poet's patriotic impulse is seen as validation for the invasion of Iraq.

I will suggest, following Jacqueline Rose's review of *Specimen Days*, that it is precisely this reading of Whitman that Cunningham counters in this novel (Rose 2005). To be sure, Cunningham does not engage directly in the debate about the political meanings of Whitman's text, nor does he address neoconservative appropriations of the bard. However, by calling his novel *Specimen Days*, Cunningham rejects facile interpretations of the poet's patriotism and offers to read Whitman in a very different light. Cunningham entitles his own novel *Specimen Days* after Whitman's *Specimen Days & Collect*, published in 1882.[3] Whitman's book gathered, among other biographical elements, the poet's account of his experience as a nurse working in military hospitals during the Civil War, taking us back to a time when his visions of the United States were far from proud and optimistic. Indeed, this is how Cunningham explains why he "decided to put Whitman into [his] novel" (Cunningham 2005b, 15):

> [H]e [Whitman] and America lived through the Civil War, when the American Dream fuelled by the labour of slaves, began visibly to tarnish. Whitman went south to nurse and comfort the wounded, and in the editions he published after the war we can see his vision beginning to take on shadows, as the nation itself began to realize that it might not, and might never have been, possible for all its citizens to live freely and equally, in peace, each according to his or her beliefs and needs. (2005b, 14)

Cunningham invites us to travel with Whitman to a wounded and frightened nation. In a section from *Specimen Days* significantly called "The Real War Will Never Get in the Books," the poet justifies his book of memoirs in terms of the factual legacy which needs to be passed on to the new generations: "Future years will never know the seething hell and the black infernal background of countless minor scenes and interiors [...] the real war will never get in the books" (Whitman 2004, 555). Whitman reveals, throughout this volume, a loathing for the machinery of war as well as an immense compassion for its real victims:

> Of that many-threaded drama, with its sudden and strange surprises, its confounding of prophecies, its moments of despair, the dread of foreign interference, the interminable campaigns, the bloody battles, the mighty and cumbrous and green armies, the drafts and bounties—the immense money expenditure, like a heavy-pouring constant rain—with, over the whole land, the last three years of the struggle, un unending universal mourning-wail of women, parents, orphans—the marrow of the tragedy concentrated in those Army Hospitals [...] those forming the untold and unwritten story of the war—infinitely greater (like life's) than the few scraps and distortions that are ever told or written. (Whitman 2004, 556)

With *Specimen Days* as his main reference, Cunningham takes us back, through poignantly visual portraits, to a time of internal fracture. In the context of the military and political events which surround Cunningham's book, this image gains further critical resonances. It not only conveys a far from optimistic image of the United States but also presents us with images of internal conflict fracture, at a time in which the ongoing bloodshed in Iraq, which ensued from the US invasion, continued to be described by many in the media as a "'civil' conflict."[4] It is with these ironic juxtapositions in mind that the three novels in Cunningham's book challenge the United States to see through its own sense of danger: "We learned several years ago that New York is under threat," says Cunningham in an interview. "My fear," he explains, "is that the US, in its shock and outrage, will elect to destroy the rest of the world. I wrote the book with that sense and I live with it after having finished the book" (Cunningham 2005c, 4).

Public images and visual politics: Visions of democracy?

Cunningham's Whitman is, thus, not the ecstatically optimistic bard we are accustomed to encounter in literary anthologies. Whitman's desire to embrace everyone and everything in US society forced him to change, contradict, and reinvent himself throughout his work. In his book, Cunningham plays with these contradictions and their role in the projection of the bard's public image. Whitman's desire to reach his audience is almost painfully physical. Indeed, Whitman built his image as a poet, quite literally, opening his arms to all his readers: "Camerado, this is no book,/Who touches this touches a man [...] It is I you hold and who holds you,/I spring from the pages into your arms" (Whitman 2004, 235). Whitman, however, sprang from the pages of *Leaves of Grass* not only through the power of his words but also through the physical presence conveyed by the daguerreotypes which he included in several editions of his work. In fact, as it is well known, the first edition of *Leaves of Grass* does not include the name of the author in its title pages: the only element that identifies Whitman as the writer of the text is a daguerreotype (Figure 4.1).

This daguerreotype appeared in many subsequent editions of *Leaves of Grass*.[5] In the 1881 edition, he positioned it next to "Song of Myself" claiming that the portrait "is involved as part of the poem" (cited in Folsom and Price, 110). Known as "the carpenter," the image presented the poet outdoors (not "sitting" but "standing" for the photographer), in working clothes, as a proud working-class figure. His friend William O'Connor liked the picture,

Figure 4.1 Walt Whitman. July, 1854. Steel engraving by Samuel Hollyer of daguerre-otype by Gabriel Harrison. Bayley/Whitman Collection, Ohio Wesleyan University Libraries.

Whitman said, precisely "because of its portrayal of the proletarian—the carpenter, builder, mason, mechanic" (Traubel 1914, 13). Whitman recalled that when *Leaves of Grass* first came out, the portrait "was much hatchelled by the fellows at the time—war was waged on it: it passed through a great fire of criticism" (cited in Folsom and Price, "Image 003" in *The Walt Whitman*

Archive). Whitman would later disparage this portrait for being "so damned flamboyant—as if I was hurling bolts at somebody—full of mad oaths—saying defiantly, to hell with you!" (cited in Folsom and Price, "Image 003"). Behind the working-class pride the portrait hides not anger, but defiance and perhaps a touch of cursing madness ("mad oaths") which the older more mature poet would not feel the need to endorse. These darker traits of Whitman are explored by Cunningham in his book. However, before examining these issues more closely, it is important to stress how visual texts offered Whitman not only sophisticated means of self-portrayal but also important tools to reflect about social and political landscapes.

Whitman's work was profoundly influenced by nineteenth-century visual culture. As several scholars have pointed out, the revolution in visual culture that Whitman experienced during his lifetime strongly influenced the poet's own approach to writing.[6] In the preface to the first edition of *Leaves of Grass*, Whitman reveals how poetry can be equated with a privileged form of visuality when he presents the poet as "a seer...he is individual...he is complete in himself—the others are as good as he, only he sees it and they do not" (Whitman 2004, 335). He adds, "[w]ho knows the curious mystery of the eyesight? The other senses corroborate themselves, but this is removed from any proof but its own, and foreruns the identities of the spiritual world" (2004, 335). The poet's interest in the technological developments that were revolutionizing nineteenth-century visual culture (his engagement with paintings, exhibitions, museums, and photography) has been usefully related to notions of democracy which were crucial to his work. Charles Zarobila, for instance, has linked Whitman's expansive technique and effort to "view all" (Zarobila 1979). As has been suggested earlier, the daguerreotype, which flourished in the United States of the mid-1850s, became particularly meaningfully useful to Whitman. The daguerreotype was not only a major new contender for the promise of "realism" but also a more democratic means of reproduction because it was significantly less expensive than the painted portrait. For some critics, the daguerreotype also illustrated Whitman's desire to merge with his subjects without erasing their individuality and distinctiveness. For Timothy Stiffel, the fact that the metals and glass used in a daguerreotype made it a much more substantially physical object than today's photographs turned the daguerreotype into an ideal "object of democratic union" (Stiffel 1996).

Whitman's work as a journalist rendered him particularly sensitive to the intricate relation between politics and the visual. Whitman's comments about the lack of competent portraits of President Abraham Lincoln clearly reveal the importance of this connection for the poet (Whitman 2004, 509). In attempts to counter this visual absence, Whitman includes several depictions of the president's daily movements with his cavalry or his occasional appearances in the presence of his wife. The poet discloses in both occasions his fascination with Lincoln's sober posture and "plain black, somewhat rusty and dusty" clothes that makes his look as "ordinary in attire, &c., as the commonest man" (2004, 508). He adds: "None of the artists or pictures has caught the deep, thought, subtle and indirect expression of this man's face. There is something else there." This idea is reiterated in different passages of *Specimen Days*.[7] Indeed, in his lecture "The Death of Lincoln," Whitman conveys the president's assassination as culmination of historical episodes which reach its apex pictographically: "[A] long and varied series of contradictory events arrives at last at its highest poetic, single, central, pictorial denouement" (Whitman 2007, 508). History, poetry, and visuality are weaved together in the performance of a national drama. The president's assassination evokes anxieties about the future of democracy which are carefully reworked into a highly visual "tableau" (2007, 508). Indeed, as Erkkila suggests, the anesthetization of Whitman's death makes the "meaningless seem necessary and natural as the fact of Lincoln's assassination is refashioned into a myth of national regeneration" (1989, 239). Anesthesia is thus visually induced in crucial sections of Whitman's work. This perceptive approach to the optics of history is carefully explored in the first novella of Cunningham's triptych, as we will see next.

Whitman's other images: Violent machinery

"In the Machine," set during the Industrial Revolution, presents us with a portrayal of New York poles apart from the buoyant visions of the city that we usually associate with Whitman. The first image we are offered is of a funeral: Simon, Lucas's brother, has been one of many victims of mechanical accidents. He has died, leaving his family in abject poverty. From the first pages of the story, we can see that New York is here miles away from usual readings of Whitman's "Mannahatta," his homage to the city in *Leaves of Grass*, where he traces back the aboriginal name to convey the vibrancy and organic amalgamation of forces, people, and energies he finds in the city. Yet, Cunningham offers us here a darker reading of Whitman's city. This is a landscape shaped by death, poverty, and exploitation, a picture best understood in the light of Whitman's comments on the consequences of industrial and commercial capitalism. Indeed, after the war, Whitman reacted with unease to the "immense problem of the relation, adjustment, conflict, between Labor and its status and pay, on the one side, and the Capital of employers on the other side" (Whitman 2007, 753). As the poet explains in one of the appendices to "Democratic Vistas":

> [T]he many thousands of decent working-people, through the cities and elsewhere, trying to keep a good appearance, but living by daily toil, from hand to mouth, with nothing ahead, and no owned homes—the increasing aggregation of capital in the hands of the few ... the advent of new machinery, dispensing more and more with hand-work. (2007, 753)

Twelve-year-old Lucas guides the reader through the dark narrative. After the death of his brother, he needs to feed his ailing parents. Lucas is himself noticeably disabled; he is afflicted by a congenital disorder that has left him "with a walleye and a pumpkin head and a habit of speaking in fits" (Cunningham 2005a, 4). Desperately needing a job, he takes his brother's place at "the works" (2005a, 11). He finds comfort in reading *Leaves of Grass*, his guiding book. Such guidance makes him constantly blurt out verses from Whitman's poetry as if he could not somehow keep the poet's knowledge only to himself. The only other company he has, after the death of his brother, is Simon's fiancée, Catherine.

At work, Lucas experiences the violence of the machine age first hand: he has a hazardous job feeding metal housings into a stamping machine. Seeing his colleagues working under similarly hostile conditions—next to him works a man who lost his fingers working at a windmill—he starts to believe that all machines are haunted. Whitman's concept of cyclical existence gains dark overtones here. In fact, Lucas begins to worry that his brother's ghost may be haunting all the machines around. He fears, most of all, that Simon's ghost might be trying to reach Catherine by haunting sewing machines in the factory where she works. Disoriented, Lucas walks around Manhattan trying to find a way to prevent Catherine from going to work. At this point, Whitman appears to Lucas in the middle of Broadway. Whitman is wearing a "broad brimmed hat," and the first thing that Lucas notices about the poet is his working-class boots: "a pair of boots that seemed familiar, though he had never seen them before. They were workingman's boots, dun-coloured, stoutly laced" (Cunningham 2005a, 66). His face is both bright and defiant:

> Here was his grey-white cascade of beard, here is broad-brimmed hat and the kerchief knotted at his neck. He was utterly like his like-ness. He smiled bemusedly at Lucas. His face was like brown paper that had been crushed and smoothed again. His eyes were bright as silver nails. (66)

Whitman tells him to go north. Walking up to Central Park, he feels the grass and watches the stars. There, he finds reasons not to fear death: "This was his heaven … It was grass and silence; it was a field of stars. It was what the book told him, night after night. When he died he would leave his defective body and turn into grass" (Cunningham 2005a, 72). Indeed, Whitman's visionary influence is literally embodied by Lucas. He saves Catherine by sacrificing himself, turning his defective body into something else: when he violently crushes his hand at the works, Catherine is forced to take him to hospital, where his hand will need to be amputated. Yet, as they realize later, Lucas's loss becomes Catherine's salvation. The great Mannahatta factory, where Catherine would have been working had she not been forced to accompany Lucas to hospital, was now on fire. Lucas and Catherine look up to see the other seamstresses jumping from the windows:

> The woman stood in the window, holding to its frame. Her blue skirt billowed. The square of brilliant orange made of her a blue silhouette, fragile and precise. She was like a goddess of the fire, come to her platform to tell those gathered below what the fire meant, what it wanted of them. From so far away, her face was indistinct. She turned her head to look back into the room, as if someone had called to her. She was radiant and terrifying. She listened to something the fire told her […] She jumped. (Cunningham 2005a, 89)

Reminiscences of September 11, 2001, are obvious and immediate. This is, however, a trick employed by Cunningham cunningly. The text is, in fact, evoking the Triangle Shirtwaist Factory Fire, where on the March 25, 1911, 146 garment workers died from the fire or jumped to their death. The seamstresses working there, mainly young immigrant women, found the exits blocked and leapt from windows higher than any fire engine ladders could reach. To encourage the seamstresses to stay at their machines and to inhibit stealing, company management routinely locked the exit doors. These women worked 9–10 hours per day under these strained conditions (Stein 1962).

Figure 4.2 The Asch building. March 1911. The Triangle Shirtwaist Company was situated in the third story from the top. From the Kheel Center for Labor-Management Documentation & Archives.

Figure 4.3 Triangle fire victims. March 1911. The Triangle Shirtwaist Company was situated in the third story from the top. From the Kheel Center for Labor-Management Documentation & Archives.

Cunningham calls the factory "Mannahatta," reinforcing the fractured optimism of Whitman's celebrated poem. By giving this industrial unit the name of this important poem of *Leaves of Grass*, Cunningham reveals the other side of Whitman's fantasy of inclusion and democracy. If this name also worked, as Wyn Thomas argues, as a celebratory guarantee of the naturalness of the life of the modern city (1982, 365), Cunningham stresses the darker side of Whitman's city "of hurried and sparkling waters" (Whitman 2004, 229). Mannahatta is here the "city of spires and masts" but viciously so (2004, 229). The tragedy represented by the Triangle Waist Factory Fire is a fracture in this optimistic organic view of the city, revealing that the same violence—both social and economical—which since the colonial times had excluded Indians from New York continued, through other means, to inhabit that very space. Oppression and exclusion underwrite the history of New York, the symbolic locus of US energy, creativity, and diversity. For Cunningham, terrorism does need not fly in a hijacked plane into US territory. It is already here in various guises—through social inequalities, economic policies, work conditions, racism, and migration laws. For Cunningham, the threats grow within. By evoking this uncomfortable but sharp juxtaposition of images, Cunningham resists easy idealizations of the city and presents us the history of New York under a very different concept of terror.

Thrills and crusades: Visions of the present

The idea of inner terror is developed in the subsequent narratives of Cunningham's triptych. The "Children's Crusade," the second novella, set in post-9/11 New York, follows the perspective of Cat, a forensic psychologist who works for "deterrence units" receiving phone calls from potential bombers in the uneasy climate which followed the 9/11 attacks. Among the growing number of threats which she receives daily, Cat is particularly taken aback by a series of phone calls from children who claim to be part of a terrorist organization. To her, they announce a mission they have already started to put into practice: they go around New York, detonating their bombs randomly and killing themselves and any passerby they may encounter. These children are orphans who have been taken care of by an old woman who calls herself Walt Whitman:

> The woman was sixty or so, sitting straight as a hat rack in the grungy precinct chair. Her white hair—arctic white, incandescent white—was pulled into a fist at the back of her long pale neck [...] Her eyes were milky blue, oddly blue, albino-ish and unfocused. If Cat didn't know better, she'd have thought the woman was blind. (2005a, 168–169)

The woman is, however, far from blind. Like Whitman, she is aware of the power of images. Bombs, like suicides, are striking messages, useful symbols of a crusade. Like Whitman, the old woman is a "seer." Whitman's prophetic role is here inflated and inflamed: the woman's figure "white hair—arctic white, incandescent white" and "milky blue, oddly blue, albino-ish and unfocused" suggest untamed visions, knowledge difficult to control. Whitman, the spiritual prophet, literally embodied such visions.

Richard Maurice Bucke, one of Whitman's friends, saw in the following picture (Figure 4.4) a "Christ likeness" and signs of the poet's illumination,

Figure 4.4 Walt Whitman, 1853 or 1854. Daguerreotype probably by Gabriel Harrison. New York Public Library.

the "moment this carpenter too became seer" (cited in Folsom and Genoways 2005). The spiritual overtones of Whitman's work are obvious, but his highly personal approach to religion has been seen as essentially inclusive, regenerative, and benign. Cunningham, however, forces us to engage with a more radical and uncomfortable reading of the spirituality of *Leaves of Grass*. He does so to raise the question of religion in contemporary political discourse.

The image of child bombers has been associated in the western media with Islamic brainwashing of vulnerable youngsters: the involvement of children in Palestinian actions, and more recently, the participation of young men in the 7/7 London bombings has often been commented upon and condemned internationally. However, the very title of Cunningham's novella forces us to reconsider such associations: the Children's Crusade is the name given to a largely apocryphal historical account of events related with the Christian Crusades who purportedly took place around 1212 (Russell 1989).

According to one of the variations of this legend, a boy claimed to have been visited by Jesus began preaching in central Europe; his mission was to lead a crusade to peacefully convert Muslims to Christianity, and through a series of supposed portents and miracles, he acquired a huge number of followers, including many thousands of children. If the novella's title already brings the image of the child crusader closer to home, the development of the narrative does the rest. The children in Cunningham's text do not fight for religious purposes, and they have no national cause nor do they attempt to harm another state. On the contrary, their crusade is against the state of their own nation. As the crazy old woman, named after Whitman, attempts to explain:

> "Look around," she said. "Do you see any happiness? Do you see any joy? Americans have never been this prosperous, people have never been this safe. They've never lived so long, in such good health, ever, in the whole of history. [...] And look at us. We are so obese we need bigger cemetery plots. Our ten-year-olds are doing heroin, or they're murdering eight-year-olds, or both. We're getting divorced faster than we're getting married. Everything we eat has to be sealed because if it wasn't, somebody would put poison in it [...] A tenth of us are in jail, and we can't build the new ones fast enough. We're bombing other countries simply because they make us nervous [...] Would you say this is working out? Does this seem to you like a story that wants to continue?" (Cunningham 2005a, 171)

Despite her hallucinated rambling, the old woman's picture of the many dissonances and asymmetries which haunt the United States is unnervingly poignant. As Jacqueline Rose points out in one of the most perceptive early reviews of Cunningham's book, "America is living in a state of violent perplexity. The message is clear. [...] America is in greatest danger from itself" (Rose 2005). The narrative of homegrown radicalization in Cunningham's novella implicitly calls into question the conventional portrayal of the War on Terror, forcing the United States (and Europe for that matter) to see the terrorists threatening their cities not as religious fanatics but insurgents against a "way of life." Uncomfortably enough, Cunningham forces us, readers, to recognize that terrorists can grow not only in our homeland but in ourselves.

This identification is forced upon the reader as the connection between Cat and one of the child bombers becomes stronger. The boy reminds her of her dead son. As in a typical noir narrative, Cat decides to help the young suicide bomber escape, by taking care of him. Yet, she continues to be fearful for her life, worried that he might kill her. The narrative finishes with their escape from New York, in an unsettling closure:

> She might still want to be his mother even if it proved fatal. And he might not, after all, be waiting to do it with a bread knife or a pillow as she slept; he might be waiting to do it gradually, as children had been doing since time began. In a sense he had killed her already hadn't he? He had ended her life and taken her into this new one, this crazy rebirth, hurtling forward on a train into the vast confusion of the world, its simultaneous and never-ending collapse and regeneration, its rock-hard little promises, its owners and workers, its sanctuaries that never endured, that never were meant to endure.
> *To die is different from what one supposes, and luckier.*
> The child kept smiling his murderous smile.
> Cat smiled back. (Cunningham 2005a, 196)

The ever-present presence of death is, in fact, at the center of this novella. By stressing this morbid element, Cunningham evokes the paradoxical presence of mortality in certain sections of *Leaves of Grass*. In the final lines of "This Compost," for instance, a poem that is usually associated to Whitman's vision of nature and organic renewal, it is difficult not to find in his depiction of "the Earth" the shadow of a battle ground:

> Now I am terrified at the Earth! it is that calm and patient,
> It grows such sweet things out of such corruptions,
> It turns harmless and stainless on its axis, with such endless successions of diseas'd corpses,
> It distils such exquisite winds out of such infused fetor,
> It renews with such unwitting looks its prodigal, annual, sumptuous crops,
> It gives such divine materials to men, and accepts such leavings from them at last.
>
> > (Whitman 2004, 130–131)

Written at a time of national crisis, the poem seems to be visited by memories of the Civil War and could be easily read as one of Whitman's many attempts to associate death with democratic renewal. Betsy Erkkila suggests that though in this poem the poet "counters the spectre of personal and national dissolution in the corpse of the land with a vision of the regenerative force of nature" (1989, 140). Both delicious and terrifying, death carries a double meaning that can be felt in several other poems by Whitman. It is this composite presence of mortality, both seductive and terrifying, that is explored in Cunningham's novella, "The Children's Crusade." What is particularly striking here is that death is no longer associated with democratic struggle. It is precisely the opposite of that. The spectacle of death presented by the young bombers is carried as a sign of the betrayal of the United State's democratic potential. To an extent, the bomber's appropriation of Whitman can also be read as an elegiac song about the United States with a demand for its regeneration. The rupture of the social texture associated in Whitman's poem with the Civil War reveals now other forms of fracture. The child bombers break down the façade of internal homogeneity and union, used as a rhetorical flag by the Bush administration in the aftermath of 9/11. "Us vs. Them," the populist political slogan repeated persistently at the time, can be read here as a nationally fomented juxtaposition, whose symbolic weight the child bombers only externalize, revealing themselves as explosive products of a landscape already broken by social injustices and disparities.

Old Testament, new world, same exodus

It is precisely from a fractured and broken nation that the final novella of *Specimen Days*, "Like Beauty," departs. If the final image of "The Children's Crusade," finished with the image of an espcape (where mother and child are bound by their new life together), the last novella further develops the idea of departure, now depicted as an epic exodus. The novella follows Simon, a simulo, and Catareen, an exploited alien, in their escape from New York. As a simulo, Simon is (not unlike his homonym character in the first story) trapped in a machine. Like the characters of Philip K. Dick's novel, *Do Androids Dream of Electric Sheep?*, he looks, feels, and behaves like a human being but is merely a replica, an android. To have his anger impulses reduced, he has been programmed with poetry chips which make him cite Whitman's poetry. As he attempts to escape New York's police, he finds an accomplice in Catareen, an orange-eyed creature from the planet Nadia, who not unlike many Mexican migrants has been given the task of baby-sitting the privileged (human beings in this case). The novella follows them as they travel across a broken-down, poisoned, increasingly deserted and divided version of the United States, a country visibly undemocratic, the very opposite of Whitman's democratic ideal.

If certain sci-fi elements may seem outlandish, the landscape is still acutely familiar. One hundred and fifty years into the future, New York has been turned into a tawdry theme park where simulos, such as Simon, work by giving tourists performances of old time mugging and rapping—a picture of what the city used to be like. Everything has changed but all has remained the same. New York of the future is not an emblem of diversity, freedom, and democracy, but of difference, exploitation, and inequality. Citizens are exploited and divided into casts, and in this climate of self-imposed terror, some more than others are heavily controlled and monitored. "Why exactly do you think we *shouldn't* be nervous all the time?" Marcus, another simulo, asks Simon, acknowledging their precarious status (211). Surveillance is part of the natural landscape of the city. "Drones" are used to monitor awkward behavior:

> They had modified the [drone's] design last year, made them less sinister in response to tourist complaints. The drones were no longer spinning black balls studded with red sensor lights. They had gilded them, elongated them, equipped them with functioning golden wings. Now they were little surveillance birds. They were golden pigeons that sniffed out crime. (213)

As they head to Denver, a city beloved by Walt Whitman, they find the country had been torn apart by religious groups (mainly Christian sects) and is now feudally governed. They pick up Luke, a damaged and disabled child on the run, who had been captured by one of the sects. The United States resembles uncannily the chaos in Iraq which ensued from the US military intervention.

When they finally reach Denver, they manage to find Simon's maker: Emory Lowell, a seventy-year-old scientific engineer. He is described as a "black man," and yet, he is the physical embodiment of the good gray poet: "He must have been seventy. A cascade of smoke-colored beard spilled over his chest. He wore a battered, broad-brimmed hat pulled down to his shaggy gray brows" (274). Emory is a prophet of the exodus: he aims to take his family to another world, Paumanok. He is building a spaceship for that purpose. As we have seen

Figure 4.5 Whitman, 1862. Probably New York. Photographed by Alexander Gardner or Mathew Brady. Library of Congress.

in the previous story, it was important for Whitman to be seen as a prophetic light. Whitman, himself, found visual reflections of this role in his portraits of the time.

Whitman described himself in the above picture, as having "a sort of Moses in the burning bush look" (Traubel 1906, 330). He added, "Somebody used to say I sometimes wore the face of a man who was sorry for the world. Is this my sorry face? I am not sorry—I am glad—for the world" (Traubel 1906, 335). In the Old Testament, the vision of the burning bush gave Moses the epiphany that made him lead the Israelites out of Egypt and into Canaan. Paumanok is Whitman's new world in *Leaves of Grass*. It is therefore appropriate that Cunningham should create a narrative of exodus with the same ambiguity, a novella that leaves us both "sorry" and "glad" for the world.

The novella wavers thus between dystopia and utopia, rejecting a unified reading of the future. As a narrative of exodus, "Like Beauty" presents us with possible ways of thinking about the future of the United States, but it also reflects back on its original narratives. Lowell is going to depart to Paumanok with a crew made up of people and Nadians. This odd-looking and boldly mixed group seems at first "crazy" to Simon, but as he soon realizes "the passengers on the Mayflower had probably been like this too, zealots and oddballs and ne' er-do-wells, setting out to colonise a new world because the known world wasn't much interested in their furtive and quirky passions" (Cunningham, 293). At one level, there is in the voyage planned by Lowell and his "multicultural" crew a desire for freedom and equality that seems no longer possible in this religiously and socially oppressive vision of the United States. In that sense, their trip could have been seen as progressive. However, Cunningham's use of the term "colonize" in the above comparisons seems to extend beyond a commentary about the United States' past and enter the terrain of the future, complicating the reading of this novella. One could, uncomfortably, read the expansionism of these new colonials in light of the search for new worlds which the recent war in Iraq also embodied for the United States. Indeed, Whitman's work, and in particular his expansionist technique, has not been completely dissociated from issues of national supremacy, having recently been examined in terms of its imperial resonances.[8] Colonization, empire, freedom, and identity also become, here, unnervingly entangled in Cunningham's image of a futuristic Mayflower. For that reason, the narrative makes a crucial detour: instead of allowing the readers to embark and discover the alternative future represented by Paumanok, it leaves them behind with Simon, who decides not to get on the ship. The final image of the novella shows us Simon, crossing the Rockies on his horse. The western mythology is, again, turned upside down with the final citation from Whitman—the line which closes the book: "The earth, that is sufficient, I do not want the constellations any nearer. I know they are well where they are, I know they suffice to those who belong to them" (305). The book ends with a rejection of expansionist enterprises. This is a vital rereading of Whitman and a pressing retort to recent political appropriations of the poet.

Cosmopolitan Attempts:
Joseph O'Neill and Mohsin Hamid

The narrators of *Netherland,* by Joseph O'Neill, and *The Reluctant Fundamentalist,* by Mohsin Hamid, are two foreigners living in the United States when the 9/11 attacks take place. These two novels are only partially set in New York: the narratives depart from New York, hoping to attain a wider picture of the world. The themes of traveling and migration play an important role in these texts, as both narrators attempt to come to terms with current political events by embracing—though not always successfully—a global perspective.

Both novels, it must be noted, received a great deal of attention. *Netherland* was widely acclaimed in the United States, where it received a PEN/Faulkner Award, and in the United Kingdom it was long-listed for the Man Booker Prize. Mohsin Hamid's book also won great attention in the United Kingdom, where the novella was shortlisted for the 2007 Booker Prize[1] and won two awards—the Anisfield-Wolf Book Award and the South Bank Show Annual Award for Literature. Although the backgrounds of O'Neill and Hamid (Irish and Pakistani origin, respectively) may appear far removed from each other, their career and writing paths disclose, in fact, a very similar sort of transnational path. O'Neill, of half-Irish and half-Turkish ancestry, grew up in the Netherlands, studied law at Cambridge in the United Kingdom, and became a barrister in England, where he practiced for ten years, mainly in the field of business law. He now lives in the United States. Hamid was born in Pakistan and had studied in the United States—first Literature at Princeton and then has attended Harvard Law School. Before moving to the United Kingdom in 2001, Hamid had worked for several years as a management consultant in New York City; in 2009 he has returned to Lahore and is said to have divided his time between Pakistan, the United States and Europe (White 2014). Both authors have studied law in highly prestigious universities, and their professional careers led them to engage directly with the world of business via business law (O'Neill) and business consultancy (Hamid). Shaped by a privileged type of mobility, the Euro-American cosmopolitanism of the business class, the backgrounds of both authors compel them to reflect on the place of "America" in the world after the wars in Afghanistan and Iraq. Their novels examine the relationship between private and public "businesses" and their international configurations during the War on Terror.

Joseph O'Neill's *Netherland*

As soon as it was published, O'Neill's *Netherland* received a number of suggestive, though slightly contradictory, labels. For some, the novel carried the ambition of "a great American novel... but one with an ordinary European Everyman at its centre" (O'Hagan 2008). Others felt that both the author's mixed background and the novel's transnational themes suggested instead the hopes of a "Great-American-Irish novel" (Bacon 2008). Still, few others were more interested to the depiction of colonial experience in the novel: for instance, the critic James Wood, presented it as "one of the most remarkable postcolonial books" (Wood 2008). Public interest was further boosted when President Barack Obama announced that he was reading this "excellent novel" (Webb 2009). Directly engaged with US mythologies of success, namely the notion of the American Dream, *Netherland* can be said to be a fitting read for a president who, for better or for worse, attempted to reclaim the traditional rhetoric associated with that national ethos and was himself the author of a book entitled *The Audacity of Hope: Thoughts on Reclaiming the American Dream* (Obama 2006). However different in terms of political significance, both the election of President Obama and O'Neill's book addressed concerns regarding multiculturalism and the place of the United States in the world.

Like many other post-9/11 novels (by writers such as Beigbeder, McEwan, Safran Foer, McInerney, and DeLillo), *Netherland* focuses on the white, western, middle-class family from the point of view of an anxious male protagonist. In O'Neill's novel, however, anxiety is deliberately let loose, verging on depression. Following the 9/11 attacks, the narrator, Hans van den Broek, a Dutch equity analyst, decides that he and his family should leave their flat in Tribeca, lower Manhattan, to live further uptown in the Chelsea Hotel. Despite his efforts, his marriage slowly disintegrates. His wife, an English woman named Rachel, decides to return to London with their son, as she becomes more and more uncomfortable in New York. The announcement of the war in Iraq transforms Rachel's unease into an active repudiation for the United States, a country which she considers "ideological[ly] diseased" (O'Neill 2009, 92). Hans, however, is left in a state of emotional numbness.

Hans's apathy becomes particularly striking when he is confronted with current political and historical events. His indifference contrasts with what he sees around him: "For those under the age of forty-five it seemed that the world events had finally contrived a meaningful test of their capacity for conscientious political thought" (96). Hans is clearly disengaged from such issues; his narrative culminates with this blunt confession:

> I lacked necessary powers of perception and certainty and, above all, foresight. The future retained the impenetrable character I had always attributed to it. Would American security be improved or worsened by taking over Iraq? I did not know, because I had no information about the future purposes and capacities of terrorists or, for that matter, American administrations [...] Did I know if the death and pain caused by a war in Iraq would or would not exceed the miseries that might likely flow from leaving Saddam Hussein in power? No. Could I say whether the right to autonomy of the Iraqi people—a problematic national entity, by all accounts—would be enhanced or diminished by an American regime change? I could not. Did Iraq have weapons of mass destruction that posed a real threat? I had no idea; and to be truthful, and to touch on my real difficulty, I had little interest. I didn't really care. (O'Neill 2009, 96–97)

Hans's aestheticized disengagement, otherwise viewed with sympathy by reviewers, is slated by Zadie Smith who notes that in *Netherland*, "the nineteenth-century flaneur's ennui has been transplanted to the twenty-first-century bourgeois's political apathy—and made beautiful" (Smith 2008, 55). Hans's apathy is, in this sense, usefully indicative of a wider social dilemma, conveying how the sense of traumatic unease—brought up in this case by the events of 9/11—can impact upon one's ability to think critically. For Hans, the collapse of the towers represents the end of a world view—both private and public. The narrator finds it increasingly difficult to deal not only with current political events but also with historical events. Indeed, Hans, who is fittingly described by a reviewer as "a latter-day 'Dutch sailor' washed up on the ragged shores of lower Manhattan" (Corrigan 2008), tends to embellish the account of his time in New York by drawing on previous transatlantic crossings. If the multiple references to the Dutch's early presence in New York at first stimulate Hans, allowing for connections between past and present events, the weight of history becomes less and less comfortable as his narrative progresses. The role of the Dutch in the early history of the United States emerges as a romanticized version of Euro-American colonial encounters. This is conveyed, for instance, when Hans is describing the contents of a booklet he received from Chuck entitled *Dutch Nursery Rhymes in Colonial Times*:

> There was a song in Dutch about Molly Grietje, Santa Claus's wife, who made New Year *koekjes*, and a song about Fort Orange, as Albany was first known. There was a poem (in English) titled "The Christmas Race, a True Incident of Rensselaerwyck." Rensselaerwyck was, I surmised, precisely the district through which my train was now traveling [...] It commemorated a horse race under "The Christmas moon" at Wolvenhoeck, the corner of the wolves [...] "Down to the riverbank, Mijnheer, his guests, and all the slaves/ went trooping, while a war whoop came from all the Indian braves.../The slaves with their whale lanterns were passing to and fro,/Casting fantastic shadows on hills of ice and snow." (58)

The presence of the Dutch in New York is, thus, idealized and presented in soothing rhymes, where the fights against the Indians and the role played by slavery in the colonial enterprise are presented as romantic details within the larger frame of the Christmassy postcard. These images work, above all, to surrender Hans to a sense of "nostos," allowing him a nostalgic return to his roots by remembering his own childhood and reimagining his own relationship with his estranged son. This romantic vision of Netherlands' role in US colonial history is, however, evoked in other parts of the narrative, for example in the depiction of old Brooklyn as a "Dutch farmland." His ancestors, Hans is told, "cleared dense hickory and oak forests, and repelled the Canarsie and Rockaway Indians, and developed the pasturelands of Vlackebos and Midwout and Amersfoort" (149). However, the more information Hans accumulates about his ancestors, the harder it becomes for him to know how to react to these accounts of the past and to position himself in history. Facing the graves of Brooklyn's original settlers, he admits: "I had no idea what to feel or what to think, no idea, in short, of what I might do to discharge the obligation of remembrance that fixed itself to one in this anomalous place, which offered so little shade from the incomprehensible rays of the past" (149). Hans is unable to confront the past. For Hans, private and public histories are burdensome realities that complicate his own view of the world. Instead of granting him with a position and perspective, the past threatens to displace Hans further, reinforcing his sense of disorientation and personal ennui.

Ramkissoon, Gatsby, and other drowned creatures

It is Hans's apathy that attracts him to Chuck Ramkissoon, a charismatic Trinidadian immigrant living in New York whom he meets in his cricket club. Feeling adrift, after the separation from his wife, Hans is seduced by the optimism and sense of purpose of this self-made entrepreneur. As most reviewers were quick to point out, Chuck is an inescapable reference to Jay Gatsby in Fitzgerald's canonical novel (Corrigan 2008; Kakutani 2008; Orlebeke 2010). He holds on to the promises of the American dream, simply and unself-consciously. An eclectic entrepreneur whose motto is "think fantastic," he is involved in a number of unlawful moneymaking schemes, but his buoyancy fascinates Hans. He is also a lover of cricket; for him the sport is a green field where the promises of the American Dream are bound to flourish. Chuck wants to create a New York Cricket Club. By building the first New York cricket stadium, he believes he can lay down a new ethical ground: "Cricket is instructive, Hans. It has a moral angle. I really believe this. Everybody who plays the game benefits from it. So I say, why not the Americans?" (2009, 204). The game represents, for Chuck, the ideal of a successful multicultural society: "I say, we want to have something in common with the Hindus and Muslims? Chuck Ramkissoon is going to make it happen. With the New York Cricket Club, we could start a whole new chapter in U.S. history. Why Not?" (2009, 204). The energy of this other "green light" infuses Hans's empty soul. Indeed, Chuck's tales—his Trinidadian narratives—interrupt momentarily and refreshingly Hans's transatlantic domestic drama and Euro-American narration (populated by conflicting references to European expansion and colonial history of the United States). Chuck's social discourse on cricket may remind some of us of C.L.R. James's theories on the reappropriation of the Victorian sport (see Malik 2001). For James, cricket could be more than a symbol of imperialism: the game could be rescued and appropriated by colonial people as a performance of anti-imperialist consciousness and patriotism. Yet, Chuck is not an anti-imperial activist, the same way that Gatsby is no socialist. As an emigrant in the United States, Chuck places upon himself the "responsibility to play the game right" (13). He does so by reinventing his social status: feeling as noble in white as Gatsby felt wearing his glamorous colored shirts. At a superficial level, Chuck embodies for Hans the fantasy of a joyful multicultural society at a time of a clash of civilizations. Chuck only makes explicit the need for inclusion experienced by Hans himself when he describes playing cricket as part of a truly multicultural team. This fantasy is central to the novel and evoked in the epigraph to the main narrative, a stanza from Whitman's *Leaves of Grass*:

> I dream'd in a dream, I saw a city invincible to
> the attacks of the whole of the rest of the earth;
> I dream'd that was the new City of Friends.[2]

The dream of a city "invincible to the attacks of the whole of the rest of the earth" gains specific connotations in light of the climate of anxiety that shapes this novel. Whitman, the poet of plurality and democracy, is, once again, evoked in the context of a 9/11 novel to articulate a desire for "a city of friends." The dream of peaceful but plural communality, which opens the novel, is problematized and contested as the narrative develops. This is aggravated by Hans's inability to come to terms with the real history of the United States. This negation is conveyed, for instance, in the way Chuck's character is presented. If examined carefully, Chuck's bright entrance into the novel seems to suggest, from the outset, signs of a potential demise.

Chuck's narrative is, at first, weaved with Trinidadian motifs and colors that interrupt Hans's solitary and mournful narration. The atmosphere of the "raucous" Caribbean boulevard where Chuck lives is vividly described, contrasting with Hans's own version of New York: "its 99-Cent stores and discount clothing outlets and solo sellers of cocoa butter and its grocery stores displaying yams and green bananas and plantains and cassava and sweet potatoes, had given way to a neighbourhood unlike any other [he'd] seen in New York" (150). A confluence of architectural styles suggests the possibility of a peaceful multicultural coexistence: we find here a "plantation house with huge neoclassical columns" next to a "Germanic place with dark green window frames"; there is a "sprawling yellow manor" close to a "Japanese-style mansion with upturned eaves and a cherry tree in photogenic blossom" (150). Moreover, the colorful landscape found in Chuck's garden corresponds only too well to exotic portraits that we often find in literary constructions of the colonial West Indies: "Manhattan seemed far away. Lilacs bloomed, a cardinal flashed through the trees, and a serpentine hose lying in Chuck's flower beds dribbled water out of hundreds of holes in its coils. The day itself was perforated by the rattle of a woodpecker" (151).

However, this exotic portrait soon gives way to a darker reality. This reality is symbolized by the creature found in Chuck's garden: "the most enormous and repulsive frog [Hans] had ever seen" (151). The monstrous frog frightens the narrator, suddenly awakening him from his sense of an idyll:

> [Chuck] returning at the moment from the house shouted out happily. He bent down and picked up the monstrous fat torso and the long, uncannily flippered legs; it seemed, in fact, as if he grasped a tiny, rotund frogman. "This is an American bullfrog," Chuck said. "It' ll eat just about anything. Snakes, birds, fish…." I followed him to the plastic fence […] Lodged in the fence, I saw, were the corpses of other neighbourhood frogs that had died trying to migrate into the garden with the water. Chuck dropped the bullfrog where he belonged. (151)

Like Chuck, the American bullfrog is proudly presented as a species capable of "[eat]ing just about anything." The animal is, however, not completely free of movement or choices, and he is ultimately unable to migrate into "the garden" of earthly delights. Instead, it is left where it belongs, alongside the corpses of other animals; their attempted migration frustrated. Like Jay Gatsby, Ramkissoon attempts to jump outside his borders but ends up drowning in the process.

Through the image of the drowned frog, this excerpt takes us back to the very first pages of the novel where we first read about Chuck. It is the news of Chuck's death that triggers the main narrative by means of an analepsis. A newspaper reporter informs Hans that Chuck was the victim of a murder and that his body was found with handcuffs around his wrists in the Gowanus Canal, in the borough of Brooklyn. Chuck's body was, significantly, discovered by an urban diver, a frogman. It lay "in the water by the Home Depot building for over two years, among crabs and car tires and shopping carts" (4). The drowned remains of Chuck's body announce, thus, from the beginning of the novel, a history of violence which can only be understood if we dare to dive into murky waters.

Traumatic images and narratives of mourning

The analepsis, mentioned above, unveils the violence at the core of the narrative. If the novel is apparently shaped by personal trauma, it is collective trauma that underpins its overall structure. Although I have contested the dominance of trauma theory in 9/11 fiction, I believe concept of trauma should be revisited in relation to a number of texts, and it should certainly be reconsidered in relation to this specific novel. The term "trauma," derived from ancient Greek, conveyed a strong physical and organic root, meaning injury or wound, akin to the Greek *titrōskein*, to wound, and *tetrainein*, to pierce. Borrowed from medicine and surgery, the word refers originally to injuries "where the skin is broken as a consequence of external violence, and the effects of such an injury upon the organism as a whole" (Laplanche and Pontalis, 466). By adopting this term, psychoanalysis carried three main ideas from the field of medicine into the psychoanalytic field: the idea of a violent shock, the idea of a wound, and the idea of consequences affecting the organic organization of the individual (466).

These three ideas are at work in a passage of *Netherland* that I have named the "Danielle episode," where history is boldly presented as an open wound. One evening, Hans is approached by a young woman of Anglo-Caribbean extraction at a Manhattan diner. Her name is Danielle. She recalls to Hans that they had briefly met before in England. Even though Hans did not recall that specific episode, he seemed to have made an impression on Danielle, who considered him a "complete gentleman" (109). Following their reencounter, Hans takes Danielle to his room at the Chelsea hotel where they have sex and where, with a rather purposeful tone, Danielle tells Hans she wants him "to be gentleman again" (110). In order for Hans to assume that noble status, this is the performance required of him:

> I took the belt, a length of black leather that was at once familiar and strange, and saw Danielle laying face down on the bed, and began to perform *the act I understood her to need*. Every lash was answered by a small moan. If this gave me some unusual satisfaction, I can't remember it now. I do recall a

tunneller's anxiety as to where and when it would all end, and at that my arm began to tire, and that eventually, as I worked at beating this woman across the back, and the buttocks, and the trembling arms, I looked to the window for some kind of relief [...] I was not shocked by what I saw—a pale white hitting a pale black—but I did of course ask myself what had happened, how it could be that I should find myself living in a hotel in a country where there was no one to remember me, attacking a woman *who'd boomeranged in from a time I could not claim as my own.* (111; italics mine)

Trauma is reclaimed here to its original meaning, assuming physical as well as psychological overtones. Danielle forces Hans to reenact an image, which literally embodies the violence of colonial history. In Danielle's fetishistic fantasy (the image of a "pale white beating a pale black"), Hans is the gentleman (from the Latin *gentīlis*) who can resurrect for her a historical marker of his "superior" cast and her "inferior" race. By forcing Hans to perform an act that "boomeranged from a time that [he] cannot claim [his] own," Danielle selects Hans as an unwitting descendant of a particular episode which had been historically repressed. She awakens, thus, what has been called a "transgenerational phantom," a symptom of devastating trauma which unlocks an unspeakable but consummated desire (Abraham and Torok 1994).

In this sense, Danielle's fetishistic reenactment of racial violence can also be understood in the context of the present time, namely the war in Afghanistan and in Iraq, which haunts the main narrative of *Netherland*. Indeed, the act Hans is forced to perform for Danielle may remind us of the Abu Ghraib images where torture and abuse (physical and sexual) were theatrically reproduced by referring to iconic images of racial oppression. Indeed, as several commentators pointed out, some of the Abu Ghraib photographs evoked the practice of lynching, which survived in the United States till the 1960s. More specifically, Susan Sontag suggested that

if there is something comparable to what [the Abu Ghraib] pictures show, it would be some of the photographs of black victims of lynching taken between the 1880's and 1930's, which show Americans grinning beneath the naked mutilated body of a black man or woman hanging behind them from a tree. The lynching photographs were souvenirs of a collective action whose participants felt perfectly justified in what they had done. So are the pictures from Abu Ghraib. (Sontag 2004)

Figures 5.1 and 5.2 Photographs depicting physical, psychological, and sexual abuse of prisoners held in the Abu Ghraib prison in Iraq. Released in 2006.

Danielle's Jamaican background, like Chuck's Trinidadian roots, is, thus, highly significant in the context of Hans's wavering narrative. Placed at the heart of colonial American history, the Caribbean islands tell a very different version of the early Euro-American encounters from that presented in the romanticized accounts of Dutch-American experience shared by Hans and Chuck. Christopher Columbus came across the island of Trinidad in 1498 and Jamaica in 1499. Jamaica was a Spanish colony until 1655 when the English took over the last Spanish fort. Trinidad and Tobago were also first ruled by Spain until the Dutch, as well as the Courlanders (the inhabitants of modern-day Latvia), established themselves in Tobago in the sixteenth and seventeenth centuries, producing tobacco and cotton. In the eighteenth century, Trinidad became a British crown colony with a French-speaking population and Spanish laws, where colonial rule relied heavily on slavery and indentured labor. This history of violence is, however, left out of the main narrative and erupts, almost accidentally, in the figure of Danielle. Danielle is, in this sense, a double to Chuck's optimistic persona, his uncomfortable "other." Her fetishistic needs convey the violence of colonial history that Chuck, himself, attempts to sublimate by wearing his white cricket shirts and embracing, in his own style, the myths of entrepreneurial success associated with the "American dream." Hans's ability to overcome his melancholia depends upon his capacity to mourn and to come to terms with these transgenerational ghosts. In psychoanalytic terms, Hans has to incorporate the past, in order to deal with the present. Indeed, while Freud was first inclined to believe that successful mourning depended upon the substitution of an object for another, he then goes on to suggest, in later works, that successful mourning depends upon incorporation (Freud 1957; Freud 1961). Chuck is, in this latter sense, someone whose symbolic identity Hans needs to integrate. The story of Chuck, which frames the novel, corresponds, then, to Hans's more or less successful attempt to mourn the end of a worldview by integrating a historical narrative that he had estranged from himself.

Globalization, economy, and worldview

Read in light of some of the early readings of Fitzgerald's novel, Chuck can be seen to follow in Jay Gatsby's footsteps: his tragic death seen as a result of a tarnished or corrupt version of the US dream. However, in the larger political and economical context conveyed by the novel, Chuck and his betting operations are only but a minute expression of the larger system they inadvertently mirror—the financial game or "casino economy" to which Hans is professionally engaged as a financial analyst. Hans understands the workings of the financial world and therefore tends to see corporations as "vulnerable, needy creatures, entitled to their displays of vigour" (19). Instead of being examined as a significant phenomenon in itself—with potential changes to the global economy and the life of millions of citizens around the world—the universe of finance, from which Hans makes his living, is presented here as an illustration of Hans's feelings of private breakdown. Hans acknowledges that he is "liable to misplace his sensitivities" (19) and reduces the vulnerability of the financial economy by projecting into it signs of his private depression. More disturbing is the fact that, within the world of finances, Hans is specifically involved in the analysis of oil futures. This, of course, has a particular resonance at the time the narrative is set, during the US invasion of Iraq, yet the ethical implications of his job are always left unquestioned. With this note, O'Neill hints at the ways in which a very postmodern imperial angst can quietly take over anxieties surrounding colonial history, without either of these ever being seriously confronted or examined.

The way in which the world of finances is entangled with the narrator's private world is also clearly conveyed when Hans describes the financial agreements of his separation from Rachel: "The loft would be sold and the net proceeds, comfortably over a million dollars, would be invested in government bonds, a cautious spread of stocks and, on a tip from an economist I trusted, gold" (28). Here, we have the exchange of one type of bond for another. The declared precision of Hans's financial investments contrasts, more boldly here, with his blindness about ethics. Indeed, his ability to see and foresee economic trends contrasts both his emotional skills and his political vision. O'Neill's narrator recognizes his lack of self-inspection as a "symptom of moral laziness" (2009, 231). He treads and trades cautiously through the emotional chaos created in the post-9/11 context, unwilling or incapable of forming judgments about these events and exasperating his wife Rachel who finds in his lack of engagement an acknowledged sign of conservatism.

This inability to see, to question, or to take a position is also present in the multiple cartographic references conveyed by the narrative. The novel presents itself clearly, and from the beginning, as a book about international movements, transoceanic journeys, and global transactions, and it is in this global context that the presentation of Hans as "a latter-day 'Dutch sailor'" (Corrigan 2008) gains real significance. The main structure of the novel depends upon a number of transatlantic movements, mainly between New York and London via The Hague, and although there is an attempt to change that trajectory (through references to "other" realities and narratives such as those conveyed by the Trinidadian motifs), these incursions are never fully explored. A real cosmopolitan approach is frustrated, and what is achieved, instead, is a limited sort of cosmopolitanism. Hans's attempts to track his family in London via Google's technology exemplifies this:

[F]lying on Google's satellite function, night after night I surreptitiously travelled to England. Starting with a hybrid map of the United States, I moved the navigation box across the North Atlantic and began my fall from the stratosphere: successively, into a brown and beige and greenish Europe bounded by Wuppertal, Groningen, Leeds, Caen (the Netherlands is gallant from this altitude, its streamer of northern isles giving the impression of a land steaming seaward): that part of England between Grantham and Yeovil; that part between Bedford and Brighton; and then Greater London, its north and south pieces, jigsawed by the Thames, never quite interlocking. From the central maze of mustard roads I followed the river south-west into Putney, zoomed in between the Lower and Upper Richmond Roads, and, with the image purely photographic, descended finally on Landford Road. It was always a clear and beautiful day—and wintry, if I correctly recall, with the trees pale brown and the shadows long. From my balloonist's vantage point, aloft at a few hundred metres, the scene was depthless. My son's dormer was visible, and the blue inflated pool and the red BMW; but there was no way to see more, or deeper. I was stuck. (119)

From the post-bohemian nostalgia of the Chelsea Hotel to the affluent borough of Richmond in the United Kingdom via a gallant image of the Netherlands, Hans's vision is flat. His difficulty to see beneath the signs of middle Europe or of white, upper-middle-class reality is made clear. His vision stops at his son's dormer. Hans acknowledges that there is something else beneath that surface, there are realities concealed from view beyond the signifiers of middle-class normality. But these are inaccessible to him, the scene remains depthless. Hans cannot see his son the same way that he cannot read his own trajectory in a global map.

This inability to see also explains the blind spot left open by Hans's vision of New York as a "city of friends." Hans's desire to see New York as an "invincible" city or a multicultural urban utopia neglects the fact that "other" cities have been completely obliterated from his map. Indeed, cities like Kabul and Baghdad remain outside Hans's field of vision, lacking any visibility within the narrative. The impossibility of Hans actually "seeing" Baghdad is revealed by the way the narrator (an expert on oil futures analyst) avoids the subject of war throughout his narrative. In fact, the Iraqi reality is reduced to a virtual reality in almost Baudrillardian terms: "[O]n television, dark Baghdad glittered with American bombs" (2009, 118). This is all that we are told about the Iraqi capital. What concerns Hans is an idealized vision of western multiculturalism, and it is this vision that demands the romanticized figure of Chuck Ramkissoon as a protagonist. Hence, when later in the novel Hans realizes that Chuck was involved in a number of illegal activities and was using him to run his business, the polish of identity politics that had allowed for the aggrandizement of Chuck in Hans's eyes disintegrates, erasing with it Hans's dream of a "city of friends."

Google Earth provides us, thus, with a metaphor for the need for perspective and the problem of the worldview embodied by the protagonist. Google Earth attempts to map the earth through the superimposition of images obtained by satellite, aerial photography, and geographic information systems. Not unlike early visual developments such as the panorama, which we referred to in Chapter 4, this technology also depends on the process of image-stitching. The sewing of images is precisely the process through which *Netherland*'s narrative is constructed: the novel starts *in media res* and travels backward and forward in time and place in a crafted tapestry of memories where Hans hopes to find himself. Indeed, this is also what Eliza, Chuck's mistress, does by creating and ordering photo albums for her clients: "People want a story," she plainly points out (126). Unable to "see" his son, Hans asks Eliza to create an album for the boy, hoping to find in it both meaning and a narrative he himself has failed to read.

Hans's inability to see deeper, more profoundly, is however far from a mere private malaise, as it reflects a generalized social problem and a global predicament. The last image of the novel reenacts a cartographic nexus through a movement which takes the reverse direction to that described above. We travel from London to New York via another optical tool, the London Eye. The Eye is the biggest Ferris wheel in Europe and the most popular tourist attraction in the United Kingdom. At the end of the novel, we find Hans, Rachel, and their son reunited and traveling together in one of the Eye's pods. The image of the London Eye, which closed Ian McEwan's *Saturday*, returns here to mark the ending of this 9/11 novel. Indeed, as in McEwan's novel, the aim here is to recover a more cohesive vision of the world in the face of global anxieties and insecurities.

The British capital, from where Hans's reminiscences depart, is still marked by salient icons of imperial power, the "Natwest Tower" standing beside "Tower Bridge," but, as the narrator explains, "the higher we go the less recognisable the city becomes" (246). Instead of examining the resonances of such mis-recognition, Hans retracts from his panoramic sightseeing and is taken back to childhood memories marked by other "towering" visions. He describes seeing Manhattan from the Staten Island Ferry when he was traveling with his mother. The Twin Towers emerge as symbols of promise, the US dream:

> The structures clustered at its tip made a warm, familiar crowd, and as their surfaces brightened ever more fiercely with sunlight it was possible to imagine that vertical accumulations of humanity were gathering to greet our arrival. The day was darkening at the margins, but so what? A world was lighting up [...] a world concentrated most glamorously of all, it goes almost without saying, in the lilac acres of two amazingly high towers [...] I wasn't the only person on that ferry who'd seen a pink watery sunset in his time, and I can state that I wasn't the only one of us to make out and accept an extraordinary promise in what we saw—the tall approaching cape, a people risen in light. (247)

The allusion to the ferryboats of Fitzgerald's *Great Gatsby* is inescapable here. By adopting the tone of Nick Carraway's voice, Hans's recollection directs the novel toward an equally melancholic conclusion. While Hans's final memories seem to allow a more direct relation with private phantoms of his past (namely through a reencounter with the memory of his mother), other public ghosts are more difficult to exorcize: Chuck, the legacies of colonial experience, the war in Afghanistan and Iraq, and its imperial connotations seem to be kept away from the circular movement and the memorial grandeur with which the novel appears to end. In the very last sentence of the novel, there is, however, a slight breakthrough in the self-serving circularity of the narrative—a final sentence that works as a sign of recognition. Still in the London Eye, Hans's son calls out to him forcing him to meet his gaze, challenging his inward drift and, therefore, demanding his attention. Cautiously, Hans first tests his immediate alliances "looking from him to Rachel and again to him [his son]" (247). Then, in the very last line of the novel, he dares to do what he had been unable to accomplish throughout the narrative: "I turn to look for what it is we're supposed to be seeing" (247). Only then does he recognize the need for a position, a vision, a perspective.

Mohsin Hamid's *The Reluctant Fundamentalist*

Like Joseph O'Neill's *Netherland*, the narrative structure of Mohsin Hamid's *The Reluctant Fundamentalist* depends on a number of cultural exchanges and transoceanic crossings that help us to think about the relations between displacement, mourning, and globalization in light of 9/11. Although Hamid's novel does not have the aesthetic ambition or narrative depth of *Netherland*, positioning itself more bluntly than O'Neill's book within the thriller genre, it is, however, an intelligent and skillfully written text that challenges the conventions and expectations of early 9/11 novels.

The novel addresses head-on the "clash of civilisations" debate revived since 9/11. While in *Netherland* it is the secondary character of Chuck Ramkissoon that introduces a cultural fracture to the Euro-American discourse of Hans's narrative, here cultural difference is personified by the narrator himself, shaping his discourse from the very beginning of the novel. The narrative also starts *in media res*: Changez, the narrator, is a Pakistani man (a bearded and suspicious looking man) who approaches a US stranger at an outdoor Lahore cafe. The novel takes place during the course of that encounter and corresponds to the story confided by Changez to his US interlocutor. The narrative wavers, thus, between our reliance, as readers, on the credibility of Changez's narrative and the sense of insecurity and distrust ignited, from the beginning of the text, between the narrator and his listener.

Changez's story is one of infatuation and frustrated love with the United States, which comments on the limitations of the American dream. Like Chuck, Changez is a go-getter, although he comes from the more privileged background and status of émigré rather than emigrant. Changez wins a scholarship to study at Princeton where he excels as a student; after graduating at the top of his class, he is instantly hired by "Underwood Samson," an elite firm that specializes in the economic assessment of companies. Around this time, he meets and eventually falls in love with Erica, a beautiful young woman from a wealthy US family. They become acquainted in Greece, during a group holiday organized by some Princeton students. Changez notices, then, how part of the Greek setting already figured a historical separation between East and West which had not been completely healed by time. The island of Rhodes becomes particularly emblematic of this: "Its cities were fortified, protected by ancient castles; they guarded against the Turks, much like the army and navy and air force of modern Greece, part of a wall against the East that still stands" (26). Changez knows well that he "grew up on the other side," (26) but that knowledge, previously veiled by the meritocratic ethos of elite universities and businesses, starts to torment him as he attempts to conquer Erica's affections.

The novel is loaded with symbols and can be read as a parable. As several reviewers and critics were quick to point out, Erica can be seen as an allegory for "(Am)Erica," that is, the United States after 9/11. Although she used to be a charismatic girl, Erica has lost her youthful optimism. She has become a fragile and melancholic young woman. The reasons behind Erica's vulnerability and subsequent difficulty in developing a relationship with Changez are justified in terms of a traumatic past event: the early death of her first boyfriend, Chris. An allegorical triangle, then, quickly emerges from the pile of symbols and bold signifiers accumulated by the narrative: (Am)Erica mourns Chris (the demise of an early Christian culture associated with European conquest; Christopher Columbus, thus, seen as an early conqueror) and now faces Changez (a changed relation to the East, brought about by globalization).

Imperial melancholia

Other significant similarities between *The Reluctant Fundamentalist* and *Netherland* are quick to emerge. Let us consider, first, the profession of both narrators. In *Netherland*, Hans was a financial analyst working for an investment bank, while in this novel Changez works as a management analyst specializing in the cold-blooded appraisal of companies (many of these foreign businesses) targeted for takeover. The fact that these two 9/11 novels depend upon narrators who are involved in trade valuations is no doubt meaningful. Both novels have a bold precedent in Nick Carraway, the narrator of *The Great Gatsby*—a classic that both novels directly allude to. Indeed, in Fitzgerald's novel, Carraway was an apprentice Wall Street trader in the rising *financial* markets of the early 1920s. It is therefore interesting to note that both O'Neill and Hamid return to this motif just before the financial collapse which marked the end of 2008. By engaging with the meaning of the crisis created by the terrorist attacks, both writers highlight the need to examine recent globalization processes in light of economical and financial concerns. In *Netherland*, Hans, as an investment banker, perceives a loss of confidence felt in Wall Street in the aftermath of 9/11, but the narrator never reflects upon the mechanisms of global capitalism. In *The Reluctant Fundamentalist*, however, Changez's occupation plays a more straightforward role in the narrative and has a preponderant part in the narrator's self-questioning (and in the resulting "change" of heart that justifies his emblematic name). This is illustrated by the role of traveling in the narrative. Changez travels to Chile and the Philippines on business to evaluate companies based in these two countries. Traveling has a clear geopolitical significance here, mapping the extent of US business abroad and stretching the concerns of the novel beyond East/West relations. Indeed, it is significant that Manila and Valparaiso, the cities whose businesses Changez has to evaluate, have a long and profound colonial history from early European rule to later US domination. What strikes Changez is not, however, the obvious presence of colonialism but the decline of Valparaiso's strategic role within the imperial cartography. This decline in strategic investment reminds Changez of his own country, Pakistan:

> Moreover, Valparaiso was itself a distraction: the city was powerfully atmospheric; a sense of melancholy pervaded its boulevards and hillsides.

I read online about its history and discovered that it had been in decline for over a century; once a great port fought over by rivals because of its status as the last stop for vessels making their way from the Pacific to the Atlantic, it had been bypassed and rendered peripheral by the Panama Canal. In this—Valparaiso's former aspirations to grandeur—I was reminded of Lahore and of that saying, so evocative in our language: *the ruins proclaim the building was beautiful.* (163)

Changez's depiction of Valparaiso's "former aspirations of grandeur" suggests a nostalgic yearning for a lost privileged position within a global chart. Like the Philippines, the other country where Changez was assigned a job, Chile suffered different waves of colonial occupation, marked by Spanish, British, and American rule. The ruins of Valparaiso's signal the end of the golden age of commerce after the opening of the Panama Canal during US period. Nostalgia is thus associated, at several points in the narrative, with losses of power and status. Indeed, this is how the narrator describes his own family's situation in Lahore: "I did not grow up in poverty. But, I did grow up with a poor boy's sense of *longing*, in my case not for what my family never had, but for what we had had and lost" (81). He explains how "imagined memories" enthused the lives of those around him: "*Nostalgia* was their crack cocaine, if you will, and my childhood was littered with the consequences of their addiction: unserviceable debts, squabbles over inheritances, the odd alcoholic or suicide" (81).

As a good investor, Changez is sensitive to economic decline and trained in finding solutions for such problems. The fact that Erica belongs to a privileged and well-established US family fits well into the investment models Changez has learned at Princeton. Not only could she restore Changez to an economical and social status which had been lost by his family in Lahore, but their partnership would work, in terms of the geopolitical symbolism of the narrative, as a significant transnational alliance, reinforcing Pakistan's relationship with this powerful nation.

This preoccupation with status and the rendition of characters' relations as representing "bonds" and "transactions" are at the heart of *The Great Gatsby*, a novel that O'Neill's *Netherland*, like Mohsin Hamid's *The Reluctant Terrorist*, also alludes to. As one of the most famous novels associated with the romantic trappings of the "American dream," Fitzgerald's book discloses the socioeconomic staging of this national myth: as a token of conspicuous leisure for her class, Daisy with her voice "full of money" could reclaim a particular stage in Gatsby's own social transformation. Status and social mobility are both romanticized and exposed by O'Neill's and Hamid's novels, particularly in what concerns the experience of migrant or foreign characters. Whereas Chuck seems to embrace US mythologies straightforwardly, if not naively (with Cricket standing in for the dreams and aspirations of Gatsby's Green light), for the middle-class Changez, personal aspirations become tangled up with mixed feelings about international politics.

Changez alludes to Fitzgerald's novel when he visits the house of one of his colleagues at the Hamptons: "a magnificent property that ma[kes him] think of *The Great Gastby*. It was beside the beach—on a rise behind a protective ridge of sand dunes—and it had a swimming pool, a tennis court, and an open-sided white pavilion erected at one end of the lawn for drinking and dancing" (48). Jim Wainwright, Changez's senior colleague, comes from a white, working-class background, which allows him to recognize in Changez the feeling of being "out of place" (48). Indeed, during the course of that evening at the Hamptons, Changez keeps "wishing [...] that Erica were there" (50). Changez needs (Am)Erica to confirm his social integration. While in Fitzgerald's novel we find that Gatsby's desire is commodified and Daisy Buchanan is herself translated into a "commodity" (Godden 1990, 83), in Hamid's novel it is Changez who, more clearly, becomes a commodity essential to the functioning of a system. Wainwright's house is, thus, the materialization of a successful and proud assimilation of corporate "values."

Here, as in O'Neill's novel, the social transactions established between characters are conveyed in nostalgic terms. In both novels, "Nostos" is not only associated with an idea of home which has disappeared, but with a home whose splendor has been lost. The "ruins" of Valparaiso and Lahore were for Changez a nostalgic symbol of the decline of "aspirations of grandeur" associated with imperial structures. Similarly, in the aftermath of 9/11, he discovers such melancholic symptoms at the very heart of US territory. In this context, however, it becomes easier for him to recognize the dangers inherent in the mobilization of mourning in times of crisis:

> Possibly this was due to my state of mind, but it seemed to me that America, too, was increasingly giving itself over to a dangerous nostalgia at that time. There was something undeniably retro about the flags and

uniforms, about generals addressing cameras in war rooms and newspaper headlines featuring such words as *duty* and *honor*. I had always thought of America as a nation that looked forward; for the first time I was struck by its determination to look *back*. Living in New York was suddenly like living in a film about the Second World War; I, a foreigner, found myself staring out at a set that ought to be viewed not in Technicolor but in grainy black and white. What your fellow country-men longed for was unclear to me—a time of unquestioned dominance? of safety? of moral certainty? (130–131)

Erica's melancholia can thus be understood in these terms: a yearning for a more powerful, more confident past. Erica is a nation in mourning, whose rapid decline prefigures, in Changez's management analysis, symptoms of a profound crisis. The immediate reaction to that sense of crisis—namely US bombing of Afghanistan, a neighbor country to Pakistan—brings the sense of threat closer to home for Changez, marking the beginning of his self-questioning. During a business meal in Valparaiso with the head of the publishing company he is supposed to evaluate, Changez realizes he is becoming a "janissary." As it is explained to him then, janissary corps were infantry units used in the Ottoman Empire of the fourteenth century formed by Christian children from conquered countries:

> "They [janissaries] were Christian boys," he explained, "captured by the Ottomans and trained to be soldiers in a Muslim army, at that time the greatest army in the world. They were ferocious and utterly loyal: they had fought to erase their own civilizations, so they had nothing else to turn to" [...] "How old were you when you went to America." (171–2)

Changez recognizes, then, that his financial valuations have been disrupting lives and businesses throughout the world for the profit of corporate clients. He realizes he has turned himself into a "modern day-janissaire." In Changez's awkward monologue, the coming of age narrative is greatly shaped by this acknowledgment—a recognition which is sparked by the War on Terror: "There really could be no doubt: I was a modern-day janissary, a servant of the American empire at a time when it was invading a country with a kinship to mine and was perhaps even colluding to ensure that my own country faced the threat of war" (173). As we have seen, the juxtaposition of children and terrorism has attracted a number of authors since 9/11. While in Michael Cunningham's book, *Specimen Days*, the image of child crusaders speaks about inbred terrorism in the United States, in Hamid's novel, the figure of the young janissary illustrates the way corporate neoliberalism is internalized independently of one's ethnicity or background.

Fundamentalist terrorism and global capitalism

As a way to undo his role as a "janissary," Changez goes back to Lahore where he finds a job as a university lecturer, "making [his] mission on campus" (103) to criticize US foreign policy, particularly in light of India's impending threat to Pakistan: "The threat of war with India reached its highest point the summer after I returned from New York. Multinational corporations on both sides of the border ordered senior employees to leave, and travel advisories were issued throughout the nations of the First World, counseling their citizens to defer nonessential trips to our region" (201).

Changez's poise during narration of this story suggests, thus, a radical transformation from one form of fundamentalism to another: from the capitalist fundamentals that guided his early work in Underwood Samson to the threatening embodiment of Islamic fundamentalist terrorist tactics. At the end of the novel, his gestures toward the US tourist become more threatening, assuming—perhaps parodically—the role of abductor or murderer. As a reviewer noted, the expectation is that Changez is moving toward "the dark side of Islamic fundamentalism, and is possibly, even as he speaks, orchestrating some Daniel Pearl-like execution of his perhaps literally captive audience" (Lasdun 2007). The reader never actually knows if Changez really aims to kill or threaten his interlocutor, or if he is merely mimicking the poise of a terrorist, as he remains an unreliable narrator until the very end of the narrative. The conclusion of the novel provides a climax to the suspense plot, without ever resolving or disclosing the real nature of the interaction between the narrator and his listener. The last paragraph of the novel assumes, then, the style of a persecution scene: Changez insists on following the American tourist to his hotel and suggests that they are being followed. The conclusion reenacts the climate of fear exacerbated by 9/11 but hints at other sources of violence.

Indeed, as a response to the sense of threat, the US tourist reaches into his pocket for what seems to be a gun—but the nature of the object remains ambiguous: "[W]hy are you reaching for your jacket, sir?" asks Changez. He then adds, perceptively: "I detect a glint of metal. Given that you and I are now bound by a certain shared intimacy, I trust it is from the holder of your business cards" (209).

This finale intensifies the juxtaposition between terrorism and corporate capitalism. The real crime can thus be seen as a result of a business transaction, the culmination of the "shared intimacy," the "trust" or "bond" established between these two men. Protected by the metal holder, the business card unveils the inscription of a system and its all-pervasive logic. Indeed, during his first days at Underwood Samson, Changez is told by his colleagues to "focus on the fundamentals" (112). This was Underwood Samson's guiding principle: "[I]t mandated a single-minded attention to financial detail, teasing out the true nature of those drivers that determine an asset's value" (112). At this point, the irony implicit in the title becomes clearer. It is the logic of persuasion of financial fundamentalism, rather than that of Islamic terrorism, that moves the novel. Indeed, in an interview, writer Mohsin Hamid—who worked for many years as a management consultant in New York and London—stressed that he did not mean to attack the United States but criticize a particular type of corporate logic: "There is a corporate or a financial fundamentalism, which is broader than just America—it is a global thing… It is a reduction of people to units of value, which happens all over the world, and increasingly often" (cited in "Writer Hamid focuses on Fundamentals"). The climate of fear and paranoia that builds up in the last pages of the novel, and which turns every character into a potential murderer, stages only too well the ways in which global capitalism becomes a mirror image of transnational terrorism— emerging from everywhere and nowhere. Like terrorism, global capitalism can be seen to be ruled by all-pervasive operations which nevertheless remain unseen, concealed, and mysterious.

For some readers, the pervasiveness of capitalist discourse is so entrenched in the construction of Changez's character that it undermines the given motifs for his transformation. The reviewer James Lasdun suggests that Changez's "repudiation of America in the wake of the September 11 attacks is a curiously frictionless, voluntary event, leaving one with an odd sense that his decision to quit is ultimately just the superior opportunism of a well-trained appraiser of ailing companies, who knows which way the wind is blowing" (Lasdun 2007). This, again, can be explained in terms of the novel's allegorical structure. Indeed, like pawns in a chess game, the characters in this novel do not offer themselves to deep psychological readings. Narrator and interlocutor can in this sense be seen as two sides of the same coin. When asked if as a writer he identified with the character of Changez, Mohsin Hamid commented: "I wonder why they never ask if I am his American listener. After all, a novel can often be a divided man's conversation with himself" (Hamid 2007). Here, Joseph Conrad's the *Heart of Darkness* emerges as another important allusion. Drawing on the figure of Kurtz in the *Heart of Darkness*, Žižek suggests that, like the corporate financier, the fundamentalism of the Islamic radical can be seen as a product of our times not of primitive traditions. In his reading of *Apocalypse Now*, Žižek asks: "Is it not significant that Kurtz [...] is presented not as a remainder of some barbaric past, but as the necessary outcome of modern western power itself? Kurtz was a perfect soldier—as such, through his overidentification with the military power system, he turned into the excess which the system has to eliminate" (Žižek 27). Changez, the quasi-perfect janissary, answers that question for us in his final encounter with the silent American. The specter of international terror reflects global capitalism, collapsing narrator and interlocutor in the very last pages of the novel.

Far from an exclusively US product, neoliberalism flows smoothly into new international contexts and is seamlessly internalized by individuals independently of their backgrounds. Neoliberal multiculturalism can, of course, make use of old mythologies of success to fuel social, cultural, and political practices and policies that use the language of markets, efficiency, consumer choice, transactional thinking, and individual autonomy. The flatness of Hamid's characters exposes how such logic shifts risk from governments and corporations onto individuals and extends this kind of market logic into the realm of social and affective relationships. Whereas in *Netherland* Chuck Ramkissoon can be seen—no doubt simplistically— as an unprincipled businessman who, not unlike Gatsby, finds a tragic death as a result of his shady approach to the US dream, in *The Reluctant Fundamentalist* it is not so much the individual but the system and its principles (the "fundamentals") that are exposed and examined. Both novels, however, struggle with a search for vision and position in a society which is still grieving. Faced by the political mobilization of mourning, post-9/11 New York becomes a setting that accommodates uncomfortably the "otherness" of characters such as Chuck or Changez in their various forms of displacement. If for O'Neill the difficulty in finding a wide enough vision, capable of embracing the disparate realities that impact upon the life of his characters, forces his narrator to retract into the personal, for Hamid ideological, economical, and postcolonial forces shape the very sense of identity of his characters, reducing them, rather uncannily, to mere positions and poises. Overall, both novels struggle with the possibility of achieving a genuine, cosmopolitan perspective regarding the changes brought about by 9/11: they reject the clichés associated with multiculturalism by political discourse and they expose the need to scrutinize new multicultural formations in light of colonial legacies and the new global economy.

Terror in the European Periphery: Ricardo Menéndez Salmón and José Saramago

El corrector, by the Spanish author Ricardo Menéndez Salmón, and *Seeing*, by Portuguese writer José Saramago, published in 2009 and 2004, respectively, offer poignant critiques to current notions of terror, articulated from a specific geopolitical location—the so-called European periphery.[1] Both books were published after Portugal and Spain became major allies of the United States in George W. Bush's War on Terror and explore with particular insight Europe's engagement with international security practices at a time when national sovereignty was becoming increasingly fragile. On March 17, 2003, the prime ministers of Portugal, José Manuel Barroso, and Spain, José Maria Aznar, met with the US president George Bush and the UK prime minister Tony Blair in the Lajes Air Base, a multi-use airfield in the Azores, for a one-day summit ("Allies to attend summit on Iraq"). The official justification for the meeting was Iraq's failure to comply with the disarmament process, based on the assumption that the country possessed weapons of mass destruction which constituted an imminent threat to international security—a supposition that proved to be unfounded. Faced by the hesitations of leaders of other European countries such as France, Germany, Russia, and China, who urged that the inspection processes be allowed more time, the Azores meeting had the aim of accelerating and reinforcing transatlantic relations and significant European support for the launching of the war in Iraq, which was indeed put into full military practice four days after this meeting, on May 20, 2003.

For Portugal and Spain, this meeting had strategic motives which had little to do with specific information gathered about Iraq's weaponry. These motives were clearly pointed out by Manuel Barroso in the speech with which he opened the summit. For the Portuguese prime minister, the meeting in the

Azores revealed "the importance of transatlantic relations, and also shows the solidarity among our countries" ("Full text" 2003). As Barroso clearly explained, the agreements made at the summit were twofold: "one statement on transatlantic relations, and a declarative statement on Iraq" (2003). The geopolitical symbolism of the Azores islands was highlighted by Barroso, who stressed the importance of staging the meeting "in this territory of the Azores that is halfway between the continent of Europe and the continent of America." For Barroso, the position of these islands had "a special meaning— the beautiful meaning of our friendship and our commitment to our shared values" (2003). This willingness to reinforce transatlantic relations in terms of military and security practices was also highlighted by Aznar: "[T]he expression of this commitment is essential, by way of guarantee of peace, security and international freedom" (2003); the Spanish president also highlighted the distinctiveness of the Atlantic bound: "[T]here is no other alternative to the expression of the Atlantic commitment in terms of security" (2003). What was at stake was the projection and international visibility of two peripheral states on a wider international stage. If we bear in mind the political and economic interests of the parties involved, it becomes clear that military operations depended upon the exhibition of credible diplomatic relations. The prime ministers of Portugal and Spain were, certainly, interested and ready— unlike other European countries, most notably France and Germany—to present themselves, alongside the United Kingdom, as the first partners of the United States in its "coalition of the willing."[2]

This context, and the larger meanings of these engagements, was bound to be reworked, more or less directly, in the work of politically perceptive writers such as Ricardo Menéndez Salmón and José Saramago. While *El corrector* deals with this immediate context directly, *Seeing* frames it within a wider picture of the failures and perversions of current democratic practices. Both novels, however, explore the need to "re-read" and "revise" the recent history of their respective countries. The trope of vision becomes central to these two novels, as the authors feel the need to rethink and revise the place of their countries in the grand global narratives in which these have been inscribed. Moreover, the motifs of vision and revision are also part of a larger intertextual strategy for both authors. Both novels, *El corrector* and *Seeing*, have been presented as sequels to the authors' previous novels. These books revisit issues about the future of liberal democracies, which had always concerned both authors, but which are reexamined here in light of current notions of terror.

El corrector (The proofreader)

Since the Madrid train bombings in March 2003 (also known in Spain as the "11M attacks"), we find in Spain a number of novels that deal with terrorism and its impact on social relations and urban life, often employing these issues to revise or intensify personal anxieties which prefigured the events. Among these, we find *La Piedra en el Corazón* by Luis Mateo Díez (2006), *Donde Dios no Estuvo*, de Sonseloes Ónega (2007), *Madrid Blues* (2008) by Blanca Riestra, *La Vida Antes de Marzo* (2009) by Manuel Gutiérrez Aragon, and *El Mapa de la Vida* by Adolfo García Ortega (2009).

Like their US, English, and French counterparts, many of these narratives depend upon cartographic mappings of the city. In Spanish novels, Madrid is naturally the privileged setting for most narratives. The novel *Madrid Blues*, for example, emblematizes well this transnational genre: it depicts the city of Madrid in great detail until the moment before the attacks, leaving the reader with elegiac cartography of a city supposedly about to disappear. The foreign title and its reference to the city's "blues" highlights how this premature nostalgia cannot avoid being read as a translation from abroad. Efforts to calibrate the relationship between the local and the national are illustrated by the insistent search for topographic points of vision. The novels also show how global pressures affect, directly and indirectly, the private lives of its citizens. Indeed, if Ian McEwan's *Saturday* and Joseph O'Neill's *Nederland* use the motif of the London Eye as an emblem for their protagonists' search for focus (between local and global visions; between past and present), in Spanish novels such as *El Mapa de la Vida* by Adolfo García Ortega this paradox is intensified by the visual reference to a roller coaster—a mechanism through which hyper-reality and the discrepancy between the global and the local are enacted though faster and even more repetitive movements.

El corrector by Menéndes Sálmon offers the reader a different perspective on these events because it faces political issues directly. Rather than merely portraying the emotional response to the attacks or embarking on a mournful mapping of the city, the book uncovers the political and ideological layers that shape our view of the attacks. *El corrector* (The Proofreader) is the final novel of what became known as Menéndez Salmón's "trilogy of evil," initiated with the publication of *La Ofensa* (2007) which was followed by *Derrumbe* (2008). Being the first book in the trilogy, *La Ofensa* is a novel set during the Second War World, focusing on a German soldier's capacity to bear witness to horrendous acts—a narrative that, as the author suggested, can be transposed to the present in relation to the war in Iraq (Menéndes Salmón cited in Coutinho). The second novel, *Derrumbe*, is set in a fictional coastal town which has been suffering a spate of crimes and acts of vandalism; through an intricate plot that explores the role of fear in contemporary society, the narrative also dwells on the voids left open by our global culture of consumption. Last, but not least, *El corrector* turns its attention to the recent history of Spain by focusing on the terrorist attacks in the Atocha railway station and the ensuing political manipulation of those events. Although the three novels were only considered a trilogy after Menéndes Salmón's last book was completed, the word "evil" used to depict and promote the triptych is highly significant in the context in which these novels were written. It evokes Hannah Arendt's analysis of the "banality of evil," her examination of how ordinary people under totalitarian regimes are willing to participate in immoral enterprises—a reference that, again, invites us to revisit lessons from the Second World War in the light of contemporary military projects.

This allusion also implies a necessary revision of the term "evil" as employed by contemporary political powers. Indeed, at the time when Menéndes Salmón was writing his novels, this word was used again and again in the political speeches made by both George Bush and Tony Blair as a way to promote the war in Iraq. Throughout his presidency, George Bush often invoked the dichotomy of good versus evil. It was this specific terminology linked to religious imagery, recurrent in Bush's speeches, that shaped the rhetoric of the War on Terror since its early days. On September 11, 2003, Bush concluded his televised address to the nation by reading the following quote from Psalm 23: "Even though I walk through the valley of the shadow of death, I fear no evil, for you are with me" (Bush 2001). This rhetoric will persist through his speeches and culminate in the "State of the Union Address" where he employed the term "axis of evil" to describe Iran, Iraq and North Korea (Bush 2002).

Despite the polemic caused by Bush's terminology, on the other side of the Atlantic, UK prime minister Tony Blair was keen to follow in Bush's footsteps, also resorting to the term "evil" as part of a similar rhetoric. In fact, on the day of the attacks on the World Trade Center, the UK prime minister also gave an emotional televised broadcast where he stated that "mass terrorism is the new *evil* in our world today" (Blair cited in White and Wintour, emphasis added). Blaire explained "[i]t is perpetrated by fanatics who are utterly indifferent to the sanctity of human life, and we the democracies of this world are going to have to come together and fight it together" (2002). It is not surprising that a writer like Ménendes Sálmon, sensitive to both the philosophical and the historical resonances of discursive practices, should feel the need to revise the semantics of this dichotomous language.

The *diegetic* time of *El corrector* starts with the first explosion in Atocha Railway Station in Madrid, precisely at "7:38" on March 11, 2004 (also known as "11M"), three days before Spain's general elections. It finishes at midnight of the same day. This approach to chronological time is comparable to the techniques used by post-9/11 novels which offer a minute-by-minute account of the time preceding or following these events. However, unlike the narrators of McEwan's *Saturday* and Beigbeder's *Windows on the World* who narrate their account from the heart of their respective metropolis (i.e., London and Paris), the narrator of *El corrector* is subject to a double distancing effect. He is narrating his account from the Asturias, rather than from the Spanish capital, Madrid. This distancing effect intensifies the view of Madrid as a peripheral metropolis, as well as of 11M as a poor simulacrum of 9/11. Moreover, the first accounts of the attacks offered by the Spanish government contrasted greatly with the information circulating in the international media. While the Spanish government was blaming ETA for the bombing in Atocha, there was information circulating in foreign media (particularly US television stations) that suggested that an Islamic fundamentalist group, inspired by al-Qaeda, was behind the attacks. This information was supported by the fact that the targets of the bombings—civilians travelling by train in the morning to go to work— diverged from the usual targets chosen by ETA, more often directed at the military, armed forces, or policemen. Menéndes Sálmón highlights the sense of estrangement experienced by the Spanish people at the time: "We were receiving life information but always through filters and simulacra: phone, television, net. We were being informed about what happened in our country through foreign media" (Menéndes Salmón cited in Coutinho). He explains how this confusion damaged Spain's view of itself; it was as "if the world had been receiving trustworthy information, truthful and veridical before the protagonists of that event which was us, the Spanish. In those days there was a feeling in the country that all the world was in Madrid." The Spanish people become protagonists in an event whose plot was being written abroad. Vladimir, the novel's narrator, considers that it was a problem both political and linguistic:

> The record of what happened between the 11th and 14th of March 2004 is a tremendous example of the versatility of our politicians in the art of lying. Forced to face a terrifying success, a trauma of colossal proportions, many of them chose to lie. Or, as it is usually said nowadays, to "not tell the truth." Not even a sophist can beat their Lordships at the game of dialects. No one has perverted so profoundly the meaning of words, of all words, like the politician; not even the most obstinate fideist.[3]

For Vladimir, the narrator of *El corrector*, language has been hijacked and distorted by political powers. Vladimir is a published writer, who has stopped writing fiction and has become a professional proofreader. Vladimir's attention to linguistic detail invites the reader to consider language as a place where failures (manipulations, errors, misreadings) occur and where revisions, proofreadings, and corrections are always necessary. Vladimir is editing a translation of Dostoyevsky's *The Demons*. The act of translation informs the oblique movement through which the narrator provides the reader with information about the Madrid train bombings. Vladimir lives in the Asturias rather than in Madrid (like Menéndes Salmón, himself) and, therefore, only experiences the attacks from afar. His experience of the bombings is made indirectly, through different media—telephone conversations, televised images, teletext—and different voices—conversations with his editor Urbesalgo, his friend Robayma, and his girlfriend Zoe. These exchanges help Vladimir to organize his own reactions to the bombings.

He relies most crucially on Zoe to provide him with an anchorage to everyday reality. Zoe is an artist who restores old paintings. Vladimir depicts her as someone who searches for authenticity and integrity in a world where images easily change and where deceit tarnishes private and public relations. In the iconoclastic language of the mass media, the search for the truth about the Madrid train bombings becomes reduced to a specific gesture: the rummage around the ripped carcass of the trains for remains of the actual bodies of the dead. Unlike the attacks on 9/11 where images of bodies were hidden away, as part of a careful ideological staging and visual virtualization of the tragedy, in Spain televisions continuously discharged images of "cadavers, cadavers, cadavers."[4] The narrator writes that on the day of the tragedy "[...] it was all of us that were there, lying in the train tracks, walking like living dead, or sat down on the municipal flower beds with the perplexed look of one who wakes up in a country of cannibals."[5] Rather than being an expression of patriotism in the face of the tragedy, this plural subject acknowledges that the Spanish people are already half-dead. The inhabitants of Madrid are neither real beings nor actual citizens: they are depicted as "living dead" or "cannibals." The search for the bodies in Atocha's station becomes tied up with a search for Spain's self-portrayal—a figure which has been buried under foreign images, globalized narratives. Madrid ceases to be, in this novel, a city depicted in real colors, to incorporate the ubiquitous neutrality of simulacra. By failing to provide convincing justifications for the bombings, Spanish politicians reinforce the generalized sense of uncertainty. Doubts about the bombings grow into interrogations about Spain itself. There is a generalized feeling that Spain is no longer the same—it has become something else. Vladimir's narrative shows how the bombs in the four commuter trains, travelling between Alcalá de Henares and the Atocha station, did not simply reach Madrid. They reached a station, a country without clear boundaries.

On the day of the bombings, Vladimir's inability to recount his own reaction to the events is further stressed by the way he literally searches for a reflection of the events, which became known as "11M," in the faces of his co-citizens:

> I guess that on that day I looked at my neighbor's faces searching for a mark, a proof, a sign of the ages. The faces around us also have hermetic qualities. And what was I able to find in them? Nothing, or better said, yes, I found the economy of our daily occupations, the cents of small hopes, of small tributes, of little great deeds. Not a trace of attrition. Not a shadow of funereal melancholy. Not a hint of mourning. Some were even laughing. Not slyly, like in a funeral, but frankly as if to a child. [...] But I swear that I

didn't find the pathos of evil by wandering around my neighbors as if I were a Homeric god facing the walls of Troy.[6]

The lack of pathos revealed by this collective mass of nameless faces contrasts with the ceremonial of individual photos, names, candles, and flags organized after the attacks in New York in 2001. The narrator's unease about the lack of emotional response conveys the incredulity and generalized confusion felt by the Spanish population, following the official stance made by the government after the attacks. If, in order to mourn, Spain needs to search for meanings abroad, Vladimir's view of himself as "an Homeric god facing the walls of Troy" becomes particularly meaningful. While this image confirms and reiterates the trope of the captivity narrative (which dominated most 11M and 9/11 novels), it also reveals the double nature of the danger lying outside the city's "walls," raising the question as to whether Islamic terrorism really is the main threat to the citadel, or whether Madrid has been threatened by the military and economic bonds established with powerful nations such as the United States. The reaction of Madrid's population is symptomatic of the conflicting pressures experienced by Spain in a global map shaped by different sources of terror.

What strikes Vladimir is not only the lack of signs of bereavement ("no hint of mourning") but also the awkward reaction of his neighbors. Some people "were even laughing" (65), he explains, "not slyly, like in a funeral, but frankly as if to a child" (65). The representation of children in the face of a crisis gains additional meanings in the novel. At this point, Vladimir makes a confession which will disturb the solid image of his relationship with Zoe. Vladimir lets the reader know that children he saw on the street that day offered him a "reflection of [his] beloved son, Eric" a child he only knew from posted pictures (65). Vladimir confesses, thus, that during a brief period of separation from Zoe, he had had a son by another woman. He received news and photos of the boy but, oddly enough, he had never met the child, who lived with his mother in Australia. Vladimir kept this secret hidden from Zoe and somehow disconnected from his everyday life—as if the child existed only in pictures, as a simulacrum, a trace of another life. At the time when the narrative takes place, Eric is already five years old and lives more than ten thousand miles away from Europe. Eric conveys, thus, Vladimir's asynchrony with the world—a discrepancy felt in terms of time and place. The child also represents the displacement of Spain's political future.

Political demons

Vladimir's confession redirects the reader to the novel's main intertext, Dostoeyvsky's *Demons* (1872), one of Dostoevsky's more openly political novels. Set in Russia in the early 1870s, it depicts a time of great economical changes, radical movements, and violence. During the late nineteenth century, Tsarist Russia was becoming a major economic power, even though large parts of the population were still living in poverty and serfdom. Despite its autocratic rule, Russia is not deaf to rumors of revolutions coming from abroad. Dostoevsky stages the clash of ideologies arising in Russia with particular wit in *Demons*. The novel takes place in a small town where a loose gang of revolutionaries, democrats, liberals, and anarchists have, for some time, been conversing, scheming, and spreading revolutionary propaganda. When Nikolai Stavrogin and Pyotr Verkhovensky, two of its members, return home—after a long period abroad—the group of left-wing idealists turns to action. These two young men personify two very different sides of radicalism. Stavrogin has a shady and manipulative personality (in *El corrector*, Vladimir calls him a dark prince). Verkhovensky is a revolutionary willing to do anything for his ideas. Under their leadership, Russia's future becomes terrifying.

This dark but humorous novel was inspired by a notorious political murder that shook Russia in 1869, and it provides a fascinating narrative about Dostoyesky's conflicting feelings about radicalism. In 1849, when he was thirty-eight years old, Dostoyevsky was imprisoned and sent to Siberia for supporting revolutionary ideals (he had been given a death sentence which was cancelled at the very last minute). When he resumed his career almost ten years later, he moved to the opposite side of the political spectrum, becoming known as a leading reactionary and slavophile. Nevertheless, his deep identification with radicalism remains a staple of his writing. This identification was acknowledged by the author himself, as Adam Kirsch relates: "In a surprising admission near the end of his life, Dostoyevsky said that, even if he had advance knowledge of a plot to kill the tsar, he could not bring himself to denounce the plotters to the police, so deeply bred was his loathing of all informers: 'the liberals would never forgive me. They would torment me, drive me to despair'" (Kirsch 2008). As Adam Kirsh also points out, it is this ambivalence, "this recognition that he has fundamental principles in common with the terrorists he loathes, that allows Dostoyevsky to write so penetratingly about them in *Demons*" (2008).

Nikolai Stavrogin and Pyotr Verkhovensky are sons of two main figures who open the novel and represent, in their turn, different facets of Russian society at the time: Varvara Stavrogina is a widow with high social standing and active participation in local politics and Stepan Verkhovensky, a philosopher, intellectual, and westernizer. Their children, Nikolai Stavrogin and Piotr Verchovjensky, were literally "estranged" from their parents, having travelled, studied abroad, and adopted foreign ideas. In Dostoyevsky's slavophile view, Russia's beloved children had grown to become the country's own "demons." The association of the image of the child with ideas about the political future has always had a long history in fiction. In this novel, the demonic sons are not a symbol of political hope but of despair, of political terror itself. These terrifying sons of old Russia are as dangerous as the terrorist children in the second story of Michael Cunningham's *Specimen Days*, "The Children's Crusade." Like the children in the second novella of Cunningham's trypctich, Dosteyevsky's "demons" embrace terror as a way to achieve change.

Unlike what happens in *The Demons*, Vladimir's child in *El corrector* does not return "home." He has never visited Spain and never met his father. Nor has his father ever travelled to Australia to meet his son. Vladimir's child, who is only reached virtually through photographs, represents the idea of a future that remains unclaimed and uncannily disconnected from the Spanish citizens themselves. Fear becomes, thus, for the narrator the main flagship of our time:

> Every age has its symbols, its flags, its conspiracies. Ours has made fear its banner, its axis of pain, its firmament. Argonauts in the galaxy of suspicion, sullen, wary, resenting others, those of us that in a day not distant in time felt attuned with the end of history but that today, just like someone short-sighted in a building, whose façade had changed during the night, wanders in search of a crack in the wall through which one may escape from this unbearable cyclic time that haunts us. In that arriving station in which we lived for less than a decade, since the fall of the Soviet Union and the marvelous achievement of a sweetener-free capitalism, and until the day

when some faithful ones that prayed to Allah, the Compassionate, decided to enter the windows of Paradise by plane and to put the clocks in motion once again, all of us—men and women, Argives or Trojans, laborers and bourgeois, destitute or monarchs—had been grouping in the multitude of markets that celebrated the plasticity of our culture and the versatility of our talent.[7]

Fear is a banner that has been made global, turning western subjects into "Argonauts in the galaxy of suspicion." The image wall (in "a building whose façade has been changed during the night") confirms the persistence of narratives of captivity which are here, ironically, associated with the end of the Cold War (the end of traditional walls) as a way to expose another, more enduring type of entrapment: the image of "cyclic time," reinforces an idea of history trapped within the logic of advanced capitalism where human desires, far from embodying the spirit of change, become a mere confirmation of that which has been anticipated and projected onto its subjects: "Everything that we had dreamed of [...] had already been invented by someone [...] alchemy was a trait of the market; bankers were the new necromancers."[8] "Cyclic time" derives not only from this haunted temporality but also from the phantasmagoria of the spatial simulacrum through which Spain has entered the language and logic of globalization—these temporal and spatial elements reinforce the erasure of Spanish history/identity in the novel.

Vladimir presents us history in philosophical terms. These lines are written in the third person plural, a subjectivity haunted by the loss of a collective identity, neither clearly Spanish nor European. The subject of the sentence that starts in "all of us" ("man and women, Argives or Trojans, laborers and bourgeois, destitute or monarchs") is a collective pronoun whose specific history seems to have been erased and replaced by "the multitude of markets that celebrated the plasticity of our culture and the versatility of our talent" (124). Vladimir's own name (a sign of his father's admiration for Dostoyevsky) reinforces the transnational projection, as it underscores the estrangement of Spanish identity, while alluding to a nineteenth-century Russian novel clearly anxious about revolutionary Europe. Attempting to translate the language of fear into logical terms, the narrative becomes philosophical and essayistic. Not unlike Saramago's novelistic essay—which we will examine next—there is an effort here to interpret the otherwise perplexing events in a clear, direct language which is, nevertheless, also highly allegorical because its intent is to subvert old political metaphors and revise their ideological content. The narrator attempts to translate and correct what is hauntingly repetitive but apparently new.

The many observational and reflective paragraphs which punctuate the narrative convey how the narrator's view of history is deeply tied up with his cultural and literary experience. The recurrent use of images and anecdotes which are employed to depict a world made of surfaces also direct the reader to a number contemporary, if not postmodern, literary references. Indeed, if the narrator alludes to Dostoyevsky in his approach to characterization, it is to Don DeLillo, the contemporary US author, that the narrator relates to in terms of the essayistic penchant of the narrative. Vladimir not only presents DeLillo as his favorite living author but he does so by admitting that he cherishes a photo of the author (a significant replica, this time, of his virtual "father", not unlike the one he kept of his son), taken outside a restaurant in New York (86). It is ironic and highly significant that Vladimir's admiration for DeLillo should be visually fetishized, as this writer was one of the first authors to openly explore the relationship between photographic image and terror (*Mao II* and *Libra*). In *El corrector*, "White noise," an expression first used by the narrator very early in the novel to mean "background noise of the relentless breath of that cosmic death that lurks behind everyday sounds"[9] is a constant reference to media and an open allusion to DeLillo's novel with the same title. However, two novels recently published by DeLillo, *Cosmopolis* (2003) and *Falling Man* (2007), are also worth mentioning in the context of Vladimir's revision. By offering different but parallel and integrated versions of security in contemporary US society. *Cosmopolis* presents an insecure and dangerously illusive basis for financial capitalism which sustains not only the economic stratum but also the very values of contemporary western world; *Falling Man* is concerned with the iconoclastic nature of acts of terrorism portrayed through the mass media. Both novels suggest a point of contact between two important historical formations which Vladimir also attempts to juxtapose. The violence embedded in mass-produced images shapes to a great extent the second part of Menéndes Salmón's novel. The last chapters purposefully dislocate the anxiety created by the attacks to other sources of global terror. In the final section of the text, we find Vladimir watching the news via teletext while having dinner with Zoe. The television screen, where visual reality is now translated into words, presents two different but equally meaningful press releases: "The first was that the Abú Hafs al-Masri brigades claimed the attacks, in the name of Al Qaeda, in a letter sent to the Arab newspaper *Al Quds Al-Arabi*."[10] The letter maintained that the attacks had been a way to "settle old accounts with Spain, a crusader and an American ally in its war against Islam."[11] It is, however, a second piece of news that closes the novel, wrapping up the narrative with a poignant blow: "[A] press-release sent at 21.57h gave notice of the New York Stock Exchange fall because of the investor's anxieties: Wall Street registered a drop of 168.51 points, some 1.64 per cent; and Nasdaq, an electronic business in which most of the technology stocks change hands, went down 20.26 points, some 1.03 per cent."[12] The novel finishes by anticipating the inevitable: a greater burst than that generated by the terrorist attack had reached New York markets and would very soon hit Europe as well. In a final attempt to escape the tension sustained by the media, Zoe and Vladimir switch off the TV and go out to look at the sea. The transatlantic fluxes of the Cantabric Sea that bathe the Asturias can be, however, cruel reminders of the fluxes of the stock exchange. The oceanic currents that transport masses of water from the Gulf of Mexico to the North Atlantic cannot avoid reminding us of the impact of financial and political fluctuations in the so-called European periphery.

José Saramago's *Seeing*

Saramago's novel, *Seeing*, was published in 2004. If in Spain the year 2004 was marked by the Madrid bombings, in Portugal it witnessed significant political implosions. Prime Minister Manuel Barroso resigned from his role as the head of the Portuguese government to assume the position of the twelfth president of the European Commission. Barroso's nomination was not fortuitous. According to Jorge Sampaio, the Portuguese president at the time, Durão Barroso's participation as host in Cimeira das Lajes in 2003 was one of the reasons why the Portuguese politician found support from a number of European leaders to become president of the European Commission elected by the Union's council.[13] Barroso's role as the head of the Union Council—at a time when this executive body had been remodeled to assume more powers—was seen by some politicians as prestigious and beneficial for Portugal. The prime minister's resignation was also symptomatic of the growing crisis in Portuguese politics. Throughout the 1990s, Portugal had greatly benefitted from European funding and was believed to have achieved financial and economic "integration" in the euro zone. However, at the turn of the century, the country was already approaching economic stagnation and there was a growing pessimism concerning the country's political future.

Seeing (2004) explores the lack of trust in the political system and the mechanisms of terror which persist at the heart of western democracies. The novel returns to the setting and themes of Saramago's earlier and highly acclaimed novel, *Blindness*, published in 1995. Unlike Menéndes Salmón's trilogy, where the dialogue and the links between the three novels are merely oblique and have no interference in terms of the diegesis, Saramago's second book refers directly to events set in the same fictional universe of the earlier novel. A brief depiction of *Blindness* may therefore be of interest here: the novel depicted the occurrence of an epidemic of blindness afflicting almost the entire population of a city. It focused on a group of characters affected by this outbreak who are quarantined in a heavily guarded asylum. Among these are a doctor and his wife (two characters who will reappear in *Seeing*). While the government implements repressive measures to control the disease, life at the overcrowded asylum becomes abject: internees are faced with starvation and lack the minimum conditions of hygiene or privacy. Abuse, exploitation, and violence also become recurrent, as some internees wish to acquire privileges and power over others. *Blindness* finishes, nevertheless, with a note of hope concerning the survival and reconstruction of the unnamed city—where the events of *Seeing* take place.[14]

Like in *Blindness*, the name and location of the city of *Seeing* are never identified.[15] Concerns regarding contemporary forms of authority link the two novels, but there are important distinctions between the two narratives: the narrative of the earlier novel focuses on the community and its citizens, while the later novel focuses on the politicians and other official agents of the "polis." *Seeing* revisits the city of *Blindness*—a city where democracy has been valiantly fought for and restored—only to find out that the majority of its citizens decided to cast blank ballots in the most recent parliamentary elections.

Due to the mediatic attention given to Saramago—who obtained Nobel Prize in 1998—the novel's reception in Portugal became immediately tied up with political debates engendered by the novel. Saramago was himself quite willing to present the novel in political terms. Facile readings of the novel's main metaphor were endorsed not only by the media but also by the author's blunt public positions. Democracy was the novel's main target, and Saramago was happy to make that clear: "in the world everything is arguable, everything is object of debate, but democracy comes out as pure, unreachable, untouchable [...] it is economic power that really governs, using democracy to its favour" (Saramago cited in "Para Saramago" 2004).[16] These comments, offered by an author well known for his ongoing ties with the Portuguese Communist Party, put off many readers and reviewers, who did not find in the novel the literary rigor of his previous works. Comparatively, the novel was better received outside Portugal, where Saramago's text was not so overexposed to the mediatic attention surrounding the book's publication or to simplistic readings of the author's comments.

Rather than reading the book solely as a grand manifesto against shortcomings of neoliberal democracy, I will show how this text specifically stages national and global pressures, by reemploying contemporary discourses about terrorism, exacerbated after 9/11, 7/7, and 11M. A close reading, attentive to metafictional and metapolitical references, will show how the text also acknowledges the shortcomings of the author's own path in a system dominated by party politics. In order to do this, I will demonstrate how certain elements of the narrative—the two distinct parts that apparently do not connect, a drifting and highly evasive narrative, and the lack of obvious protagonists—challenge simplistic ideological readings of Saramago's work.

While the public persona created by Saramago in order to deal with political issues (Communism, Iberianism, European Community, the role of religion in society, and so on) often tended to assume a severe and rigid posture in front of TV cameras or newspaper journalists, the narrative voice of Saramago's texts is, as is well known, highly ironic, sardonic, and caustic. His narrators are famous for double entendres and ambiguity through which straightforward readings of Saramago works are necessarily challenged. The very beginning of *Seeing* starts with a trickery:

Terrible voting weather, remarked the presiding officer of polling station fourteen as he snapped shut his soaked umbrella and took off the raincoat that had proved of little use to him during the breathless forty-meter dash from the place where he had parked his car to the door through which, heart pounding, he had just appeared. I hope I'm not the last, he said to the secretary, who was standing slightly away from the door, safe from the sheets of rain which, caught by the wind, were drenching the floor. Your deputy hasn't arrived yet, but we've still got plenty of time, said the secretary soothingly. With rain like this, it'll be a feat in itself if we all manage to get here, said the presiding officer as they went into the room where the voting would take place. (Saramago 2007, 1)

"Weather" is a translation of the Portuguese "tempo," which means both weather and time. "Terrible voting weather" thus also implies quite ironically: "terrible time to vote." The rain falls with a ploy, a false start. This may remind us of the famous beginning of Charlotte Brontë's *Jane Eyre*: "There was no possibility of taking a walk that day."[17] The question Saramago raises here is similar: was there a possibility to vote *that* day? *Seeing* is, not unlike Brontë's book, a narrative about agency. Both *Jane Eyre* and *Seeing* depart from the notion of impossibility, unfeasibility, or hopelessness to highlight the singularity of desire, action, active possibility. The weather would suggest a high rate of voter abstention. However, as also happens in *Jane Eyre*, the narrator of *Seeing* immediately rectifies the readers' expectations by presenting them with *agency* of a very singular type. Citizens dare to face the weather and translate their desires into votes, but it is the specific character of their inscription—that blank vote—that surprise the politicians at the voting tables. While the "terrible" voting weather will not prevent people from going outside, this gesture of agency is translated into a blank, which reiterates the emptiness of the choices provided and the nullity of the election process itself.

Unwilling to understand the reason behind the blank-vote majority, the government promotes police operations which involve imprisoning certain citizens, submitting people to lie detectors, and leaving the city in a state of siege. Following these drastic measures, a bomb explodes in the subway killing several people. The government, helped by the media, attributes this action to the group supposedly behind the blank voters (immediately tagged as terrorists), but signs indicate that the bombing was actually orchestrated by government officials as a means to implicate the blank voters. The government, then, decides to abandon the city, transferring the capital to another place and leaving the population without basic provisions. An anonymous letter reaches the prime minister, offering a theory that government officials readily adopt: it suggests that the doctor's wife (the only person not to go blind in the epidemic described in *Blindness*) may be the person leading the supposed "terrorist movement." The government sends, thus, three undercover agents to search for the leaders of the blank-vote rebellion. This search becomes the second part of the book. If the first part of the novel had focused on the intrigues and scheming of politicians during and after the elections, the second part focuses on the activities of three policemen as they enter the city and initiate their investigation. The agents of the law are told by the interior minister that they should bring "results"—"I won't ask by what means you obtained them" (184). The double structure of the novel is, thus, directed by different agents of the "polis"—the "politicians" and "policemen"—none of whom are ultimately able to connect, understand, or represent its citizens. In *Seeing* we find a city without citizenship, where power is totally detached from the community.

While the parabolic nature of the narrative defies national borders, the text makes specific references to Portuguese history and politics. Early in the novel we find a direct reference to the Portuguese history and its people in a speech given by the nation's president—a reference which is immediately retracted and presented as a "merely" illustrative example by the sardonic narrator:

> My dear compatriots, or Esteemed fellow citizens, or even, were it the moment for playing, with just the right amount of vibrato, the bass string of patriotism, that simplest and noblest mode of address, Men and women of Portugal, that last word, we hasten to add, only appears due to the entirely gratuitous supposition, with no foundation in objective fact, that the scene of the dire events it has fallen to us to describe in such meticulous detail, could be, or perhaps could have been, the land of the aforesaid Portuguese men and women. It was merely an illustrative example, nothing more, for which, despite all our good intentions, we apologize in advance, especially given that they are a people with a reputation around the world for having always exercised their electoral duties with praiseworthy civic discipline and religious devotion. (82–83)

With this tongue-in-cheek reference to (and denial of) the Portuguese political "reputation"—a reminder of paternalistic and religious basis of the Portuguese dictatorship—the idea of authoritarianism is both localized and displaced, conveyed as national and global. While the narrative certainly conveys a distrust in Portuguese party politics, which will be reflected in the actual increase in blank votes in Portuguese legislative elections of 2005,[18] the text also presents the reader with a global allegory, a parable about current trends in western democracies.

Ursula Le Guin's review of the novel offers a frank and revealing example of how Saramago's novel was read by liberal intellectuals in the other side of the Atlantic. Le Guin's review starts by conveying her concerns about the way electoral apathy helped to promote conservative governments in both England and the United States: "In a functioning democracy, one can consider not voting a lazy protest liable to play into the hands of the party in power (as when low Labour turn-out allowed Margaret Thatcher's re-elections, and Democratic apathy secured both elections of George W. Bush)" (Le Guin 2006). She explains: "[I]t comes hard to me to admit that a vote is not in itself an act of power, and I was at first blind to the point Saramago's non-voting voters are making. I began to see it at last, when the minister of defense announces that what the country is facing is terrorism" (2006). Le Guin's use of the visual metaphor in the above citation ("I began to see at last") is also significant for the way it recognizes a blind spot in western liberal thought. The novel's dominant metaphor becomes, thus, clearer to Le Guin, and to most reviewers, when the narrative becomes directly more concerned with depicting how official discourse about terror has been used to legitimize authoritarianism. This discourse, easily recognizable in both sides of the Atlantic, has been reproduced and reinforced transnationally in the past decade, having become the new common language shared by political elites all over the world. By placing and displacing the unnamed city in the novel and by literalizing and generalizing the notion of *polis* in the text, *Seeing* sheds light on the means through which such discursive constructions depend upon the intersection and cross-fertilization of local and global fictions.

Headless capital: Two sides of the spectrum

In *Seeing* (as in *Blindness*), the character that most clearly embodies the possibility of vision is the wife of the doctor. In *Seeing*, she becomes, as I have previously mentioned, the person accused of heading the movement of blank voters. She is conveniently seen by official agents as the "head" of a movement which in fact has no leader. Indeed, the more estranged, alienated, and physically detached from the city are the politicians, the more obsessed they become in the search for a figure, the face of what they call "terrorism." The irony of such a quest becomes all the more apparent if we remind ourselves that etymologically *capital* derives from the word "head" in Latin (caput, capitis). The "search" for a "head" ordered by the politicians and performed by the police agents conveys, thus, the lack of substance of the agenda of the political leaders who end up abandoning the capital. This incongruous state of affairs is reinforced by the coded conversation that takes place between the interior minister and the superintendent, one of the police agents ordered to initiate the "search," in the second part of the novel:

> Hello, puffin speaking, Hello, puffin, replied albatross, First contact made with local bird life, friendly reception, useful interrogation with the participation of hawk and gull, good results, Substantial, puffin, Very substantial, albatross, we got an excellent photograph of the whole flock, tomorrow we'll start identifying the different species, Well done, puffin, Thank you, albatross, Listen, puffin, I'm listening, albatross, Don't be fooled by occasional silences, puffin, when birds are quiet, it doesn't necessarily mean that they're on their nests, it's the calm that conceals the storm, not the other way round, the same thing happens with human conspiracies, the fact that no one mentions them doesn't mean they don't exist, do you understand, puffin, Yes, albatross, I understand perfectly, What are you going to do tomorrow, puffin, I'm going to go for the osprey, Who is the osprey, puffin, explain yourself, It's the only one on the whole coast, albatross, indeed, as far as we know, there has never been another. (205–206)

By calling themselves "albatross" and "puffin," minister and superintendent assume their roles in a farce which is meant to parody the fine line between identity and disguise which the process of espionage, not unlike that of party politics, entails. As it will become clear to the superintendent, the "osprey" that the ministers are searching for is the wife of the doctor—who will soon become prey of the national media, power's influential appendage in times of conceptual void.

We should note, at this stage, that the narrative also briefly depicts another female figure that functions, to a certain extent, as the double or nemesis of the doctor's wife. That character is the wife of the prime minister. Easily overlooked by readers, this character's fleeting presence in the text performs nevertheless a significant role. We meet her when we follow the prime minister into his private quarters: she is listening to her husband's plans to take on the portfolios of defense and interior in the name of a national emergency. She suddenly imagines herself as the wife of this self-promoted "savior of democracy," the only man supposedly able to contain the subversive movement of blank voters. With this vision she slithers close to her husband in a "mixture of carnal desire and political enthusiasm" (140). Yet, her yearning is rebuffed through poetry by the political man,

> her husband, conscious of the gravity of the hour and making his the harsh words of the poet, Why do you grovel before my rough boots?/Why do you loosen your perfumed hair/and treacherously open your soft arms?/ I am nothing but a man with coarse hands/and a cold heart/and if, in order to pass,/I had to trample you underfoot/ then, as you well know, I would trample you underfoot, abruptly threw off the bed clothes and said, I'm going to my study to keep an eye on developments, you go back to sleep, rest. (140–141)

Although the author of the poem is never acknowledged, the lines that start in "Why" and finish in "underfoot," are translations of verses written by the Portuguese poet, Mário Dionísio.[19] They are part of a little known poem, entitled "A Carne é Fraca" (The Flesh Is Strong), published in the book *Solicitações e Emboscadas* ("*Solicitations and Ambushes*") in 1945, during the Portuguese dictatorship which lasted from 1933 to 1974. In a double-language aimed at deceiving the censors, the poem is an account of resistance in the form of a lover's complaint. Many of the poems in this collection became known for the earnest way in which, despite the censorship, they accounted for the everyday of militants—the death of communist comrades, forced exiles, and lives gone underground.[20] Like Saramago himself, Mário Dionísio was a member of the Portuguese Communist Party. Yet, unlike Saramago, he left the party in 1962 due to pressures regarding the orientation, and time devoted to, his art.[21]

The scholar Cristina Ribeiro has pointed out that as a love poem, the style, images and metaphors, and the brawny masculinity of the poetic subject do not resonate with other amorous poems by the same author. The inversion of the religious expression "the flesh is weak" (*New International Version*, St Matthew 26:41) into its opposite suggests an overturning of meanings associated with strength and power.[22] The male subject in the poem strikes us due to his defensive and potent poise—a position which is anchored in "rough boots" (Dionísio 1982). This type of footwear, used for shielding one's feet and legs and for providing ankle support for strenuous activities, such as those engaged by the military, can easily conjure up images of authoritarian power, such as those one would associate with the Portuguese dictatorship. Yet, in this poem, the idea of power is reversed and the expectations of the readers are frustrated: the power of the flesh stands, here, for the efforts of the resistance, rather than of hegemonic power. The lure of hegemony is, instead, presented as a woman with loose and perfumed hair. Dionísio show us "in the flesh" both the struggles and temptations of those who fought for democracy during António de Oliveira Salazar's authoritarian regime.

So what happens when we read Dionísio's poem as part of Saramago's narrative? Saramago turns upside down the already twisted metaphors of Dionísio's text. By placing the poem in the mouth of an authoritarian prime minister, Saramago reverses the ideological position of the poetic subject and places the rough boots back on the feet of dominant power. Saramago's minister wears the boots of power but speaks as a destitute political poet. The two sides of the political spectrum are reversed in an aim to highlight the parodic mirrors of party politics. Saramago's ministers are capable of lying, creating scapegoats, and staging criminal acts as a way to maintain power but they do so with a fine self-consciousness, an almost sentimental acknowledgment of their own mask. By revealing what authoritarian tendencies in liberal democratic societies have in common with Fascist and Stalinist regimes, Saramago also unveils political tensions which have shaped his political path. The novel discloses, thus, tensions between the principles set out by the Portuguese Communist Party, to which the author was always publicly faithful, and the trespassing of those codes demanded by his writing. The undermining of the vote (which placed Saramago at odds with the agenda of the Communist Party in the election campaigns of 2004 in Portugal)[23] is merely one of such forms of infringement enacted in *Seeing*.

The novel does a lot more than to reiterate old dichotomies—"seeing" is not a naive double to "blindness" nor are the "politicians/policemen" mere doubles to the "terrorists."[24] There is a more profound level of doubling at work in the text. This twofold movement is best exemplified by the space that brings together and separates "husbands" and "wives" in the novel. One may associate this space with Derrida's notion of *différence*, since the figure of the wife here becomes the sign of a fantasy whose meaning is always "deffered" or postponed and also stands for a binary opposition which may radically change the meaning of the text. We have two sets of couples: the minister and his wife and the doctor and his wife. Interestingly, the minister and the doctor are, in more senses than one, less "visionary" than their wives. The minister's wife stays in bed, engaging more fully with the fantasy of power her husband is not completely able to embrace. The doctor's wife, the only person that never lacks vision in *Blindness*, is also the promise of radical freedom in *Seeing*. While none of the two wives fulfills their wishes within the symbolic, the novel revolves around the desire they both personify. They also embody a space outside codified politics and in that sense they correspond to visions which can hardly be obtained in official politics and can only be seized through other types of *vision*, more akin to that of art. At the heart of the novel, the ambivalence between husbands and wives leaves the narrative in a limbo—within and without the political system—in a movement that lacks resolution.

As soon as the narrative breaks into two parts (and politicians and policemen become engaged in the search for a nonexistent leader of the blank-vote rebellion), the city emerges as a fractured body and a headless capital. The city has been emptied out of political life as well as of economic and cultural capital. It has become a space where citizens have lost their essence (citizenship) and can, now, be considered potential terrorists. The made-up destination of where the three policemen will find accommodation in the city, "Providential ltd" is significantly described "a bogus insurance and reinsurance company which a complete dearth of clients, whether local or foreign, had not yet managed to bankrupt" (184). The media assumes its role at the side of the estranged political classes, substituting facts for spectacular images. The wife of the doctor is therefore exposed by the main newspapers as the leader of the movement, finally giving face to "striking headlines, in letters the colour of blood." The headlines read: "Revealed At Last—The Face Behind The Conspiracy" (278). The use of *capital* letters in these headlines, which the narrator transcribes to the readers, is both ironic and somber since it prefigures a profound *decapitalization* of the polis which accompanies the decapitation of the leaderless movement. Indeed, following this episode, the wife of the doctor, the last symbol of vision, is shot by one of the policemen and blindness is restored to the city:

The woman goes over to the iron balustrade, places her hands on it and feels the coolness of the metal. We cannot ask her if she heard the two successive shots, she is lying dead on the ground and her blood is sliding and dripping onto the balcony below. The dog comes running out, he sniffs [...] Then a blind man asked, Did you hear something, Three shots, replied another blind man, But there was a dog howling too. Its stopped now, that must have been the third shot, Good, I hate to hear dogs howl. (307)

Conclusion: The beheaded polis

Written after the launching of the War on Terror, *El corrector* and *Seeing* challenge current notions of "terror" from the standpoint of peripheral democracies. If in Menéndes Salmón's novel there is a distancing of the main protagonist from the Spanish capital, in Saramago's novel that estrangement is more radically transformed into an erasure, the decapitation of the social body, itself. The cities of both *El corrector* and *Seeing* are not only places without capital, but also capitals where the lack of political *capite* inevitably leads to an erasure of economic and cultural sovereignty. Through the use of politically loaded intertexts by Dostoyevsky and Dionísio, respectively, Menéndes Salmón and Saramago expose the distorting mirror of neoliberal democracies and the way it contributes to the self-imposed captivity of peripheral countries. Lacking political weight, the cities of both novels become poor and minor versions of the "polis." In Menéndes Salmón's displaced approach to *Madrid* and Saramago's blank vision of Lisbon, we find capitals under siege. They have been captured not by terrorists but by a terrorizing discourse. They are headless capitals—spaces that depend on *estranged* notions of "terror" and "democracy." By unveiling these beheadings, Menéndes Salmón and Saramago challenge current notions of terrorism and—from the standpoint of a peripheral economies—expose other sources of violence which are bred and propagated in neoliberal democracies.

Beyond the Transatlantic Nexus: Salman Rushdie and J.M. Coetzee

This chapter explores the relationship between colonial history and contemporary global politics by examining works by Salman Rushdie and J.M. Coetzee—two celebrated novelists whose writing conveys how colonial legacies are intricately implicated in current definitions of terror. Moreover, if the debates about 9/11 literature usually depart from a very specific geopolitical perspective shaped by US and European realities, writers such as Rushdie and Coetzee contribute to a significant displacement of the focus of terror away from the "West," challenging dominant Euro-American perspectives. These authors not only depart from very different geopolitical positions, but also are able to historicize and revise the roles of western politics worldwide when examining key moments in the history of the Indian subcontinent and South Africa. Both authors engage with ideas of "state terror" which cannot be dissociated from the legacies of colonialism and have, thus, important implications for the construction of notions of "international terrorism." These connections are poignantly explored in the two novels which I will examine here: Salman Rushdie's *Shalimar the Clown* (first published in 2005) and J.M. Coetzee's *Diary of a Bad Year* (2007).

Let us start by paying close attention to Salman Rushdie's work. Rushdie was never afraid to engage with controversial and openly political issues: after the publication of his first and highly celebrated novel, *Midnight's Children*, Rushdie wrote *Shame* (1983), a clear allegory of the political turmoil in Pakistan. His third book, *The Jaguar Smile: A Nicaraguan Journey* (1987), is an essayistic work about Nicaragua which recounts the author's travels to the country in 1986, as the United States waged a covert war against the Sandinistas. It was, however, his fourth novel, *The Satanic Verses* (1988), which became Rushdie's most polemic work, receiving accusations of blasphemy and provoking protests from Muslims in several countries. Rushdie received several death threats and, in 1989, Ayatollah Ruhollah Khomeini issued a fatwa requiring Rushdie's execution. This forced Rushdie to issue an apology; its refusal by Khomeini's office then led the author to a life in hiding, under permanent security watch. This tense relation with Islamic fundamentalism had profound effects in Rushdie's life and view of the world, as his novel autobiographical book *Joseph Anton: A Memoir* (2012) would show. In an interview about this autobiographical book, Rushdie stated: "[T]he same mindset, the same extremism that attacked those buildings in New York and Washington was the one that attacked me." The author sustained: "[P]eople didn't really understand it in the West, because they couldn't set it into a narrative that they understood" (Rushdie 2012).

Shalimar the Clown (2005) focuses on the India–Pakistan conflict over Kashmir, offering the West a narrative through which the War on Terror can be understood. The book engages with the legacies of postcolonialism in Southeast Asia by examining several contexts of terror: terrorist acts promoted by jihadist organizations as well as state-endorsed terror. *Shalimar* redirects postcolonial paradigms by examining transnational terror networks and their regional and international impact on global politics. In the style of a thriller, the first chapter introduces a murder: Maximilian Ophuls, a charismatic figure of US counter-terrorism who worked as US ambassador in India, is murdered by his Muslim chauffeur, a mysterious figure, called Shalimar. As a whodunit, the narrative travels back in time to the subcontinent. The plot is propelled by events taking place in the village of Pachigam in Kashmir before, during, and after the conflict between India and Pakistan over the region. Like a number of 9/11 novels examined in this study, *Shalimar the Clown* engages directly with the thriller genre. But the novel is more than a thriller; it is also a historical novel, where the documentary is intersected by a bold magical realism that embraces different continents while it travels in time. The narrative starts in Los Angeles but moves to the subcontinent, stopping briefly in London and Paris among other cities on a journey of circumnavigation, which concludes by returning to Kashmir and, finally, Los Angeles. This strained geographical path covers several meaningful periods in the twentieth century from the Second World War to the War on Terror via the Cold War. The geographical and chronological itinerancy—explored by other 9/11 novels such as O'Neill's *Netherland* and Hamid's *Reluctant Terrorist*—conveys the novel's ambitious purposes. This is a novel that clearly sets out to explore how the legacies of colonial history and international politics have led to explosive configurations in the globalized world such as Islamic terrorism and the War on Terror.

Rushdie's inflammable view of globalization is conveyed in the very first chapter of the novel, when we are first introduced to India (née Kashmira) and her Russian landlady Olga Volga (née Simenovea): "Everywhere was now a part of everywhere else. Russia, America, London, Kashmir. Our lives, our stories, flowed into one another's, were no longer our own, individual, discrete [...] There were collisions and explosions. The world was no longer calm" (Rushdie 2006, 37). In order to create such an ambitious historical and geographical panorama, the role of magical realism is stretched to its limits here, intersecting with elements of the thriller—a genre which, as we have seen in previous chapters, is particularly well suited to the climate of fear and international conspiracy which has emerged since 9/11. One reviewer called this novel "the story of everywhere: California, India, France, Britain, Pakistan, Algeria, the Philippines." The result, he suggested, is a "cross between a piece of magic realism [...] and the contemporary international thriller" (Tait 2005).

The heart of the narrative and the root of the "crime" can, however, be traced to Kashmir. Described with great vitality and an eye for local idiosyncrasies, Kashmir is firstly presented as a secular, ideal community where Hindu and Muslim traditions coexist pacifically. *Kashmyriat*, or Kashmiriness, is described as "the belief that at the heart of Kashmiri culture there was a common bond that transcended all other differences" (Rushdie 2006, 110). The peculiarity of Pachigam is further explained in these terms: "Most bhand villages were Muslim but Pachigam was a mixture, with families of pandit background, the Kauls, the Misris, and the baritone singer's long-nosed kin—sharga being a local nickname for the nasally elongated—and even one family of dancing Jews" (110). In other books by Rushdie, Kashmir as a place of multicultural harmony corresponds more to an ideal than to a historical and geographical reality. Yet its recurrence in the authors' oeuvre reveals the importance of such fantasy—a significant heterotopia, a place of affirmation of difference and escape from authoritarianism and repression. *Shalimar*'s Kashmir, is more than an "imaginary homeland."[1] As the author noted in an interview, although the beginning of *Midnight's Children* (1981) is set in Kashmir, and his book of children's stories, *Haroun and the Sea of Stories* (1990), is also, according to the writer, "a fairy tale of Kashmir," none of these novels actually tackle the intricate political and social reality of the region (Rushdie 2005a). In fact, Rushdie felt he "never really addressed Kashmir itself" before writing *Shalimar the Clown* (2013).

The ideal of religious and cultural coexistence, embodied in this early version of Kashmir, is consummated in the passionate relationship between a young woman, from a Hindu Pandit family, named Boonyi Kaul and Shalimar, a young man from Muslim family, who trained and worked as the village clown. This relationship is, however, doomed as the two epigraphs which introduce the novel readily announce: an excerpt from Agha Shahid Ali's *The Country without a Post Office* and another from William Shakespeare's *Romeo and Juliet*. Shalimar and Boonyi's bond is threatened, and ultimately destroyed, soon after their marriage due to the appearance of the US ambassador to India, Max Ophuls, who begins an affair with the ardent young Boonyi. This rupture comes to symbolize the divide between India and Pakistan, unraveling the geopolitical allegory that structures the novel. In the words of Shakespeare, which are replicated in the epigraph of the novel this will mark the beginning of "a plague on both [...] houses" (Epigraph of *Shalimar the Clown* Rushdie 2006).

Attracted by the wealth, power, and cosmopolitan lifestyle represented by Max, Boonyi leaves her husband and the small village of Pachigham to become the ambassador's lover. Boonyi is the last in a string of lovers seduced by Max, who is officially a married man. Formally, he remains the husband of Margaret (Peggy) Rhodes, the English woman Max first met during the Second World War when they worked together as members of the French resistance. The passion that brought Max and Peggy together dissipated over the years. In the eyes of Max, Peggy loses the appeal she once had as a wartime heroine, and she learns to accept her husband's lustful adventures. Max is eager to spoil his new lover with everything money can buy. He offers her an apartment in Delhi, dance lessons, dreams of stardom, and a glamorous lifestyle which will only be materialized in the confines of their love nest:

She also craved the women's fashions of 1966, not the boring Jackie Kennedy pillbox-hat-and-pearls styles but the looks in the magazines she devoured, the Pocahontas headbands, the swirling orange-print shift dresses, the fringed leather jackets, the Mondrian squares of Saint Laurent, the hoop dresses, the space-age catsuits, the miniskirts, the vinyl, the gloves. She only wore these things in the privacy of the love nest, dressing up eagerly for her lover, giggling at her own daring, and allowing him to undress her as he pleased, to take his time, or to rip the clothes roughly off her body and leave them in shreds on the floor. (193–194)

As a parody of conquered territory, Boonyi becomes increasingly isolated and can only dedicate her commodified existence to other forms of consumption; she becomes addicted to certain drugs and obsessed with food. As time goes by, Boonyi's dreams are dispelled; she becomes obese, dishevelled, and maniacal. Her physical appearance only heightens the increasingly negative image of US power abroad during the 1960s, undermining Max Ophuls' mission: "America was trampling over southeast Asia, Vietnamese children's bodies were burning with unquenchable napalm fire, and yet the American ambassador had the gall to speak of oppression" (198). The Indian media starts to condemn the double standards of US foreign policies: "'America should put its own house in order,' thundered India's editorial writers, 'and stop telling us how to take care of our own land.'" At this point, Max Ophuls' aide, Edgar Wood, identifies Ophuls' lover as "the source of the ambassador's problems" and "decide[s] that Boonyi Noman had to go" (198).

The conquering and swift discarding of Boonyi represents well the modus operandi of the US foreign policy. As the scholar Andrew Teverson suggestively put it, "America's power seduces, its affections imprison, its commodities corrupt and it abandons once it has taken what it wants" (Teverson 2008). When Boonyi gives birth to a baby she calls Kashmira, the child is seized away from her by Max's wife Peggy, who then takes the baby with her to England. Boonyi, now a pitiably fat woman suffering from several destructive addictions, is sent back to Pachigam where she will remain an isolated and ghostly presence until the end of her days. Betrayed, Shalimar changes from a caring and joyful young man into someone who lives only for pain: "I am killing because it is what I have become," he tells Boonyi, "I have become death" (298). Swearing revenge, desiring to kill his wife, her lover, and their child, Shalimar is drawn into one of the many jihadists groups emerging in the troubled region between India and Pakistan. Rushdie unflinchingly captures the profound devastation and violence inflicted upon Muslim and Hindu communities by both Islamic militants and the Indian army. Islamic insurgents are led by the iron mullah, Bulbul Fakh, a prophet said to be made of scrap metal. Their fight, as the mullah explained, was not primarily motivated by worldly desires, but by what they believed to be true: "Economics was not primary. Ideology was primary" (265). Rushdie predicts with vivid detail the everyday life of the militants, their rituals, and the many activities inherent to the operations. The destruction caused by Islamic fundamentalism is thoroughly depicted by Rushdie, but it is not presented as the only source of terror in the region. Indeed, it is the reaction of the Indian army and the escalation of state-endorsed terror that is more painfully depicted in the novel. Rushdie shows with heartbreaking precision how the military not only fails to care for the life of the Hindu pandits in Pachigam but also takes revenge against the villagers accused of protecting Islamic extremists. The Indian army finds its own version of exceptionalism to justify extra-judicial killings. The military uses torture, pillaging, and rape as their weapons of choice. The moment when Shalimar's father is tortured and his mother is gang-raped by the Indian army is one of the most agonizing moments of the narrative:

> Who killed the sarpanch? Who broke his hands? Who broke his arms? Who broke his ancient neck? Who shackled those men? Who made those men disappear? Who shot those boys? Who shot those girls? Who smashed that house? Who smashed that house? Who smashed that house? Who killed that youth? Who clubbed that grandmother? Who knifed that aunt? Who broke that old man's nose? […] Who poisoned the paddies? Who killed the children? Who whipped the parents? Who raped that lazy-eyed woman? Who raped that grey-haired lazy-eyed woman as she screamed about snake vengeance? Who raped that woman again? Who raped that woman again? Who raped that woman again? Who raped that dead woman? Who raped that dead woman again? (308)

Fundamentalism, on the one hand, and nationalism on the other, are both responsible for the destruction of Pachigam. Rushdie boldly presents these two forces side by side, highlighting how state-endorsed violence can also achieve the status of terrorism. However, Rushdie's most important accomplishment in this novel is not only to denounce how terror is propagated by the state (by making a clear connection between the Indian army and the US army, as similar agents in the War on Terror) but to dramatize the historical emergence of these two sources of terror (Islamic insurgency and military terror), by taking into account the wider geopolitical interests that fuelled them both.

Indeed, if the relationship between Boonyi and Shalimar works as a significant allegory, its meanings can only be properly understood in the light of other symbolic bounds which frame the narrative. It is the appearance and interference of Max Ophuls and his wife Peggy Rhodes that complete the overall geopolitical allegory, widening the scope of Rushdie's novel and structuring it as a narrative of globalization. Critics were quick to point out that the figure of Max represents "a parable of the carelessness of American intervention on the subcontinent" (Cowley 2005). The role played by the United States is indeed central in this narrative, as I will show next. Yet the roles played by Europe in the novel have eluded most of the critics. This is hardly surprising since the figure of Margaret (Peggy Rhodes), the wife of Max Ophuls, is presented as an elusive character. The reader is told that Max first met Peggy in Marseille; she was then nicknamed the "Grey Rat" for her work in the resistance. He is struck by her disheveled appearance and her desire to conceal her beauty: "That the Rat was beautiful was obvious enough, even though she did her best to hide it. Her shock of fair hair looked like it hadn't been washed for a month and stuck out behind her head like a bottle brush [...] She looked like a vagrant, Max thought, a buttoned-up hobo who had somehow strayed into the secret passages of the war" (168). The Second World War is a period through which the War on Terror is insistently reassessed in this novel. Not only is this conflict an important historical precursor of the Cold War, whose alignments will ultimately annihilate Kashmir, but it also evokes a notion of resistance which contrasts greatly with the way certain insurgency movements are perceived today. As Rushdie himself noted, "the resistance, which we think of as heroic, was what we would now call an insurgency in a time of occupation. Now we live in a time when there are other insurgencies that we don't call heroic—that we call terrorist" (Rushdie 2005a).

Despite her upper-class background and aristocratic posture, Peggy's disheveled and destitute appearance conveys the vulnerability of post–World War Europe: a continent devastated by its own internal conflicts; an old colonizing power about to lose its outposts overseas. Peggy becomes a shadow of her continent's grandiose past. With the decline of her marriage, Peggy is stuck to her past, unable to assume meaningful roles for herself or form substantial connections with others. Without descendants and neglected by her husband, she becomes desperately attached to the love child of her husband and his lover Boonyi, baby Kashmira, which she rechristens India as a reminder of England's greatest colony. Peggy is not only a version of England as an old colonial power in demise, but also stands for Europe at large, a continent which despite many efforts never recovered its projection worldwide and continued to be dependent on the United States.

Maximilian Ophuls' own history is also, significantly, shaped by the Second World War. Max is born in Strasburg. Like Peggy, he is also a war hero. Yet, in contrast to his wife, Ophuls epitomizes energy, glamour, and a capacity for reinvention epitomized by the United States—a country which after the demise of Great Britain becomes a major player in world politics with clear interests in the Indian subcontinent. He is described as a man of enormous vigor and formidable intellectual capacities. Max Ophuls represents the idealized New World in more senses than one: he is a privileged type of US migrant—a Euro-American. The character borrows his name and some of his cosmopolitan path from the famous German-born director with the same name. The real "Max Ophüls" started working in Germany but fled to France in 1933 due to the rise of Fascism in his home country. After the fall of France to Germany, the director travelled through Switzerland and Italy to reach the United States in 1941. Rushdie's Max is, like his homonym, a Jew, a cosmopolitan, a creator of fictions, and a master of self-renewal.[2]

As a police investigator tells India, after Max's death, "*your father served his country in some hot zones, he swam for America through some pretty muddy water*" (335; italics in the original). Although Max's role as an ambassador to India culminates with a number of scandals, the charismatic man returns to the United States unscathed and, after the end of the Cold War, his role is quickly recycled as he goes underground in order to reemerge with a secret role in US counter-terrorism:

> Here is drowned Max, the invisible man. Underground Max, trapped in a
> subterranean Edgar Wood world, a world of the disregarded, of lizard people
> and snake people, of busted hustlers and discarded lovers and lost leaders and

dashed hopes. Here is Max wandering among the high heaps of the bodies of
the rejected, the mountain ranges of defeat. But even in this, his newfound
invisibility, he is ahead of his time, because in this occult soil the seeds of the
future are being planted, and the time of the invisible world will come, the
time of the altered dialectic, the time of the dialectic gone underground, when
anonymous spectral armies will fight in secret over the fate of the earth. A good
man is never discarded for long. (212; italics in the original)

Max's reincarnations, transformations, and secret missions emblematize only
too well the changing interests of the United States in the Indian subcontinent
as the Cold War gives way to the War on Terror. Rushdie works hard to highlight
these historical connections, as a way to historicize the present, showing
ultimately how western powers, and the United States in particular, have been
implicated in different contexts of terror. Indeed, more than Shalimar, it is Max
himself who defines our time. He is after all the "maker of our time" (213). The
puppet masters of the US foreign policy, such as Max, have always had as much
power in "the invisible world" (213) as terrorist groups, such as al-Qaeda.

By stressing the malleable and highly contradictory character of Max
Ophuls, Rushdie creates a powerful personification of the changeable nature
of US foreign policies as they shape not only the Indian subcontinent but also
the world. While the superficiality and lack of coherence and depth of Max
were noticed by early reviewers, these traits were often seen as major flaws of
the novel. Writing for the *New York Observer*, David Thompson, for instance,
states that "Max is as hollow as Shalimar" (Thomson 2005), and he sees this
as "a fatal sign of Mr. Rushdie's uneasiness with male characters when they're
meant to carry a great deal of narrative energy" (Thomson 2005). Likewise,
Pankaj Mishra, writing for *The New York Review of Books*, states that "Rushdie
barely lingers over the inner lives of his characters, or the everyday experiences
that might constitute his basic material" (Mishra 2005).

Yet, it is precisely this flatness that turns Max into a powerful embodiment
of the US foreign policy. If all characters in this novel serve Rushdie's
allegorical purposes, the superficiality of characters such as Max and
India is further reinforced by the spatial settings they end up inhabiting,
namely in Los Angeles. While the promise and the demise of Kashmir is
painted with incisive brushes and striking colors, European cities such as
Strasbourg, Paris, and London are depicted with a sepia tint of the past.

However, the most hyper-real city of all is, obviously, Los Angeles, Max and India's chosen city and Max's final home. The fact that the novel begins and ends in the capital of postmodern urbanism is certainly not arbitrary. Los Angeles is described as a city with "no focal point" (21). In fact, Max admires the city, rejecting "the idea of centre [which] was in his view outdated, oligarchic, an arrogant anachronism" (21). For Max, "[t]he decentred promiscuous sprawl of this giant invertebrate blob, this jellyfish of concrete and light, made it the true democratic city of the future" (21). Democracy is, thus, parodically reduced not only to its lack of center but also to its clear lack of direction. This heartless city with its "hollow freeways" and "bizarre anatomy, which was fed and nourished by many such congealed and flowing arteries" contrasts quite drastically with the sensuous, fervent, and, ultimately, bleeding streets of Kashmir, the city which will remain the heart of the novel. Los Angeles, the city of angels and devils is, after all, for Max and India, a virtual replacement of the paradise lost which was Kashmir itself.

The interference of bold and highly conceptual postmodern tropes in Rushdie's magical realism is highlighted by Teo Tait, who compares Rushdie to DeLillo by stating that the Indian author exhibits in this novel "a DeLillo-ish concern with the limousine-borne power-brokers who shape our world, and the secret networks that underlie it" (Tait 2005). According to the critic, Max is "given to essayistic fugues on modern America, uttered in a spirit of 'half-humorous perversity'" (2005). However, for Tait, this essayistic positioning has its limitations: "Max and India may have started out as cool and conceptual, but they end as a fantasy of sophistication and omni-competence that would make Ian Fleming blush" (2005). If a postmodern mismatch of styles weakens the novel's conclusion, it is interesting to notice how this fantasy of omnipotence can be read as a parodic portrayal of the United States (and of the author's path), which the novel had been trying to weave since the very beginning.

Shalimar the Clown depicts how power can turn characters—their personal and national traits—into caricatures: the iron mullah, on the one hand, and general Kachhwaha, on the other, are excellent examples of this. But be it in Max (the United States) or in India/Kashmira (Rushdie's inescapable doppelgänger), the reader finds Rushdie's most painful caricatural depictions.

In the final pages, we see Kashmira ready to challenge Shalimar, who has magically escaped from prison. The last pages bring together the postmodern thriller genre and magical realism, making it clear to the reader that we are in an unashamedly fantastic, and indeed fictional, universe. Yet, this is a fantasy that needs to be taken seriously. The last words of the novel, "There was no India. There was only Kashmira, and Shalimar the clown" (398), stage a desire for an idealized place of tolerance—both political and autobiographical, while acknowledging the impossibility to revert to such reality. After all, Kashmira is now more American than she will ever be Kashmiri (although nostalgic about her mother's birthplace, she rarely returns to the subcontinent and lives, like Rushdie himself, surrounded by bodyguards and security paraphernalia). Kashmira has had her freedom stolen from her not only through the bellicose claims of Pakistan and India, but also, and more profoundly, by the imperial powers who adopted her for their own interests. By staging the desire to reclaim the land of his grandparents, Rushdie exposes a primal fantasy which has been at the heart of his fiction but that is here frustrated by the politicized history of subcontinent. As Rushdie points out in an interview written after the publication of *Shalimar*:

> At the height of the British Empire very few English novels were written that dealt with British power. It's extraordinary that at the moment in which England was the global superpower the subject of British power appeared not to interest most writers. Maybe there's an echo of that now, when America is the global superpower. Outside this country, America means power. That's not true in the United States itself. There are still writers here who take on politics—Don DeLillo, Robert Stone, Joan Didion, and so on. But I think many American writers are relatively uninterested in the way America is perceived abroad. As a result there's relatively little written about the power of America. (Rushdie, 2005a)

To be sure, Rushdie continues to retaliate against Islamic fundamentalism, as can be seen by his 2005 contribution to the *New York Times*, entitled "India and Pakistan's Code of Dishonor" and in his articles about the reform of Islam (Rushdie 2005b; Rushdie 2005c).[3] However, more than jihadist terrorism, it is the US control, as the great global superpower, which is more strikingly parodied in this novel. By highlighting the place of Kashmir in global geopolitics, the novel unveils the historical role played by colonial and imperial history in several contexts of terrorism in Southeast Asia. Ultimately, the novel also explores the ambivalence between omnipotence and clownish helplessness which sustain jellyfish empires, either jihadist or democratically endorsed, that continue to assert their influence across the globe.

Diary of a Bad Year

In terms of style and tone, Coetzee's *Diary of a Bad Year* (2007) could be seen to be poles apart from *Shalimar the Clown*. While *Shalimar the Clown* is a boldly ambitious work which explores interconnected narratives, moving from place to place and time to time, as it attempts to embrace transnational flows, *Diary of a Bad Year* is a slighter book, shaped by a strong sense of impotence and isolation in the face of global tendencies. Yet the core concern of these novels is, surprisingly, similar. As often happens in Coetzee's works, in *Diary*, the voice of the main character, JC, purposefully confuses itself with that of the author as a way to interrogate the relations between individual subjectivity, authorial power, and to scrutinize, through the intertwining of fiction and facts, totalitarian tendencies in contemporary society. Like Coetzee himself, the narrator is an old South African writer who is living in Australia, and the author of the celebrated novel, *Waiting for the Barbarians*. The protagonist is however seventy-two years old, five years older than the author when he published *Diary* (in 2007 Coetzee was sixty-seven years old). The extra years enhance the weariness and vulnerability of the aging novelist (JC seems to have Parkinson's disease, his eyesight is deteriorating, and he finds it more and more difficult to type) adding a memorial tone to the *Diary*. However, both the novel's authorship and its genre keep being called into question throughout the process of writing and revision. As the protagonist announces, halfway into the first part of his strong opinions: "[This] is a collection of opinions I am committed to, not a memoir. A response to the present in which I find myself" (Coetzee 2007, 67).[4]

The book is divided into two chapters, "Strong Opinions" and "Second Diary." The first chapter, which borrows its title from Nabokov's collection of interviews and essays published in 1973, presents some of Coetzee's bold and, arguably, controversial views on the state of the world. According to the narrator, his "opinions" were commissioned by a German publisher with the aim of bringing to light some of his (JC's) thoughts on current political, social, and cultural trends. These opinions include topics apparently as diverse as the formation of democratic states, the inconsistencies of political life in Australia, Bush and Blair's War on Terror, the trends and practices of academic life, commentaries on musical and literary works, and JC's views on torture.

The opinions collected in the first diary and in the "Second Diary" are followed by elliptical thoughts by JC (different in tone from his earlier comments), narrative fragments of his interaction with his typist Anya, as well as direct comments made either by Anya herself or by her boyfriend, Alan. These other voices break the page into two or three sections, often stealing the attention of the reader from JC's "strong opinions" to the opinions or actions taking place "below." These new sections often disrupt, always fracture, and sometimes comment upon the essays which open each page. These voices force the narrator-writer to review them through the eyes of characters that do not correspond to his typical readers, but whose resistance challenges the writer's sense of authority, forcing him to reflect on his role in an increasingly fractured society. Coetzee's essay on J.S. Bach, whom the protagonist calls, toward the end of his "Second Diary," "[his] spiritual Father" (222), suggests some of the ways to understand the book's structure. Bach's music is marked by contrapuntal strands which, although autonomous and distinct, present interesting relations with their counterparts—a configuration that is evoked in the tripartite structure of *Diary*. Indeed, as Andrew Riemer points out, "*Diary of a Bad Year* is laid out like a three-part musical score in which the notation for each 'voice' is printed on a separate staff, though in performance all are sounded simultaneously" (Riemer 2007).

Anya, JC's first interlocutor, is an Australian-Filipina who is described, from the outset, as an object of sexual desire. She is presented, in the first pages of the novel, as a "startling young woman" (3) with a "derrière so perfect as to be angelic" (8). The narrator meets her for the first time in the laundry room of their tower block, while watching the "washing go round" (3). As the setting of their first meeting suggests, Anya emerges as a possible disruption to the cyclical, repetitive, and self-deprecating nature of JC's train of thought and a possible intrusion into his intimate space (as the popular expression goes "the airing of [his] dirty laundry in public"). Anya's piquant depiction says much about the narrator's persona—a man whose aging body is no longer at its best, whose masculinity and vigorous intellect are made more fragile due to a growing feeling of powerlessness in relation to the general state of affairs of which the War on Terror is representative. Indeed, the notion of fragile and ailing masculinity evoked by the protagonist reminds one of 9/11 novels such as Phillip Roth's *Exit Ghost* and Auster's *Travels in the Scriptorium*, both also published in 2007, where the reflections on aging, mortality, and loneliness intersect with feelings of authorial impotence in the face of a disconcerting historical and political climate.

Anya embodies a concern which in Coetzee's novels is often translated sexually: the propinquity between power and abuse. This anxiety is explored in several novels by Coetzee, most forcefully in *Disgrace* (1999) and *Waiting for the Barbarians* (1980). While in *Disgrace* the protagonist forcibly seduces one of his students and consequently loses his reputation and his job, in the earlier novel, *Waiting for the Barbarians*, the protagonist, a magistrate, develops an intimate relationship with a girl who has been tortured by the military of his own "Empire." In both novels—as will happen in *Diary*—the female body (the bodies of both Lurie's daughter and the "barbarian girl") emerges as a fantasy of containment where the narrator's guilt regarding his own authority is projected. *Diary* also invites us to reread Coetzee's previous novels (and *Waiting for the Barbarians* in particular) as a wider reflection on state authority, which is inextricably linked to the ongoing metafictional revisions of Coetzee's oeuvre. In *Diary*, as the protagonist's "strong opinions" insist on highlighting, contemporary politics continues to embrace—and to attempt to rework globally—theories and practices which are, treacherously, not very different from those more openly used in South Africa during the apartheid system. As we will see next, *Diary* follows the ghostly path of *Waiting for the Barbarians*: it is a book haunted by the continued existence of practices such as torture which call into question the political legitimacy of so-called democratic states and of humanist discourse itself.

Torture and barbarism

In Coetzee's award-winning novel, *Waiting for the Barbarians*, the narrator is an official, a "magistrate," in a small frontier town under the jurisdiction of a political entity known only as "the Empire." A state of emergency is declared following fears that Empire may be under attack. After the killing, capture, and torture of a group of "barbarians," the magistrate begins to question imperial practices and procedures, and he nurses a "barbarian girl" who had been tortured and left partially blinded by her torturers. The complex and ambiguous relationship established between the magistrate and this girl (whom the magistrate both desires and wants to "keep" but ultimately ends up taking back to her people), stages the contradictions of those who, more or less reluctantly or passively, felt forever trapped in their role as accomplices in a highly discriminatory and authoritarian system of government. By demanding a reaction, an emotion from the barbarian woman, and forcing her to "speak," the magistrate reenacts the act of torture himself and hence substantiates his own guilt, erasing the distance between himself and her torturers. I highlight the plot of this early novel here because torture is a place—a dark place, indeed a "dark chamber"—to which the author will return again and again in his fiction, and very explicitly in *Diary*.

Some of Coetzee's reflections on torture were also translated into an essay entitled "Into the Dark Chamber: The Writer and the South African State," first published in 1986, where the author acknowledges that torture has exercised "a dark fascination" on himself as well on other writers from South Africa because "the relations in the torture room provide a metaphor, bare and extreme, for relations between authoritarianism and its victims" (Coetzee 1992, 363). The aim of torture "exerted upon the physical being of an individual in a twilight of legal illegality" has the purpose "if not of destroying him, then at least of destroying the kernel of resistance within him" (363). However, as the author also perceptively points out, its representation poses a number of problems and pitfalls: realistic depictions of tortures may serve the torturer's own intents by reproducing the techniques of the State, by divulging its terrorizing methods and, indirectly, adding to the climate of fear promoted in the name of security: "[H]ow to treat something that, in truth, because it is offered like a Gorgon's head to terrorize the populace and paralyze resistance, deserved to be ignored?" (366). However, to simply disregard torture could be seen as a form of silent connivance toward such practices. For Coetzee, then, "the true challenge is how *not to* play the game by the rules of the state, how to establish one's own authority, how to imagine torture and death on one's own terms" (364; italics mine). Coetzee concludes his article by stating that he hopes for

> a time when humanity will be restored across the face of society, and therefore when all human acts, including the flogging of an animal, will be returned to the ambit of moral judgment. In such a society it will once again be meaningful for the gaze of the author, the gaze of authority and authoritative judgment, to be turned upon scenes of torture. (368)

This conclusion seems, however, painfully anachronic, when read today. Twenty years after the publication of Coetzee's essay, torture continues to play a role in activities promoted, not by isolated or "underdeveloped" countries, but by one of the most powerful nations in the world with the endorsement of its allies. Torture has not only been a vivid staple of the War on Terror, but it also has been a practice promoted by the US government through a number of surgical operations and disingenuous clippings to the law. Indeed, as Coetzee was writing his *Diary*, the US Congress gave final approval to the renewal of the Patriot Act which, according to its supporters, gave "law enforcement the tools necessary to stay on the offensive in [the] fight against terrorism."[5] The act, originally signed by President Bush in 2001 following the attacks of September 11, abridged restrictions in law enforcement agencies' gathering of intelligence within the United States and increased the Secretary of the Treasury's authority to regulate financial transactions concerning foreign individuals and entities. The act also expanded the capacity of law enforcement and immigration authorities in detaining and deporting immigrants suspected of terrorism-related acts. More significantly, this piece of legislation expanded the definition of terrorism to include domestic terrorism and, by doing so, it enlarged the number of activities to which its law enforcement powers can be applied. This enlargement has tended to continue with the endorsement of subsequent heads of state. In fact, on May 26, 2011, President Barack Obama signed the Patriot Sunsets Extension Act of 2011, a four-year expansion of three key provisions in the USA Patriot Act.[6]

But 2006 was also the year when US president George W. Bush promised to close the US prison camp at Guantanamo Bay—a promise which was never fulfilled. As is well known, the disregard for human rights in the treatment of prisoners continues to take place in Guantanamo, despite some efforts made by President Obama to close this facility. Drawing on the imagery surrounding the pornography of war, JC suggests in his "Diary" that "someone should put together a ballet under the title *Guantánamo, Guantánamo!*" and depicts the haunting images playing in his mind:

> A corps of prisoners, their ankles shackled together, thick felt mittens on their hands, muffs over their ears, black hoods over their heads, do the dances of the persecuted and the desperate. Around them, guards in olive green uniforms prance with demonic energy and glee, cattle prods and billy-clubs at the ready. They touch the prisoners with the prods and the prisoners leap; they wrestle prisoners to the ground and shove the clubs up their anuses and the prisoners go into spasms. In a corner, a man on stilts in a Donald Rumsfeld mask alternately writes at his lectern and dances ecstatic little jigs. (37)

The physical depiction of the prisoners' bodies gains resonance in a diary, which is also about coming to terms with the physiological limitations of its aging author; a text whose protagonist feels himself incarcerated in a body whose pathetic limitations—"the physical mechanism deteriorates" (181)—only exacerbate his inability, as a writer, to react to the events he sees being played out on the international stage. Moreover, it should be noted— though this is not referred to by JC in his *Diary*—that many images from Guantanamo and Abu Ghraib were, indeed, reworked and performed not in a ballet but in an opera, composed by Philip Glass, based on Coetzee's *Waiting for the Barbarians*. The opera, named after Coetzee's novel, was part of a project Glass had in mind back in 1991, although the opera was completed in 2005, two years before *Diary* was published. Depictions of torture have, since the War on Terror, proliferated in both high art and popular culture. While some films, such as Paul T. Scheuring's *The Experiment* (2010), critically examine torture by highlighting the links between the abuse of prisoners in the Abu Ghraib pictures with the famous 1971 Stanford prison psychology experiment, others, such as the highly polemic *Zero Dark Thirty* (2012), directed by Kathryn Bigelow (2012), have been criticized for their graphic and politically ambivalent representation of torture. Although it is quite likely that representations of torture will continue to flourish by adopting more or less critical stances, Coetzee's suggestion that authors should question the rules of the game and "imagine torture and death on one's own terms" (Coetzee 1992, 363) can be said to gain, in this context, a fresh and powerful resonance.

Anya and the middle voice

Although Anya is not subject to the oppression of the "Barbarian woman" in *Waiting for the Barbarians* (who is both the object of torture and of sexual desire), the depiction of Anya's body also suggests the image of a threatened space, reinforcing the metaphor of invasion or occupation which dominates so many novels by Coetzee. Like *Waiting for the Barbarians* and *Disgrace*, Anya's relationship with "El Senõr C" is, from the outset, presented as a relationship based on power and hierarchy where sexuality plays an ambiguous role. After all, the reader knows that Anya has certainly not been hired for her intellectual capacities or her organizational skills. Indeed, at first, Anya seems to present herself as nothing more than a body, a vessel, a container, a medium (typist) for the circulation of the writer's words and as an object of his sexual desire. However, throughout the process of typing and commenting upon JC's works, she proves to have more integrity, more of a sense of perspective and, surprisingly, a broader worldview than her own employer. She also unveils the narrator's sexualized obsessions as part of a ritual of self-humiliation which speaks about his difficulty in understanding the world as it is. Indeed, JC puts himself purposefully in a role that is doubly dangerous: his relationship with Anya is always-already fraught by the idea of potential abuse, and this is precisely what attracts the protagonist. The possibility that abuse can either come from JC (from the old but horny employer) or be directed toward him by Anya and her ruthless lover, Alan (an opportunist and financier of sorts, who is willing to steal from JC's bank account), is a necessary risk entailed by JC's revision of his own life and work. This possibility of abuse, which is ultimately never fulfilled, creates, nevertheless, a useful fantasy set-up for the aging author—a masochist scenario where positions of power are necessarily questioned and subverted.

Coetzee knows only too well that writing is in itself a practice which entails power. The author uses his characters to engage in metafictional strategies to reenact societal pressures as well as violent dynamics of control. Teresa Dovey argues that all Coetzee's novels are "always making reference to the self of writing," and that they "exploit the notion of the divided subject of Lacan, the split between text and narration, or utterance and enunciation, in order to gesture toward the possibility of escaping complicity with the dominant discourses" (Dovey 1998, 19). The white woman is particularly pertinent to this metafictional strategy, as a number of critics have highlighted. Fiona Probyn states that "Coetzee represents his marginality, his 'writing without authority,' in the characters of his white women narrators who construct 'their' texts (or 'story' in the case of Susan Barton, 'letter' in the case of Elizabeth Curren, and 'pastiche diary' in the case of Magda) from a position of marginality in relation to the canon, its recognized literary forms, and its masculinist dominance" (Probyn 2002). These female characters become necessary "middle-voices" through which Coetzee can interrogate his own privileged position (2002). If this self-questioning is clear in Coetzee's South African novels, where the white woman embodies an ambivalent status between the colonial master and the colonized, in *Diary*, Anya's intermediate role is no less patent. Framed within the distance that separates her boyfriend (an advocate for neoliberalism) to her employer—in Alan's words, "an old-fashioned free-love, free-speech sentimental hippy socialist" (Coetzee 2007, 92)—Anya is also necessarily a medium between two competing worldviews.

Anya will play an important role in encouraging JC to revise his opinions. The most central concern of the novel is the issue of shame, an issue that dominates his South African novels during the apartheid and post-apartheid era and which is here relived due to actions of the United States and their allies since the launching of the War on Terror. To examine this problem, JC quotes Demosthenes: "Whereas the slave fears only pain, what the free man fears most is shame" (39). The main concern for JC can be articulated in the following questions, presented earlier on in the novel: "[I]n the face of this shame, to which I am subjected, how do I behave? How do I save my honor?" (39). The issue of Australia's keen participation in the "coalition of the willing" and active support for the war leads JC to rework the question of national guilt in national terms. He wonders:

> Is dishonor a state of being that comes in shades and degrees? If there is a state of deep dishonor, is there a state of mild dishonour too, dishonour lite? The temptation is to say no: if one is in dishonour one is in dishonour. Yet if today I heard that some American had committed suicide, rather than to live in *Disgrace*, I would fully understand: whereas an Australian who committed suicide in response to the action of the Howard government would risk seeming comical. The American administration has raised vengefulness to an infernal level, whereas the meanness of the Australians is as yet merely petty. (43–44)

Coetzee goes back and forward on the question of disgrace and dishonor but is, ultimately, unable to relieve himself from the burden of collective guilt, which due to the history of his country, he has carried most of his life. He is unable to translate this differentiated view of national guilt to the personal sphere and therefore returns to a definition made in more absolute terms. One of the sentences used to described this novel in book blurbs and reviews is therefore a poignant statement, made after the above quote and halfway into the novel, that "when you live in shameful times shame descends upon you, shame descends upon everyone, and you have simply to bear it, it is your lot and your punishment" (96). Anya, however, who does not share JC's special status as renowned intellectual, challenges his sweeping and indiscriminate notion of collective guilt. She tells JC a "story" to make her point: she recounts how she and a friend were raped in Cancún. They had been invited by three young American college students to go sailing in their yacht: "[T]here were three of them and two of us, and they must have decided that we were just a couple of bimbos, a couple of *putas*, whereas they were sons of doctors and lawyers and what have you" (97). The touristy setting of Anya's story gives an ironic twist to notions of global mobility, unveiling some of the conflicts behind the positive clichés of globalization: "They were taking us cruising on the Caribbean, so we owed them, so they could do what they liked with us" (97). The police chief, however, refers to honor and guilt in the very same terms pronounced by Coetzee: "You are sure you want to do this (meaning, are you sure you want this story to get out), because, you know, dishonour, *infâmia*, is like bubble gum, wherever it touches, it sticks" (100). Yet, Anya takes the opposite choice to that taken by the daughter of the protagonist in JC's previous novel *Disgrace*, who decided not to present charges against the men who raped her. Anya metafictionally presents a powerful reversal (or revision) to JC's previous narratives on honor. She retorts, "This is the twentieth century, capitano (it was still the twentieth century then). In the twentieth century, when a man rapes a woman it is the man's dishonor" (101). After exposing her case, she directs herself to her employer, whom she also calls "señor C":

> When you tell me you walk around bent under your load of dishonour, I
> think of those girls from the old days who had the bad luck to get raped
> and then had to wear black for the rest of their lives—wear black and sit in a
> corner and never go to parties and never get married. You have got it wrong,
> Mister C. (103–104)

For Anya, the problem of bending as a result of shame is not only a question of self-definition but also a problem of action and agency. Despite their horrible experience, Anya and her girlfriend report the rape, the American boys are arrested, their yacht is impounded, and unexpectedly the "story" has long-distance repercussions: "hit[ting] the papers back in Connecticut" (99). By doing that, the girls made sure the college boys' "little adventure" would have consequences: they prevented them from "[going to] look for another one [i.e., another adventure]" (98). Not convinced by Anya's argument, JC reacts to her story by stating, rather patronizingly, that he would be very surprised if down deep the boys' actions did not continue to dishonor her. Anya replies with "a ray of pure and cold rage" and the following words: "*Don't tell me what I feel!*" (115). This imperative marks the end of their relationship, as it was. Anya decides to quit her job as JC's typist; she refuses to continue to be treated as one of his characters. After typing his book, she moves to Brisbane, leaving her boyfriend Alan behind too, but most importantly, proving to her "employer" and "creator" that she can have a life of her own and free herself from his predefined plots and strong opinions.

This liberation and autonomy becomes also, paradoxically, an acknowledgment of the author's isolation. Later on, conscious of their differences in terms of intellectual status, but ultimately truthful to her worldview, she writes to JC:

Sometimes I blush when I think of the comments I made about your opinions [...] but then I think to myself, *Maybe he appreciated having a perspective from below, so to speak, an opinion of his opinions.* Because I did feel that you were taking a risk, being so isolated, so out of touch with the modern world. (196)

JC begs Anya to come back and acknowledges the role she played in the writing of his Diary: "You have become indispensable to me—to me and to the present project" (121). He realizes that since moving into "the orbit of Anya" there was a change in "[his] opinion of [his] opinions" (136). As a result he starts to write "gentler" opinions (145), about life, birds, love. Anya becomes, thus, not only his most significant connection to life but also his final companion, his guide toward death. Her "orbit" becomes the inescapable cycle of his existence, rendering the work of revision absolutely necessary. Indeed, JC begins his "Second Diary" by retelling a dream in which he "had died but not left the world yet" (157). He was in company of a woman, one of the living younger than [himself]" (157). "She was doing her best to soften the impact of death" (157). JC believes the story of Eurydice has been misunderstood: the story is about "the solitariness of death" (159). Eurydice is not Anya but JC himself. The writer becomes, thus, the wife of Orpheus "in hell in her grave clothes" (159). Abandoned, JC finds his virility questioned, his authority troubled, and his opinions softened.

Humanism and the loneliness of the public intellectual

At time when the rhetoric of humanism is used to promote the "interventions" made recently by the United States (in the name of "military humanism"), the writer who sees himself as a humanist finds himself in greater need of defending his ideas and positions and ascertain the value of humanistic principles. JC's diary makes clear that, after the War on Terror, it becomes even more pressing to pursue Edward Said's dictum: "to be critical of humanism in the name of humanism" (Said 2004, 10). This pursuit, however, is arduous and painful. Alan, Anya's boyfriend, emblematizes some of the economic and social tendencies of the twenty-first century opposed by JC. Like the narrators of *Netherland* and *Reluctant Fundamentalist*, he is an investment consultant;

he is a rude but necessary character to JC's narrative because his ruthless and manipulative approach to social relations exposes some of the connections between current military and economic enterprises. Like the narrators of novels by O'Neill and Hamid, respectively, his appearance in a narrative about the War on Terror unveils the role of recent military enterprises within the context of neoliberal globalization. But if Alan emerges as the main "antagonist" of the narrator, he is also, and most significantly, the person who voices the author's most profound misgivings about his own role as a writer. He is, perhaps not erroneously, suspicious of JC's intentions toward Anya but also of JC's premises as a public intellectual and liberal humanist. He accuses the writer of being both a "dreamer and a schemer" (196). He explains the latter:

> We are both schemers, you and I (Anya isn't a schemer at all), but at least I don't pretend. I am a schemer because I would be devoured alive if I wasn't, by the other beasts of the jungle. And you are a schemer because you pretend to be what you are not. You put yourself forward as a lone voice of conscience speaking for up for human rights and so forth, but I ask myself, If he really believes in these human rights, why isn't he out in the real world fighting for them? (196–197)

These accusations are part of the textual strategy that shapes Coetzee's argumentative narrative—a strategy that places pressure on the protagonist himself, as a way to provoke a reaction from his "anarchist quietistic pessimism" (203). The sections that divide the text into different voices split, segregate, and segment the overall body of the text, denying it unity or tranquility. Faced by the violence of the arguments it incorporates, the body of the text shudders, twitches, and hurts. By presenting a text that is thwarted, twisted, argumentative, and, in fact, hurtful toward its author, Coetzee is showing us how he cannot avoid applying strategies of torture upon himself. After all, "torture" derives from the Latin *torquere*, which comes from "to twist, turn, wind, wring, distort." The critic Barry Hill explains, quite clearly, the logic of his twisted text: "[T]hroughout *Diary* we come to a host of critical thoughts— expressed either by Alan or Anya or JC himself—which are fundamentally self-subversive: that reason cannot be potent in such dark times, that life's struggle cannot admit too many moral qualms, that any attempt to find the foundations of logic produces pompous mysticism" (Hill 2007). According to

Hill, JC becomes an "effigy into which pins can be shoved endlessly, each jab confirming his impotence" (2007).

JC's move to Australia offers no real relief from his felt complicity with systematic application of discriminatory practices and policies witnessed in South Africa. On the contrary, although Australia does not share either South Africa's or the United States' violent histories (Coetzee lived in Texas during the Vietnam war), it's duplicitous treatment of aboriginal people, adherence to neoliberal doctrines and enthusiastic part in the "coalition of the willing," led by the United States, all force the author to find, in his present, unwarranted images of his past. Indeed, *Diary* departs from the very premise that the liberal democratic state, for all its valorization of representative politics, is as authoritarian a system as any:

> If you take issue with democracy in times when everyone claims to be heart and soul a democrat, you run the risk of losing touch with reality. To regain touch, you must at every moment remind yourself of what it is like to come face to face with the state—the democratic state or any other—in the person of the state official. Then ask yourself: Who serves whom? Who is the servant, who the master? (15)

The author recognizes that "the alternatives are not placid servitude on the one hand and revolt against servitude on the other" and notices that there is a "third way, chosen by thousands and millions of people every day. It is the way of quietism, of willed obscurity, of inner emigration" (12). Yet, this option, which, no doubt, corresponds to the author's predisposition, proves to be as dangerous as its alternatives, and is ultimately more treacherous for a writer. As Anya's words suggest—"you were taking a risk, being so isolated, so out of touch with the modern world" (196)—isolation can be harmful for any man but it can entail a severe "risk" for an author who has always been engaged with the world around him. Indeed, the aging writer's impotence is heightened by the sense of entrapment and isolation which is promoted by contemporary culture, despite its global tendencies.

If the sense of isolation has been a staple of many of Coetzee's protagonists—in novels such as *Waiting for the Barbarians*, *The Heart of the Country*, *Life & Times of Michael K*, and *Age of Iron*—it gains particular resonance in this highly cosmopolitan text (a text commissioned by a German Publisher and written by a South African writer living in Australia with the help of his Australian-Filipina typist; a book which will be translated and published in different parts of the world), where transnational pressures, both political and cultural, only help to further intensify the writer's desire to withdraw. In a text which is so patently concerned with the renewal of authoritarian practices, JC's isolation is both tragic and symptomatic. As Hannah Arendt suggested in *The Origins of Totalitarianism,* "what prepares men for totalitarian domination in the non-totalitarian world is the fact that loneliness, once a borderline experience usually suffered in certain marginal social conditions like old age, has become an everyday experience of the ever-growing masses of our century" (Arendt 2004, 615). Citing Luther, Arendt also shows how loneliness promotes "self-evident logicality": a "deducing process which always arrives at the worst possible conclusions" (615). JC's felt isolation becomes, thus, aggravated at the end of his "Strong Opinions." As a way to challenge his isolating pessimism, JC devotes some of his final opinions to Harold Pinter's attack on Tony Blair in his Nobel Prize acceptance speech during which he recognizes that "there comes a time when the outrage and shame are so great that all calculation, all prudence, is overwhelmed and one must act, that is to say, speak" (127). It is also highly significant, then, the fact that in the *Diary*'s very final pages—the concluding notes of "Second Diary"—JC should present the work of Tolstoy and Dostoyevsky as major literary models. In a cold recalling of Russian authors, JC invites the West to rethink its affiliations and recognize itself in the face of its historical "others." Tolstoy and Dostoyevsky pose a number of difficult questions which make JC desire to be a "better artist." He explains, "by better I do not mean more skillful but *ethically* better" (italics mine). These authors are unique for the way they face dishonor and shame and for the way they revolve about the notion of *confession,* which is so central to the tortuous writing of this *Diary*.[7] By providing the author with a "better" kind of "diary," these writers also allow the writer a final act of liberation; a release from the captivity of his time and of his aging body: "[T]hey annihilate one's impurer pretensions, they clear one's eyesight; they fortify one's arm" (Coetzee 1992, 227).

Read side by side, *Shalimar* and *Diary* convey differently the ways in which colonial history continues to shape and inform current imperial configurations. In terms of the authors' relationships with their characters, it is as if each novel moved in different, if not opposing, directions. Rushdie makes an insightful narration of the colonial and imperial continuum and the emergence of global terrorist networks by exacerbating the urges and desires of his characters and illustrating their power through the plasticity of magical realism. Powerful historical figures become in this context both epic and pathetic. In *Diary* we are, on the contrary, faced by public and private flaws, by a fractured and often powerless narrative which interrogates the western subject's complicity with the logic of new empires. Coetzee's result is more somber but not less sharp.

In Rushdie's work there is a clear movement of projection, as the author seems to throw into the lives of his characters not only experiences and notes of temperament which are fantasies of more glamorous, heroic, but also inevitably parodic and even comical, versions of himself. The author challenges his own biography of confinement by creating a world where fear cannot ultimately trump desire. Coetzee, on the other hand, introjects the flaws, vices, and political wrongdoings. The old and aging body of the protagonist of *Diary* assumes as his own the failures of democratic liberal systems as well as of humanist liberalism. Fear of failure is the real agent of the Coetzee's self-imposed captivity. Fear in Coetzee's novel is instigated by an inner, private enemy: it is related with the alarming possibility that the author's oeuvre may not rise to the occasion. It is caused by the horror of seeing his body failing to accompany his intellect, by the anxiety of not being able to translate his felt complicity with the times into a capacity to act, that is, to write ethically.

The work of these two writers conveys a critical cosmopolitanism which is both aware of their original backgrounds as well as their privileged mobility across the US–EU nexus. Both writers faced directly the mechanisms of security imposed inside and outside their countries of origin. Yet, despite the difference in terms of their experiences with "terrorism" (state-endorsed as well as insurgent), their work converges in very significant ways. In the aftermath of 9/11, both urge their readers to examine contemporary forms of terror in light of the legacies of colonialism. Both are adamant about the importance of unveiling about the roles played not only by the United States, but also of Europe and the West at large, as part of that history.

Transatlantic Fictions: Captivity, Security, and Futurity

If examined beyond the paradigms of trauma which have dominated literary and critical responses to the attacks, 9/11 novels become something else. While many of these narratives naturally grieve the deaths and destruction caused by the attacks, most of these texts nevertheless attempt to recover sight, see through the pain, and tell their story. Bedazzled as they may be by the phenomenon which came to be known as "9/11," they disclose anxieties, aspirations, frustrations, and desires framed by their specific location; they depict and reimagine their particular contexts. They reclaim not only feelings but also thoughts, arguments, and ideas—which we are, often, led to believe to be incompatible with pain. Speaking about our age and driven by millennial apprehensions, they reflect upon the history of the West, about old colonial legacies, and new imperial enterprises. Many dwell on American fantasies and their global reach, while others expose Europe's fractured and awkward self-image. Some—as those gathered here—speak about an uncomfortable Euro-American nexus, its worldwide identifications and projections. Even when the wound is very much open and the text still visibly pregnant with anxiety, as happens with many novels written within the first five years after the attacks, these texts do not ultimately surrender to silence under the aegis of trauma's linguistic paradox. Despite common moments of muteness and hesitation, these texts also depend upon structures, senses, and meanings which depart from the current crisis to explore long-standing troubles and to ponder about the future. To attempt to read these texts otherwise implies necessarily to acknowledge their pain but to choose to depart from specific symptoms rather than from a pre-given diagnosis (i.e., trauma). To examine these texts otherwise implies acknowledging movements, gestures, and positions which have been neglected by readers and critics. It also implies recognizing that recurring pain is often correlated with older—often untreated—wounds, and that to ignore the ongoing causes for such wounds may lead to new or renewed injuries.

If the agony disclosed by these novels is usually staged in the city, it is not merely the setting or depiction of specific urban spaces that concerns these texts but also larger questions about the very notion of "polis." While representing the many faces of the besieged city, these novels interrogate the meaning of citizenship, ponder about governance, and question the law and the management of common spaces. The city, depicted in these novels, is far from a tidy political abstraction. More often than not, it emerges as messy place which exposes the paroxysm of crisis in its manifold meanings (fracture, rupture, and decision); it is above all an insecure space where *polis* is always in danger to become critical, but where *krísis* may also be the necessary action or place of departure for political ethics. In these novels, visual references to New York are often transfigured into more uncomfortable images of Kabul or Baghdad; European cities such as Paris and London absorb and react against the iconography of "American metropolis," while Lisbon and Spain address the violence of their marginal position as capitals without global capital. Further away from the Atlantic (but not beyond its reach), Kashmir and Sydney intersect with US, European, and African cities where the violence of colonial history continues to shape global maps, demanding longer views.

By extending the study of post-9/11 fiction to include international and transnational perspectives, I have aimed to show how the hegemonic grip of security discourses, exacerbated by the War on Terror, penetrates urban imaginaries from different geographical coordinates, but I have also registered significant paths, passages, and moments where the novels contest, pierce through, and decenter dominant notions of terror. My concern has focused purposefully on the EU–US nexus. Although this affiliation reemerges from time to time in public discourse, the imperial and colonial narratives that are still shared by the two geopolitical powers have received little attention by scholars of contemporary literature. Yet, this liaison projects itself materially and phantasmatically not only across the Atlantic but far beyond it. In order to understand the relation between transatlantic narratives and contemporary politics, I have observed how texts written by English, French, Portuguese,

Spanish, and Irish writers approach not only the 9/11 attacks but also the War on Terror, and with particular attention the invasion of Iraq—a war which, although largely unpopular and divisive in Europe, did not dissuade European countries to assume a key long-term role in the War on Terror and its politics of preemption.[1] The inclusion, within this literary corpus, of writers like Mohsin Hamid, Salman Rushdie and J.M. Coetzee, whose view of Euro-American relations is profoundly shaped by their own experiences of Asian and African histories, has been crucial to the sort of transatlantic approach required here, since their perspectives invite us to consider the War on Terror in light of the legacies of previous intercontinental narratives of captivity. None of the novels examined here are meant to represent to stand for a single, homogenous or "official" national perspective, even if such a thing could be attained. These are clearly localized texts which, more or less anxiously, attempt to achieve global visions, but they are also documents that clearly engage with national and international politics while assuming, if only fleetingly, positions of eccentricity without representation in formal political debates.

Novels are extremely revealing about the points of convergence and contradiction of Euro-American relations, but little work has been done to understand the conflicting, and often uncomfortable, political and cultural implications of that nexus from a literary perspective. I hope this book will show how the study of cultural and contemporary transatlantic affairs requires self-reflective and self-critical positions from both sides of the Atlantic. An understanding of American imperialism implies recognizing crucial moments when European powers have not only failed to resist US foreign policies, but have also been compliant, complacent, and active supporters of imperialist strategies. To study the cultural and literary expression of US empire entails, thus, the acknowledgment of the ways non-US texts, writers, critics and intellectuals have either contributed to, accepted, or challenged US global power, and the effort to understand the transnational fantasies which have sustained such positions.

As I have attempted to demonstrate, the sense of ongoing threat embodied by the fictional cities examined throughout this book is a key narrative motif in the fictions of white western middle-class captivity which, since the 9/11 attacks, have been resurrected with particular poignancy in both sides of the

Atlantic. These fictions, which are deep-rooted in Euro-American imaginaries, reveal the persistence of political and cultural discourses about "ourselves" (i.e., the western subject) and its "other" (potential captors) which have been updated, renewed, and expanded throughout the centuries, justifying fears and desires about territorial security, expansion, political affirmation, and consolidation. Fueled by the media, the psycho-geographical movement of self-portrayals of captivity is naturally supple and free-floating. As these narratives travel in time and space, they become highly flexible, fluid, and exchangeable accounts, adaptable to multiple crises. The mobilization of narratives of captivity has played an important role in politics. Although its usage has been intensified worldwide since 9/11, it is not a new element of political discourse. As I have suggested earlier, narratives of captivity by aliens of different kinds proliferated during the Cold War, and the captivity motif was certainly present in the Vietnam War's iconography and recurrently used in different expansionist initiatives. Nor have captivity narratives been merely a staple of conservative, right-wing political discourse. Although the framing of captivity fictions into western-genre language and narratives (rescue-revenge, *cowboy-Indian*) was a bold staple of George W. Bush's War on Terror rhetoric, one can also find, for instance, subtler versions of captivity narratives in the language of US Democratic presidents. President Barak Obama's rhetoric has been no exception. In an essay that examines Obama's own approach to the biopolitical settlement of George W. Bush's War on Terror, Donald E. Pease has luminously shown how, after having himself been the subject of a captivity narrative framed by the Tea Party, Obama managed to invert and rewrite that fantasy in his own terms (Pease 2013). If the Tea Party had created a racially loaded fantasy of President Obama as a terrorist—by, among other things, questioning his citizenship and suggesting that his health polices threatened the biopolitical security of the homeland—Obama, himself, decided to use an official and particularly mournful occasion to amend this narrative. In January 2011, Obama made an important address at a memorial service in Tucson in Arizona where a lone gunman had shot Congresswoman Gabrielle Giffords and several participants in a political rally. This tragedy, accompanied by the President's address, recalled, among other things, "a series of assassinations— of presidents and presidential candidates and charismatic civil rights leaders: Jack and Bobby Kennedy, Martin Luther King Jr., and Malcolm X" (Pease

2013, 226). This narrative allowed President Obama to present himself as the victim or captive—rather than the instigator of—an "armed terrorist's thanato-politics."[2] It can be argued that the twists in this narrative disclose more vital setbacks at the heart of Obama's presidency, more specifically the president's failure to accomplish the changes announced in his campaign. In the last five years, it has become apparent that Obama did not suspend George W. Bush's preemptive policies. Instead, President Obama renewed the legal reach of surveillance policies, failed to close Guantánamo Bay, increased the use of air strikes, and launched the bombing of military bases in Libya in 2011. Donald E. Pease shows how these policies have been accompanied by strategic metaphoric appropriations, such as those used by Obama in a speech made in Brazil in March 2011:

> In the body of his address President Obama constructed a series of dubious rhetorical analogies—correlating the "universal" human aspirations for freedom and socioeconomic justice informing the "Arab Spring" with his own grassroots movement, with his "humanitarian" intervention in Libya, as well as with his neoliberal trade agreements with Brazil—that would have been comparably unimaginable. President Obama's efforts to transpose the truly revolutionary movement taking place in the Middle East into a mirror image of his disbanded grassroots political movement rivaled the cynicism evidenced in the Tea Party's appropriative maneuvers. President Obama named his military campaign in Libya "Odyssey Dawn" so as to draw it into the imaginary orbit of the "Arab Spring," and he deployed technologies—drone missiles and special ops units—to remove those who were killed or disfigured from the field of visibility. (Pease 2013, 232)

As I am writing this conclusion, news and images of the beheading of two US journalists, James Foley and Steven Sotloff, and two British aid workers, David Haines and Alan Henning, captured by self-designated Islamic State of Iraq and Levant (ISIS), inundate the media.[3] The beheading of prisoners as a strategy to publicly exploit images of executions is far from new, but the broadcast of these videos has a powerful resonance in western media because it reinforces a number of elements typical of past narratives of captivity (such as the torture and brutal killing of well-intentioned[4] civilians by barbarian captors). The apparently self-exoticized portrayal conveyed by ISIS is meant, however, to invert the roles of *captor* and *captive* performed by its main characters. By dressing their US and English prisoners in orange jumpsuits, ISIS members turned these *captives* into reminders of Guantanamo's illegal detainees and the prison's unlawful history.[5] By extension, images of the "global homeland" are further distorted, exposed, and available for ransom.[6] In response to the murder of Steven Sotloff, the Committee to Protect Journalists (CPJ) presented a letter of condemnation for the beheadings stating that "He [Steven Sotloff], like James Foley, went to Syria to tell a story. They were civilians, not representatives of any government" ("CPJ condemns killing" 2014). CPJ's compassionate statement seems, nevertheless, to miss the point, since it is precisely *the telling of the story*, the narrative itself, that ISIS unashamedly wants to hijack. Through their grotesque visuality, these videos disclose the raw materials of war (blood, carnage, and desolation), as they respond to the air-strikes that Obama administration has attempted to keep sanitized and out of the field of vision, through the use of sophisticated military technology, restrained rhetoric, and mindful media coverage.

The narrative of "captivity" achieved in the videos of the beheadings depends upon a number of visual arrests. Like the attack on the Twin Towers which turned US cultural and economic apparatus against itself, the images of these beheaded prisoners attempted to invert the narratives of US domination by speaking directly to the masses. Indeed, the images of these captives take us back to images of DeLillo's photographer in *Mao II*, a novel where the visual image, whose reproduction is intricately connected to the desires of the "crowd," emerges as the creator and guardian of a new reality. Conscious of the multiple roles played by visual culture in the intricate relation between political and fictional narratives, most 9/11 novels tend to reproduce and comment upon the visual spectacle of this terrorizing language. Particularly important, however, are the specific passages and texts which go beyond the surface of highly mediatized images to recognize and explore the optical unconscious of War on Terror, from both sides of the Atlantic. Indeed, if we look through the recurring images of fallen towers, in the domestic setting of novels such as McEwan's *Saturday*, we find accusatory photographs of Abu Ghraib and Camp Bread Basket. If we look closer at Beigbeder's Montparnasse Tower, we will find cinematic images of an international playboy which has been bankrupt since the Cold War. The falling bodies in Michael Cunningham's "In the Machine" reveal hidden pictures of the Triangle Shirtwaist Factory and of terrors that haunt the United States from the inside. Hamid and O'Neill penetrate the virtual reality of *Google* maps and credit cards to assert the limits of their cosmopolitan visions. Rushdie and Coetzee offer us distorted maps where images of colonial history emerge. If we look closely at the photo of the displaced son of Menéndez Salmón's narrator, in *El corrector*, we find a simulacrum of Europe's future (always already elsewhere).

Saramago's *Seeing* is perhaps the novel more deeply concerned in reframing notions of visuality in light of contemporary politics, and for that reason, I will leave you with a final note about its proposition here. Facile or simplistic readings of Saramago's *Seeing* would easily equate the motif of visuality in the novel with a defense enlightened rationality. To associate an author, who always remained faithful to the Portuguese Communist party, with old-fashion notions of enlightenment would be tempting for many. However, careful readings of Saramago's novels, *Blindness* and *Seeing*, clearly show us that concepts such as *vision* and *blindness* are often not what they seem, independently of their political context. Saramago not only complicates ideas of sightlessness by introducing the idea of "white blindness," challenging the obscurity we associate with lack of vision, but he also posits the possibility of creative communal relations in his depiction of *blind* and *seeing* communities, alike (Vieira 2009). More than a defense for enlightened reason, Saramago's work forces us to engage with the perils of totalizing images, not only in mainstream party politics but also in both sides of the political spectrum. The plague of blank votes, representing as it does the rejection of simulacra, is an embodiment of terror for politicians from both "left" and "right." Visions of another—more desirable—polis are necessarily left out of the frame of the novel; the eye of the narrative captures only the simulacrum (the search for the terrorist group of blank-voters as a rescue-and-revenge narrative), and the rest can only be "seen" by the reader.

Captivity narratives seem, thus, to be omnipresent: they go back and forth; they are employed and reemployed; they help to frame arguments and retorts between public figures, having become significant staples of western imagination. Again and again, they have been appropriated not only US politicians but also, as we have seen in some of the previous chapters, by their European counterparts. Tony Blair, the grand advocate for the War on Terror, was also the main promoter of "weapons of mass destruction" captivity which justified the invasion of Iraq. Less famous but equally necessary have been also the narratives promoted by apparently minor, but always necessary secondary characters, such as those embodied by the former Portuguese prime minister Manuel Barroso. Having supported the Iraq War in the name of an Atlantic vision, Manuel Barroso became president of the European Commission in 2004 and the main representative of a "Peaceful Europe" fantasy, having received—alongside Herman Van Rompuy and Martin Schulz—the Nobel Peace Prize for the European Union in 2012. Paradoxically—or perhaps necessarily—motifs of captivity have been also reused and revised by left-wing, liberal intellectuals, and other avid critics of current political discourse and opponents of War on Terror. Indeed, as I have shown, within the literary corpus examined here, the most painful allegories of political captivity, the most forceful depictions of the stalemate of current political discourse and party politics in the West, belong perhaps to Coetzee and Saramago, in two very different texts which bravely recognize the moments when the authors' own visions inevitably fall prey to ideological traps.

Faced by the reach of captivity narratives, one may ask if it still makes sense to speak about "polis" in relation to transatlantic urban fictions. Sociological work on risk has examined the impact of modern fears, particularly in Europe and the United States, and has greatly shaped our view of contemporary urban life. The German sociologist Ulrik Beck and the British sociologist Anthony Giddens are the two authors who contributed more to the concept of "risk society."[7] Their studies have not only demonstrated the ways in which modern society organizes itself against risks, but they have also suggested that our perceptions of fear may have a positive potential. In 2001, Ulrich Beck published an article where he states that terrorism opened a "new chapter in world risk society" (Beck 2002). This new chapter has less to do with the actual dangers posed by the threat than with the state of watchfulness it promotes: "[T]he greatest danger, therefore, is not risk, but the perception of it, which releases fantasies of danger and of the antidotes to them, thereby robbing modern society of its freedom and action" (2002). Rather than seeing this *perceived threat* [sic] as a problem, he presents it as an opportunity: "A question repeatedly raised and discussed in the past was the following: what can unite the world? The experimental answer was: An attack from Mars. [...] Suddenly the rivalries between the various European nations dissolve and their common interests come to the fore, not only within Europe, but also between Europeans and the United States—a bad time for Euro-skeptics" (2002). Different views are offered by the sociologist Frank Furedi, who has responded to the work of the above authors, considering that the proposed emphasis on the political management of risk reinforces the acceptance of an irrevocable loss of trust in progress and depends upon a definition of the modern subject based on vulnerability rather than resilience. Furedi maintains that "*the tendency to offer fear as* the negative moral foundation for community renewal is underwritten by the assumption that a positive vision of the future can no longer provide the focus for the construction of social consensus" (Furedi 2006, 137). The novels examined here acknowledge and interrogate this tendency. They respond to— by absorbing, rewriting, or attempting to revise—negative utopias or, indeed, political dystopias which we have not yet been able to counter.

Contemporary narratives of captivity register and shape our structure of feeling. Throughout this book, I have paid particular attention to the social, cultural, and ideological construction of notions such as "terror" and "insecurity," and I have made use of psychoanalysis to examine concepts such as "fear," "apprehension," and "anxiety" which, although distinct from the above notions, interact directly with them offering us a more complete view of the psychosocial fabric that sustains current narratives of captivity. Studies on the rhetoric of the War on Terror tend to focus on the concept of "terror" as an ideological sublime, rather than from more tangible and localized notion of *fear* (Jacques Rancière view of terror as a mode of perception, for example, derives precisely from such a distinction).[8] However, terror can also usefully be examined in proximity with a number of other—more or less substantial or object-driven—emotional categories such as fear, anxiety, insecurity, etc. An examination of the intricate relation between these categories will allow us to better understand the social continuum that justifies in the long term the suppleness and resilience of captivity narratives. This continuum can, of course, in itself serve political purposes (after all politicians tame some fears in order to fuel others; there are also "known knowns" and "known unknowns"[9]). However, it is through mainstream cultural processes (media, art, education, etc.) that the relation between those feelings assumes a cohesive narrative and becomes part of our daily lives. Although the relations between fear, anxiety, terror, and insecurity have received some attention from psychoanalytic theorists, more notice is required from scholars working with cultural, literary, and fictional texts. Focus on the fictional, narrative, and linguistic elements that articulate and organize the above feelings and reactions will allow us a better understanding of the emotional spectrum of captivity narratives, as well as of the ways they travel from country to country, from culture to culture, from time to time.

Texts, characters, writers, and readers create, rather than merely reflect, the polis. Culture not only reproduces but can actively stimulate or subvert the narratives put forward by the politics of fear and the rhetoric of the War on Terror. The transatlantic view, proposed here, allows us to consider cultural transactions established between the United States and Europe which have been largely ignored, but more work is needed to understand all the mechanisms which underpin transnational projections. That work needs to engage necessarily with the ongoing examination and dissection of "America"—a fantasy of US centrism and expansionism which scholars have been forcefully challenging for more than two decades. However, one should not overlook the fate of another—distinctive but intimately related—fantasy, created and propagated worldwide and reinvigorated with the emergence of the European Community—the fantasy of "Europe," itself. The renewal of this fantasy, which naturally embodies historically specific and localized continental dreams, has been partly promoted in association—rather than competition—with fears and desires shaped by the United States. Such a fantasy has been reinforced by a long history of circum-atlantic movements, deeply connected to a legacy of colonial and neocolonial settlement. This is an argument which I believe is worth exploring further and that would certainly benefit from self-reflective approaches within cultural and literary studies. Finally, let me highlight that, while I believe that robust transnational, international, comparative cultural studies are certainly needed to understand the fabric of captivity narratives, these "new approaches" should not ignore the points of resistance mapped out by specific area studies, national cultural studies, and localized theories.

Narratives of captivity offer important insights about western fears and fantasies: they allow us to come to terms with narcissistic views of ourselves as both heroes and victims; they dislocate anxieties that expound paternalistic views of others; they speak about political manipulations and the recognition of our inner terrors; they speak about social stagnation and political impasse. Yet, they also reveal unexpected paths by dwelling on moments of identification with the Other or on instances of desire for something Other. Indeed, even in fearful prewar fantasies such as Ian McEwan's *Saturday*, we find instances that disrupt the conservative strain of the main narrative, such as that moment when the main character, surgeon Perowne, attempts to save his captor by trying to get "inside" the head of the thug Baxter, his *social other*. With this gesture, McEwan's main character recognizes, if only momentarily, the limiting focus of his white middle-class captivity fantasy and discards the comfort of its transatlantic reach.

To conclude, allow me to direct my words to my imagined community of readers through the plural, collective "we"—a necessary fantasy of transoceanic readership for the loose stitching of an impossible closure. Let me finish by suggesting that our way out of captivity may demand, first of all, the recognition that the possibilities of capture are manifold—we will find these fictions again and again in the many texts that cross and become part of our lives. Yet we must dare to find in them something else: a door left ajar, a crack in a window frame, a movement, or a becoming. We must dare to face up the possibilities of change—*that* postponed terror. This implies reimagining or recognizing ourselves beyond our comfortable jumpsuits, beyond the logic of preemption, beyond customized freedoms. It implies learning to read *insecurely*.

Notes

Chapter 1

1   The first two books published on 9/11 literature, *Literature after 9/11* edited
    by Ann Keniston and Jeanne Follansbee Quinn, published in 2008, and
    Kristiaan Versluys's *Out of the Blue: September 11 and the Novel*, published
    in 2009, are emblematic of the early reception of these novels. The first is an
    edited collection dedicated to 9/11 fiction. The articles in this collection draw
    on a wide range of theoretical perspectives: from trauma theory to genre
    theory and from theories of postmodernity to theories of space and time.
    Kristiaan Versluys's *September 11 and the Novel* is consistently engaged with
    trauma theory. As the first monograph devoted to 9/11 fiction, this book
    has a clear goal which it thoroughly pursues: to explore "the emotional and
    ethical impact of these traumatic events". Kristiaan Versluys. 2009. *Out of
    the Blue: September 11 and the Novel.* New York: Columbia University Press,
    17. Versluys sensitively acknowledges that traumatic discourse is loaded
    with old dichotomies which reinforce the radical "Othering" of the terrorist
    subject. He perceptively shows how some writers are able to avoid such
    dichotomies, addressing the issue of alterity while maintaining an ethical
    responsibility for the "Other" in Levinas's sense of the term. This analysis
    is, nevertheless, always framed by the paradigm of trauma that shapes the
    study. The tenth anniversary of 9/11 saw the publication of *After the Fall:
    American Literature After 9/11* by Richard Gray and *9/11 and The Literature
    of Terror* by Martin Randall, both of which benefit from the perspective of
    a longer view, disclosing more awareness of the political discourses that
    penetrates these works. Although these authors acknowledge that the War
    on Terror, 9/11, and the invasions of Afghanistan and Iraq have changed the
    climate of US literature, they do not examine how the representation of such
    events can complicate or problematize the primacy of the trauma paradigm
    which dominates critical analyses of these texts. Both authors are primarily

interested in defining the heterogeneous group of literary works on 9/11, taking into account the differences in terms of strategies and positions of the texts written in the last decade. Like Versluys, Gray welcomes those writers able to avoid the dichotomies of political discourse engaging formally with hybridity and thus resisting "the challenge of silence by deploring forms of speech that are genuinely crossbred and transitional, subverting the oppositional language of mainstream commentary—us and them, West and East, Christian and Muslim" Richard Gray. 2011. *After the Fall: American Literature Since 9/11*. Chichester, UK: Wiley and Sons, 17. It is in this fusion of voices that, according to Gray, the "bearing witness of trauma can really occur" (17). Trauma is also a concern in Martin Randall's analysis of fiction, poetry, theater, and cinema about the 9/11 attacks. Randall cites an article by Ian McEwan written immediately after 9/11, in order to highlight that the "urge to 'put into words' the personal and collective suffering endured on 9/11, to 'narrativise' the seemingly inchoate events and then in some way to be able to 'speak' of the day's trauma and therefore, however incompletely, 'heal' some of the massive loss, is redolent of Holocaust Literature." Martin Randall. 2011. *9/11 and the Literature of Terror*. Edinburgh: Edinburgh University Press, 31–32. The redolence mentioned by Randall is, however, never problematized. At the heart of Randall's concept of "literature of terror" lies the "conviction that whatever 9/11 may or may not mean for the global political situation there is little doubt that it has fundamentally and irrevocably ruptured reality" (35).

2   This comment was first made by Christopher Bollas in the Hermes Doctoral Summer School—"Fear and Fantasy in a Global World," organized by the Centre for Comparative Studies, FLUL, in Cascais, June 12–18, 2011. The comment was later written and e-mailed to me by the author, at my request.

3   For Baudrillard, 9/11 has become an iconic event—terrorism's "mother-event." Jean Baudrillard. 2002. "The Spirit of Terrorism." Trans. Michel Valentin. *The South Atlantic Quarterly* 101.2, 403. On the same topic, Jacques Derrida suggests: "The brevity of this appellation (September 11, 9/11) stems not only from an economic or rhetorical necessity. The telegram of this metonymy—a name, a number—points out the unqualifiable by recognizing that we do not recognize or even cognize, that we do not yet know how to qualify, that we do not know what we are talking about." Giovanna Borradori. 2003. "Autoimmunity: Real and Symbolic Suicides—A Dialogue with Jacques Derrida." *Philosophy in a Time of*

Terror: Dialogues with Jurgen Habermas and Jacques Derrida. Chicago: University of Chicago Press, 86.

4   For an examination of DeLillo's oeuvre in relation to the temporality of late capitalism and the millennial moment, see Peter Boxall. 2006. *Don DeLillo: The Possibility of Fiction*. London: Routledge.

5   The photograph by Tom Junod initially appeared in newspapers around the world, including on page 7 of the *New York Times* on September 12, 2001. The title "The Falling Man" is, however, the title of an article about the photograph by Junod that was published in the September 2003 issue of Esquire magazine. In 2006, filmmaker Henry Singer and Richard Numeroff made a documentary film, entitled, *9/11: The Falling Man*, focusing on the picture and on Junod's Esquire story.

6   *Mao II* (1991) is a particularly interesting example of a postmodern reworking of captivity motifs because entrapment is explored at the intersection between literature, photography, and international terrorism. In his article "Seeing Terror, Feeling Art: Public and Private in Post-9/11 Literature," Michael Rothberg highlights that Don DeLillo's novel *Mao II* reveals the writer's "prescience of large-scale, international terrorism—demonstrating that the global culture already possessed a discourse for terrorism" (123). Michael Rothberg. 2008. "Seeing Terror, Feeling Art: Public and Private in Post-9/11 Literature," in Ann Keniston and Jean Follansbee Quinn (eds.), *Literature After 9/11*. New York: Routledge, 123–142.

7   *The Sovereignty and Goodness of God*, also known as *A Narrative of the Captivity and Removes of Mrs. Mary Rowlandson*, or as *The True History of the Captivity and Restoration of Mrs. Mary Rowlandson*, was written sometime between 1676 and 1682 in the Massachusetts Bay Colony.

8   On the subject of British Captivity narratives, see, for example, Elizabeth Denlinger. 2002. "Caught Between Worlds: British Captivity Narratives in Fact and Fiction." *Biography* 25.2, Spring, 391–394.

9   See, for example, Alex P. Schmid. 2011. "The Definition of Terrorism," in *The Routledge Handbook of Terrorism Research*. London and New York: Routledge, 39.

10 For an examination of the notion of "Homeland" in relationship with the political rhetoric of the Bush administration see Amy Kaplan. 2003. "Homeland Insecurities: Some Reflections on Language and Space." *Radical History Review* 85, Winter, 82–93. See also Donald E. Pease, "The Extraterritoriality of the Literature for Our Planet," ESQ 50, 1–3: 177–221.

Chapter 2

1   Voicing an idea also expressed by several critical commentators after 9/11, Slavoj Žižek suggests that the September 11 attacks were "the stuff of popular fantasies long before they actually took place." Slavoj Žižek. 2002. *Welcome to the Desert of the Real.* London: Verso: 17.

2   In an article published soon after the September 11 attacks, McInerney, for instance, is presented as "the author of the definitive modern New York novel." Jay McInerney. 2001. "Brightness Falls." *The Guardian*, September 15: 1. In a later article, dedicated to 9/11 fiction, McInerney also presents New York as his "proper subject." See Jay McInerney. 2005. "The Uses of Invention." *The Guardian*, September 17: 4–6.

3   See Donald E. Pease. 2004. "The Extraterritoriality of the Literature for Our Planet." *ESQ* 50.1–3, 177–221.

4   The sense of ongoing malaise, paralysis, and absurdity in human relations that prevails in DeLillo's novel has much in common with Deborah Eisenberg's *Twilight of the Superheroes* (2006), a collection of stories where New York also stages critical anxieties about the future.

5   *Extremely Loud and Incredibly Close.* 2011. Dir. Stephan Daldry. Warner Brothers and Paramount Pictures. Released: December 25. Film.

6   Arad and Walker's actual memorial, "Reflecting Absense" shares a number of traits with the main competitor of "The Garden" in Waldman's novel, a design called "The Void," which is described as a somber twelve-story high black granite rectangle hospitable to ambiguity and uncertainty. When Mo is forced to withdraw from the competition, it is "The Void" that will ultimately take its place as the official 9/11 memorial. "The Void" is supported by the influential artist Ariana Montagu, which alludes to Maya Lin's pivotal support for "Reflecting Absense."

Chapter 3

1   Stephen Metcalf. 2005. "French Twist." *New York Times Book Review*, April 17: 96.

2   Laura Miller. 2005. " 'Windows on the World' by Frederic Beigbeder," March 20. Accessed: June 29, 2015, http://dir.salon.com/story/books/review/2005/03/20/beigbeder/index.html

3   Blurb from the Harper Perennial, 2005, paperback version of Beigbeder's book. In one of the first chapters of *Windows on the World*, Beigbeder not only includes McInerney in a list of his favorite US writers but also mentions having met him

in Paris. Frédéric Beigbeder. 2005. *Windows on the World*. Trans. Frank Wynne. London: Harper Perennial: 17.

4   Beigbeder, *Windows on the World*, 16–17. Subsequent references to this novel will be given in parenthesis in the text.

5   Since September 11, 2001, there has been a renewed interest in French travelogs about the United States. Alongside Beigbeder's book, another good example of this new literary trend is Bernard Henry Lévy's journey through the United States in the footpath of Toqueville. See Bernard-Henry Lévy. 2006. *American Vertigo: Travelling America in the Footsteps of Toqueville*. Trans. Charlotte Mandell. New York: Random House.

6   The French narrator invites autobiographical readings of his section of the novel by presenting, among other references, a suggestive pun with the author's surname: "My name is Frédéric Belvédère." Beigbeder, *Windows on the World*, 95.

7   While Carthew sees himself in the figure of Sinclair Lewis's George Babbitt, Frédéric finds his alter ego in Lester Burman, the protagonist of Sam Mendes's film *American Beauty*, whom he describes as a "cynical, phlegmatic guy, bored shitless with his perfect family." Beigbeder, *Windows on the World*, 39. See also Sam Mendes. 1999. *American Beauty*. Los Angeles: Dreamworks Pictures.

8   Walt Whitman's "Salut au Monde" as quoted by Beigbeder. Beigbeder, *Windows on the World*, 16.

9   Ed Folsom gives an excellent account of the ways Walt Whitman has been recently appropriated by George W. Bush's pro-war campaign. See Ed Folsom. 2005. "'What a Filthy Presidentiad:' Clinton's Whitman, Bush's Whitman, and Whitman's America." *Virginia Quarterly Review* 81. Spring, 96–113.

10   The term "axis of evil" was, famously, used by George W. Bush in his "State of the Union Address" on January 29, 2002, to describe governments such as Iraq, Iran, and North Korea, and to suggest that these countries were major sponsors of terrorism and producers of weapons of mass destruction.

11   Kristiaan Versluys. 2007. "9/11 as a European Event." *European Review* 15.1: 74. Versluys also mentions Luc Lang's *11 Septembre, mon amour* (2003) as an anti-US novel and a counterexample to Beigebder's text. Luc Lang's novel is narrated during his stay in an Indian reservation, and his novel works as anti-western. Influenced by his interest in Indian American history, Lang sees 9/11 as only the most recent in a list of mass-murders, some of which committed by the United States. Luc Lang. 2006. *11 Septembre, Mon Amour*. Paris: Stock.

12   June Namias. 1993. *White Captives: Gender and Ethnicity on the American Frontier*. Chapel Hill & London: The University of North Carolina Press: 17.

13   The female body, either covered (*hijabed*) or uncovered, has become, since 9/11, a central site for discussion of the differences between "Islam" and the "West." Regarding the references to female consumerism of Beigbeder's quotation, it is also interesting to note how characters from popular TV shows such as *Sex and the City* reiterated Mayor Rudy Giuliani's idea of shopping as a patriotic act. In the final season to the series, characters reacted to 9/11 by encouraging each other to shop even more, supposedly to encourage the city's financial recovery. Michael Patrick King. 1998–2004. *Sex and the City*. Series Six. New York City: HBO.

14   Barbara Mortimer. 2000. *Hollywood's Frontier Captives: Cultural Anxiety and the Captivity Plot in American Film*. New York & London: Garland Publishing: 5.

15   In *The Unredeemed Captive: A Family Story from Early America*, John Demos retells the story of Reverend John Williams captivity narrative of 1707. *The Redeemed Captive Returning to Zion* narrates Williams's efforts as a returned captive to secure the release of members of his family and his congregation who were captured by an alliance of Iroquois. Williams, however, is not able to secure the release of his youngest daughter Eunice, and he barely refers to her in his narrative. This silence becomes, nevertheless, a structuring pattern in Williams's narration. Yet, as John Demos significantly shows, Eunice refused to go back to her white family, having married a member of the Kahnewake Mohawk in 1713. See John Demos. 1994. *The Unredeemed Captive: A Family Story from Early America*. New York: Alfred A. Knopf.

16   Another example of a novel whose cover similarly makes use of London buildings to evoke the image of the attacks to the World Trade Center is Iain Banks's *Dead Air*. The cover of the 2003 Abacus edition of *Dead Air* depicts an image of a plane flying over the Battersea Power Station. See Iain Banks. 2003. *Dead Air*. London: Abacus.

17   Ian McEwan. 2005. *Saturday*. London: Jonathan Cape: 14. Subsequent references to this novel will be given in parenthesis in the text.

18   Laura Miller. 1998. "The Salon Interview: Ian McEwan." March 31. Accessed: June 29, 2015: http://archive.salon.com/books/int/2005/04/09/mcewan/index_np.html.

19   Joel Surnow and Robert Cochran. 2001. *24*. Los Angeles: Fox.

20   This political slogan was famously put forward by the US president George W. Bush in a news conference with the French president Jacques Chirac on November 6, 2001. George W. Bush. 2001. Cited in "Bush says it is time for action" *CNN.com/ U.S.*, November 6. Accessed date: June 29, 2015: http://edition.cnn.com/2001/US/11/06/ret.bush.coalition/

21   Susan A. Sontag points out that even though German soldiers in the Second World War took photographs of their activities in Poland and Russia,

photographs where the torturers photographed themselves alongside the prisoners are extremely rare. Susan Sontag. 2004. "Regarding the Torture of Others." *New York Times Magazine*, May 23. Accessed: June 29, 2015, http://www.nytimes.com/2004/05/23/magazine/regarding-the-torture-of-others.html. The Abu Ghraib photos can also be seen as self-portraits where the American soldiers depict a double vision of oppression and abuse, international as well as domestic. See Susana Araújo. 2006. "Propagating Images, Circulating Violence and Transatlantic Anxieties: McEwan in New York and Abu Ghraib," in George Handley and Patrick Imbert Amaryll Chanady. *America's Worlds and World's Americas*. IASA Conference Proceedings. Ottawa, ON: University of Ottawa/Legas, 196–197.

22 See, for instance, Allen G. Breed. 2004. "England Called to Explain Her 'Bit of Fun' on Her Abu Ghraib Night Shift." *The Independent*, August 4: 6. This article, which is supposed to relate the first day of a hearing to decide if Lynndie England should face court-martial, reveals an uncomfortable but compelling focus on the soldier's pregnant body.

23 "The Falling Man" is the title of the story by Tom Junod which accompanied the photograph taken by Richard Drew in the morning of September 11, 2001. Tom Junod. 2003. "The Falling Man." *Esquire*, September 1: 177–199.

24 The image of "the falling man" has not only been avidly used by the media but also been famously recreated in literature. In the last pages of *Extremely Loud and Incredibly Close* by Jonathan Safran Foer, a sequence of photos of a human figure falling from the towers is presented in reverse to give an impression that the person is flying rather than jumping. The image is also evoked in Don DeLillo's *Falling Man*. In this novel, the title refers, among other things, to a performance artist who recreates the events of 9/11 by jumping from elevated structures. Jonathan Safran Foer. 2005. *Extremely Loud and Incredibly Close*. London & New York: Hamish Hamilton. Don DeLillo. 2007. *The Falling Man*. New York: Scribner.

25 The threat which is seen to be directly posed against women in these novels—by either Islamic terrorists or lower-class "thugs"—is also presented as testing ground to their femininity and female mores. Also significant is the threat posed against children in both novels, which exposes anxieties not only about maternity but also about paternity; the latter is presented in relation to new forms of masculinity. The idea of the absent father, for instance, is conveyed in both novels: in *Windows of the World*, Beigbeder accuses himself of abandoning his child, whereas in *Saturday*, Perowne wonders about the paternal competence of Giulio, Daisy's Italian partner (a character which is literally absent from the plot). Beigbeder, *Windows on the World*, 181, 209; McEwan, *Saturday*, 275.

Chapter 4

1   Richard Chase famously criticized Whitman for viewing history as a force which is essentially predisposed toward democracy. See Richard Chase. 1955. *Walt Whitman Reconsidered*. New York: William Sloane. David Marr faults Whitman for contradicting the spirit of democratic plurality in his yearning for a unitary national literature. See David Marr. 1988. *American Worlds since Emerson*. Amherst, MA: University of Massachusetts Press. Betsy Erkkila considers that Whitman fails to achieve a convincing merge between its visionary ambition and the actual social reality that grounds his work. See Betsy Erkkila. 1989. *Whitman the Political Poet*. New York: Oxford University Press.

2   Although Sam Hamill had been one of the poets invited to Laura Bush's event, the poet declined the invitation and in response to that he organized the Poets Against the War movement. See John Nichols. 2003. "Poetic Protests against War, Censorship". *The Nation*, February 4. Available: http://www.alternet.org/waroniraq/15100/ (Accessed April 2009).

3   Much of the text that later composed the book had been published in periodicals, and most of the Civil War section had formed a book entitled *Memoranda during the War* (1875–1876).

4   See, for example, "Elements of 'civil war' in Iraq" in *BBC News*, February 2. Accessed: June 29, 2015. http://news.bbc.co.uk/2/hi/middle_east/6324767.stm.

5   This picture appears in several later US editions of *Leaves of Grass* and a cropped version of the picture was also used in 1869 by William Michael Rossetti in the British edition of Walt Whitman's poems.

6   A great amount of scholarly work has been dedicated to Whitman's relation to visual culture. See, for instance, Alan Trachtenberg. 1989. "Mirror in the Marketplace: American Responses to the Daguerreotype." In *The Daguerreotype: A Sesquicentennial Celebration*. Edited by J. Wood. Iowa City: University of Iowa Press: 60–73; Matthew Baigell, "Walt Whitman and Early Twentieth-Century American Art." In *Walt Whitman and the Visual Arts*. Edited by Geoffrey M. Sill and Roberta K. Tarbell. New Brunswick: Rutgers UP: 121–141; Ruth L. Bohan. 1992. "The Gathering of the Forces': Walt Whitman and the Visual Arts in Brooklyn in the 1850s." In *Walt Whitman and the Visual Arts*. Edited by Geoffrey M. Sill and Roberta X. Tarbell. New Brunswick: Rutgers UP: 1–27.

7   This idea is reiterated in another entry written after the death of the president. This is called, plainly, "No good Portrait of Lincoln" where Whitman describes with the same photographic eye "Lincoln's face, the peculiar colour, the lines of

it, the eyes, the expression." He adds, "[o]f technical beauty it had nothing—but
to the eye of a great artist it furnished a rare study, a feast and fascination."
Walt Whitman. 2004. *The Portable Whitman*. Edited by M. Warner. London:
Penguin, 641.

8   See Irene Ramalho Santos, *Atlantic Poets: Fernando Pessoa's Turn in Anglo-
    American Modernism*. Hanover, NH: University Press of New England, 2003.

Chapter 5

1   For biographical and bibliographical information on the author, see
    Contemporary Writers in the UK Database. Accessed: June 29, 2015, http://
    literature.britishcouncil.org/mohsin-hamid

2   From "I Dream'd in a Dream" in *Leaves of Grass* by Walt Whitman as quoted by
    O'Neill in the epigraph to *Netherland*.

Chapter 6

1   According to the European Commission, the term "EU periphery" is used to
    describe those countries "with 75% or less of the EU average GDP per capita,"
    and which "comprise the western and southern seaboards of the Union."
    European Commission—Economic and Social Research Institute. 1997. "The
    cases of Greece, Spain, Ireland and Portugal." *The Single Market Review*, Subseries
    VI Aggregate and Regional Impact, 2, Luxembourg, 9.

2   The term "coalition of the willing" had already been used in other political
    contexts (President Bill Clinton, for instance, used it to refer to advocate for
    international cooperation against North Korea's use of nuclear weapons),
    but its usage over Iraq became recurrent in US president George W. Bush's
    speeches since 2002. See "Bush: Join 'coalition of willing.'" 2002. *CNN/World*,
    November 20. Accessed: June 29, 2015, http://edition.cnn.com/2002/WORLD/
    europe/11/20/prague.bush.nato/

3   From the original Spanish text: "La crónica de lo que sucedió entre los días 11
    y 14 de marzo de 2004 es un magnífico ejemplo de la versatilidad en el arte de
    la mentira alcanzada por nuestros políticos. Enfrentados a un suceso aterrador,
    a un trauma de proporciones colosales, muchos de ellos optaron por mentir.
    O, como se dice ahora, «por no decir la verdad». Cuando sus señorías juegan

a la dialéctica, no hay sofista que les haga sombra. Nadie como el político ha pervertido tanto el sentido de las palabras, de *todas* las palabras; ni siquiera el más recalcitrante fideísta." Ricardo Menéndez Salmón. 2009. *El corrector*, Barcelona: Seix Barra: 52–53. Although *El corrector* has been translated into different languages, the book does not have an English translation. All translations presented here have been made by Nuno Marques, a researcher of Project CILM (http://www.cilm.comparatistas.edu.pt/) under my supervision.

4   In the original: "[…] cadáveres, cadáveres, cadáveres." Ricardo Menéndez Salmón, *El corrector*, 34.

5   In the original text: "[…] éramos todos nosotros los que estábamos allí, tirados entre las vías, caminando como zombis o sentados en los parterres municipales con la mirada perpleja de quien despierta en un país de caníbales." Ricardo Menéndez Salmón, *El corrector*, 34.

6   From the Spanish: "Sospecho que aquel día miré las caras de mis convecinos buscando una señal, una evidencia, un signo de los tiempos. Los rostros que nos rodean también son elementos cabalísticos. ¿Y qué hallé?Pues nada, o, mejor dicho, sí, encontre la moneda corriente de las pequenas esperanzas, los pequeños tributos, las pequenas hazañas. Ni rastro de atrición. Ni sombra de fúnebre menacólia. Ni un assomo de duelo. Incluso había gente que reía. Y no solapadamente, como en un entierro, sino com total franqueza, como ante una criatura. […] Pero juro que no descubrí el pathos del mal deambulando entre mis convecinos como un dios homérico ante las murallas de Troya." Ricardo Menéndez Salmón, *El corrector*, 79-80.

7   The original text, in Spanish, reads: "Todo tiempo posee sus signos, sus emblemas, sus cábalas. El nuestro há hecho del miedo su estandarte, su venero de dolor, su firmamento. Navegantes de la galaxia de la sospecha, adustos, desconfiados, llenos de rencor hacia el prójimo, deambulamos los que un cercano día nos sentimos solidarios del final de la Historia pero hoy, desesperadamente, como topos en una construccíon cuya fisonomía hubiera cambiado de la noche a la mañana, buscamos un resquício por el que huir de este intolerable tiempo cíclico que nos acosa. En aquella estación de llegada en la que llevábamos viviendo hacía al menos una década, desde la caída de la Unión Soviética y la conquista del mundo feliz de un capitalismo sin edulcorantes, y hasta que unos fieles que rezaban a Alá, el Compasivo, decidieron penetrar en avión por las cristaleras del paraíso y poner de nuevo en marcha los relojes, todos—hombres y mujeres, argivos y troyanos, obreros y burgueses, pies negros y sangre azul—nos habíamos ido congregando en la multitud de mercados que

celebraban la plasticidad de nuestra cultura y la versatilidad de nuestro talento."
Ricardo Menéndez Salmón, *El corrector*, 123–124.

8   From the Spanish: "Cualquier cosa que hubiéramos soñado […] ya había
     sido inventada por alguien […] la alquimia era una propiedad del mercado;
     los banqueros eran los nuevos nigromantes." (Menéndes Sálmón, *El
     corrector*, 124)

9   In the original text: "[…] ruido de fondo, del implacable hálito de esa muerte
     cósmica que acecha tras los sonidos cotidianos." Menéndez Salmón, *El
     corrector*, 35.

10   In the original text "La primera, que las Brigadas Abú Hafs al Masri se atribuían,
     en nombre de Al Qaeda, la responsabilidad de los atentados en una carta enviada
     al periódico árabe *Al Quds Al-Arabi*." Menéndez Salmón, *El corrector*, 139.

11   In the original text "ajustar viejas cuentas com España, cruzado y aliado de
     América en su guerra contra el islam." Menéndez Salmón, *El corrector*, 139.

12   In the original text "una nota de agencia fechada a las 21:57 horas, se informaba
     del hundimiento de la Bolsa de Nueva York debido al nerviosismo de los
     inversores: Wall Street anotaba una baja de 168,51 puntos, un 1,64 por ciento; y
     el Nasdaq, negocio electrónico en el que cambian de manos la mayor parte de
     las acciones del sector tecnológico, retrocedia 20,26 puntos, un 1,03 por ciento."
     Ricardo Menéndez Salmón, 139–140.

13   Jorge Sampaio. 2013. Cited in Catarina Falcão, "Cimeira das Lajes. Iraque era
     a menor das preocupações para Portugal e Espanha," *Jornal i*, March 18, 2013.
     Accessed: April 28, 2014, http://www.ionline.pt/artigos/portugal/cimeira-
     das-lajes-iraque-era-menor-das-preocupacoes-portugal-espanha

14   When receiving his Nobel prize, Saramago stated that *Blindness* was written "to
     remind those who might read it that we pervert reason when we humiliate life,
     that human dignity is insulted every day by the powerful of our world, that the
     universal lie has replaced the plural truths, that man stopped respecting himself
     when he lost the respect due to his fellow-creatures." José Saramago. 2013. Nobel
     Lecture: "De como a personagem foi mestre e o autor seu aprendiz." *Nobelprize.
     org*. Nobel Media AB 2013. Web. November 14. Accessed on: November 21,
     2013, http://www.nobelprize.org/nobel_prizes/literature/laureates/1998/
     saramago-lecture-p.html

15   When the movie director Fernando Meirelles tried to get permission to adapt
     the first novel, *Blindness*, for the screen, one of Saramago's main conditions
     was that the film should be set in a country that would not be recognizable to
     its audiences. See Martin Knelman. 2007. "Even non-TIFF movies got deals,"

Toronto Star, August 17. Accessed on: November 21, 2013, http://www.thestar
.com/opinion/columnists/2007/09/17/even_nontiff_movies_got_deals.html

16 My translation from the original text in Portuguese: "No mundo tudo se discute,
tudo é objeto de debate, mas a democracia surge como pura, inatingível, intocável,"
disse o escritor, destacando que "é o poder econômico que realmente governa,
usando a democracia a seu favor." Saramago cited in "Para Saramago, 'Ensaio sobre
a Lucidez' vai causar polêmica," *24HorasNews*, March 25, 2004. Accessed: April 14,
2012: http://www.24horasnews.com.br/noticias/ver/para-saramago-ensaio
-sobre-a-lucidez-vai-causar-polemica.html#sthash.9aCCp0FY.dpuf

17 From Charlotte Brontë's *Jane Eyre*: "There was no possibility of taking a walk that
day. We had been wandering, indeed, in the leafless shrubbery an hour in the
morning; but since dinner […] I was glad of it: I never liked long walks, especially
on chilly afternoons: dreadful to me was the coming home in the raw twilight,
with nipped fingers and toes, and a heart saddened by the chidings of Bessie, the
nurse, and humbled by the consciousness of my physical inferiority to Eliza, John,
and Georgiana Reed." Charlotte Brontë, *Jane Eyre*, first sentence of Chapter 1.

18 Saramago Freire and Marina Costa Lobo. 2006. "The Portuguese 2005 Legislative
Election: Return to the Left." *West European Politics*, 29.3, 581–588. Accessed on:
November 21, 2013, http://cde.usal.es/master_bibliografia/practicas/sistemas
_comparados/portugal.pdf

19 My translation from the Portuguese of the following verses of the poem "A Carne
é Forte": "Porque te lanças aos pés/das minhas botas grossas?/Porque soltas
agora o teu cabelo perfumado e abres traidoramente os teus braços macios?/Eu
não sou mais que um homem de mãos grossas/e coração voltado para um lado/
que se for necessário/pisar-te para passar/te pisará Bem sabes." Dionísio, Mário.
1982 [1945]. *As Solicitações e Emboscadas*, 2ed. Mem Martins, Publicações
Europa-América. I thank Fundação José Saramago for helping me find the exact
source for this reference.

20 See, for example, the poem entitled "Elegy to a Dead Companion," the poem
that immediately precedes "The Fresh is Strong," or a "Balada Dos Amigos
Separados" ("Ballad of Friends Apart"), among others. The English translation of
the titles is mine. Mário Dionísio. 1982. [1945] *As Solicitações e Emboscadas*. 2ed.
Mem Martins: Publicações Europa-América, 153.

21 In his *Autobiografia*, Mário Dionísio explains that the desire to have a more
autonomous militant role within the cultural sphere, rather than within the
maps and rules set out by the Party, was also felt by other artists at the time, such
as João José Cochofel, Carlos de Oliveira, Lopes Graça Mário Dionísio. 1987.

Autobiografia. Col. Autobiografias 3. Lisboa: O Jornal, http://www
.centromariodionisio.org/autobiografia_mariodionisio.php

22   I am very thankful to Cristina Ribeiro at the Faculty of Arts, University of Lisbon
for our discussions and her generous clarifications on subject of Mário Dionísio's
work, which were vital to the writing of this chapter.

23   Saramago publicly acknowledged that there was a "formal contradiction"
between his critique of party politics in *Seeing* and the inclusion of his name, in
the election campaigns of 2004, as a member the Coalition for Democratic Unity
(electoral and political coalition between the Portuguese Communist Party and
the Ecologist Party, "The Greens"), yet he justified this inclusion as a sign of his
historical association to the party. José Saramago. 2004. Cited in "José Saramago
apela ao voto em branco" TSF, March 30. Accessed: June 29, 2015, http://www.tsf.
pt/paginainicial/interior.aspx?content_id=768164

24   For an analysis of *Blindness* which challenges facile tendencies to equate vision with
reason, light with enlightenment (and derivative dichotomies) in Saramago's novel,
please see Patricia I. Vieira. 2009. "The Reason of Vision: Variations on Subjectivity
in José Saramago's Ensaio sobre a Cegueira." *Luso-Brazilian Review* 46.2, 1–21. I
believe that Vieira's arguments can also be applied to Saramago's *Seeing.*

Chapter 7

1   In his 1992 essay, *Imaginary Homelands*, Rushdie presents his own writing as
inevitably tied up with notions of migration, translation, and fiction, that is,
necessarily entailing symbolic losses and imaginary gains: "It may be that writers
in my position, exiles or emigrants or expatriates are haunted by some sense of
loss, some urge to reclaim, to look back, even at the risk of being mutated into
pillars of salt. But if we do look back, we must also do so in the knowledge—
which gives rise to profound uncertainties—that our physical alienation from
India almost inevitably means that we will not be capable of reclaiming precisely
the thing that was lost; that we will, in short, create fictions, not actual cities or
villages, but invisible ones, imaginary homelands, Indias of the mind." Salman
Rushdie. 1992. *Imaginary Homelands: Essays and Criticism 1981–1991.* London:
Penguin, 10.

2   Like his homonym, the German-born film director Max Ophüls, Rushdie's
character, Max also had a house in Los Angeles and has a child who becomes a
maker of documentary films. In a review to *Shalimar the Clown*, John Updike

highlighted the differences between the German Director and Rushdie's character, while inevitably also hinting at the similarities between the two: "The two have no connection save the name and a peripatetic life, including a period of Los Angeles residence and a child who becomes a maker of documentary films—the real Max Ophuls's son, Marcel, made 'The Sorrow and the Pity', and the fictional Ophuls's daughter [...] is the auteur of 'Camino Real', a filmed trip up the West Coast along the mission-planting trail taken by Fray Junípero Serra in the seventeen-seventies. The real Ophuls was born in 1902 in Saarbrücken, near the French border in the Saar region of Germany, and died in Hamburg in 1957, after an adult life spent entirely in theatrical precincts; whereas Rushdie's imaginary Ophuls is born around 1911 in the French city of Strasbourg and dies in Los Angeles in 1991, after distinguishing himself as the US Ambassador to India from 1965 to 1967 and afterward as the 'U.S. counterterrorism chief.'" See John Updike. 2005. "Paradise Lost: Rushdie's 'Shalimar the Clown.'" *The New Yorker*, September 5. Accessed on: June 1, 2013, http://www.newyorker.com/archive/2005/09/05/050905crbo_book

3   Salman Rushdie. 2005b. "India and Pakistan's Code of Dishonor," *New York Times*, July 10, 2005. Accessed on: June 1, 2013, http://www.nytimes.com/2005/07/10/opinion/10rushdie.html

4   J.M. Coetzee. 2007. *Diary of a Bad Year*. London: Vintage Books. Hereafter presented as *Diary*.

5   Republican speaker Dennis Hastert interviewed by BBC News. See "Final Approval for US Patriot Act." *BBC News*, March 8. Accessed: June 29, 2015, http://news.bbc.co.uk/2/hi/4784694.stm

6   One of the sections of the act extended by Congress is the "'roving wiretap' power, which allows federal authorities to listen in on conversations of foreign suspects even when they change phones or locations. Another section gives the government access to the personal records of terrorist suspects; it's often called the 'library provision' because of the wide range of personal material that can be investigated. A third section is known as the 'lone wolf' provision because it gives the government the authority to investigate foreigners who have no known affiliation with terrorist groups." See Lisa Mascaro. "Patriot Act Provisions Extended Just in Time." *Los Angeles Times*, May 27, 2011. Accessed on: May 2013, http://articles.latimes.com/2011/may/27/nation/la-na-patriot-act-20110527.

7   In 1985, Coetzee wrote an essay entitled "Confession and Double Thoughts: Tolstoy, Rousseau, Dostoevsky," which focused on the role of confession in the

work of both Russian authors and which is therefore fundamental to understand the writer's approach to "fiction" and "truth." See J.M. Coetzee. 1985. "Confession and Double Thoughts: Tolstoy, Rousseau, Dostoevsky." *Comparative Literature* 37.3 Summer, 193–232.

Chapter 8

1   See, for example, Marieke De Goede. 2008. "The Politics of Preemption and the War on Terror in *Europe*." *European Journal of International Relations*, March 14. 1, 161–185.

2   Donald E. Pease shows that "in Tucson, Obama turned the Tea Party into the spectral accomplices within a scenario in which he executed two significant acts of dissociation: of his movement from that if the Tea Party and of his biopolitics from an armed terrorist's thanato-politics. The memorial service also enabled Obama to use the images with which the Tea Party movement had demonized him to recover the position in between irreconcilable antagonists." Donald E. Pease. 2013. "Barack Obama's Orphic Mysteries" in Laura Bieger, Ramon Saldivar, and Johannes Voelz (eds.) *The Imaginary and Its Worlds: American Studies After the Transnational Turn*. Lebanon, NH: Dartmouth College Press, 227.

3   See, for example, Chelsea J. Carter and Ashley Fantz. 2014. "ISIS Video Shows Beheading of American Journalist Steven Sotloff." *CNN: International Edition*, September 9, http://edition.cnn.com/2014/09/02/world/meast/isis-american -journalist-sotloff/ See also Raya Jalabi. "David Haines Video Has Marked Similarities to Sotloff and Foley Killings." *The Guardian*, September 14. Accessed: June 29, 2015, http://www.theguardian.com/world/2014/sep/14/david-haines-video-similarities-sotloff-foley-killings

4   This idea is supported by interviews and visual material where aid worker David Haines is depicted helping children in Syria as part of his work in humanitarian aid campaigns. See, for example, Robert Barr. 2014. "British Aid Worker Beheaded by ISIS Helped Syrian Kids, Had 'Heart Of Gold.'" *Huffington Post*, October 5. Accessed: June 29, 2015, http://www.huffingtonpost.com/2014/10/05/alan-henning-aid-work_n_5934626.html

5   See, for example, Dan Lamothe. 2014. "Once again, Militants Use Guantanamo-Inspired Orange Suit in an Execution." *Washington Post*, August 28. Accessed: June 29, 2015, http://www.washingtonpost.com/news/checkpoint/wp/2014/08/28/once-again-militants-use-guantanamos-orange-jumpsuit-in-an-execution/

6   My use of the expression "global homeland" draws on largely on the works of Donald E. Pease and Amy Kaplan. See Donald E. Pease. 2003. "The Global Homeland State: Bush's Biopolitical Settlement." *Boundary 2* 30.3, 1–18. See also Amy Kaplan. 2003. "Homeland Insecurities: Some Reflections on Language and Space." *Radical History Review* 85. Winter, 82–93.

7   See, for example, Anthony Giddens. 1991. *Modernity and Self-Identity. Self and Society in the Late Modern Age.* Cambridge: Polity; Anthony Giddens. 1999 "Risk and Responsibility." *Modern Law Review* 62(1): 1–10. See also Ulrich Beck. 1992. *Risk Society: Towards a New Modernity.* New Delhi: Sage.

8   Jacques Rancière. 2006. "De la peur à la terreur," in *Les aventures de la raison politique.* Paris: Éditions Métailié: 275–291.

9   In reply to a question about the lack of evidence connecting the government of Iraq with the supply of weapons of mass destruction to terrorist groups, US secretary of defense, Donald Rumsfeld, articulated the paradoxes of security intelligence in the following metaphysical terms: "Reports that say that something hasn't happened are always interesting to me, because as we know, there are known knowns; there are things we know we know. We also know there are known unknowns; that is to say we know there are some things we do not know. But there are also unknown unknowns—the ones we don't know we don't know. And if one looks throughout the history of our country and other free countries, it is the latter categories that tend to be the difficult ones." Donald Rumsfeld. 2002. "DoD News Briefing – Secretary Rumsfeld and Gen. Myers U.S." *Department of Defence. News transcript,* February 12. Accessed: June 29, 2015, http://www.defense.gov/transcripts/transcript.aspx?transcriptid=2636

Bibliography

"Book Review Podcast: Steven Brill's 'Class Warfare.'" 2011. *The New York Times*, August 19. Available: http://artsbeat.blogs.nytimes.com/2011/08/19/book-review -podcast-steven-brills-class-warfare/

"Bush: Iraq War "Noble" and "Necessary." 2008. *CBS News* March 19. Available: http://www.cbsnews.com/news/bush-iraq-war-noble-and-necessary (Accessed: July 18, 2014).

"Bush: Join' Coalition of Willing." 2002. *CNN/World*. December 17, 2014. Available: http://edition.cnn.com/2002/WORLD/europe/11/20/prague.bush.nato/

"CPJ Condemns Murder of US Journalist Steven Sotloff Committee to Protect Journalists." 2014. *CPJ Website*. New York, September 2.

"Para Saramago, "Ensaio sobre a Lucidez" vai causar polêmica." 2004. *24 HorasNews*, March 25, 2004. Available: http://www.24horasnews.com.br /noticias/ver/para-saramago-ensaio-sobre-a-lucidez-vai-causar-polemica.html (Accessed: April 14, 2014).

"The Year in Books: The New New York Novel" *The New York Magazine*. Available: http://nymag.com/arts/cultureawards/2008/52752/ (Accessed: December 7, 2008).

"Writer Hamid Focuses on Fundamentals." 2007. *BBC News*, July 2. Available: http:// news.bbc.co.uk/2/hi/south_asia/6426749.stm (Accessed: March 30, 2012)

Abraham, Nicholas and Maria Torok. 1994 [1968]. *The Shell and the Kernel: Renewals of Psychoanalysis*. Vol. 1. Edited and translated by Nicholas T. Rand. Chicago: University of Chicago Press.

Adorno, T. W. 1984 [1958]. "The Essay as Form." Translated by Bob Hullot-Kentor and Frederic Will. *New German Critique* 32: 151–71.

Anon. "Elements of 'civil war' in Iraq." 2007. *BBC News*, February 2. Available: http:// news.bbc.co.uk/2/hi/middle_east/6324767.stm (Accessed: April 2009)

Anon. "Final Approval for US Patriot Act." 2006. *BBC News*, March 8. Available: http://news.bbc.co.uk/2/hi/americas/4784694.stm

Araújo, Susana. 2006. "Propagating Images, Circulating Violence and Transatlantic Anxieties: McEwan in New York and Abu Ghraib." In *America's Worlds and World's Americas*. Edited by George Handley and Patrick Imbert Amaryll Chanady. IASA Conference Proceedings. Ottawa: University of Ottawa/Legas.

Arendt, Hannah. 2004 [1951]. *The Origins of Totalitarianism*. New York. Shocken Books.

Bacon, Katie. 2008. "The Great Irish-Dutch-American Novel." *The Atlantic*, May 6. Available: http://www.theatlantic.com/doc/200805u/joseph-oneill (Accessed: March 30, 2012).

Baigell, Matthew. 1992. "Walt Whitman and Early Twentieth-Century American Art." In *Walt Whitman and the Visual Arts*. Edited by Geoffrey M. Sill and Roberta K. Tarbell. New Brunswick: Rutgers UP: 121–141.

Banks, Iain. 2003. *Dead Air*. London: Abacus.

Barr, Robert. 2014. "British Aid Worker Beheaded by ISIS Helped Syrian Kids, Had 'Heart of Gold'," *Huffington* Post, October 5.

Barroso, Manuel. 2003. "Full Text: Azores Press Conference." *The Guardian*, March 17. Available: http://www.guardian.co.uk/world/2003/mar/17/iraq.politics2

Baudrillard, Jean. 1983. *Simulations*, translated by Paul Foss, Paul Patton and Phil Beitchman. New York: Semiotext[e].

Baudrillard, Jean 2002. *The Spirit of Terrorism: And Requiem for the Twin Towers*. London: Verso.

Baudrillard, Jean. 2002. "The Spirit of Terrorism." *The South Atlantic Quarterly*. Translated by Michel Valentin. 10.2: 403–415.

Beck, Ulrich. 1992. *Risk Society: Towards a New Modernity*. New Delhi: Sage.

Beck, Ulrich. 2002. "The Cosmopolitan State." *Eurozine*, 19 February. Available: http://www.eurozine.com/authors/beck.html

Beigbeder, Frédéric. 2005. *Windows on the World*. 2003. Translated by Frank Wynne. London: Harper Perennial.

Belasco, Susan, Ed Folsom, and Kenneth M. Price (eds.). 2007. *Leaves of Grass: Sesquicentennial Essays the Sesquicentennial Essays*. Nebraska: University of Nebraska Press.

Bettencourt, Sandra. 2012. "El Mapa de la Vida e *El corrector*: Aproximações e distanciamentos das representações literárias madrilenas a Nova Iorque." *Babilónia* 12. Available: http://revistas.ulusofona.pt/index.php/babilonia/article/view/4111 (Accessed: November 26, 2013).

Blair, Tony. 2001. Cited in Michael White and Patrick Wintour. 2001. "Blair Calls for World Fight against Terror." *The Guardian*, Wednesday, September, 12. Available: http://www.theguardian.com/politics/2001/sep/12/uk.september11 (Accessed: December 19, 2014).

Bohan, Ruth L. 1992. "The Gathering of the Forces': Walt Whitman and the Visual Arts in Brooklyn in the 1850s." In *Walt Whitman and the Visual Arts*. Edited by Geoffrey M. Sill and Roberta X. Tarbell. New Brunswick: Rutgers UP: 1–27.

Bollas, Christopher. 2001. Personal email to Susana Araújo, November 17.

Bolton, Sally. "Allies to Attend Summit on Iraq." *The Guardian*, March 14, 2003. Available: http://www.theguardian.com/world/2003/mar/14/iraq.usa1

Books 55 (18) November 20. Available: http://www.nybooks.com/articles/22083 (Accessed: March 30, 2012).

Borradori, Giovanna. 2003. *Philosophy in a Time of Terror: Dialogues with Jürgen Habermas and Jacques Derrida*. Chicago: University of Chicago Press.

Boxall, Peter. 2006. *Don DeLillo: The Possibility of Fiction*. London: Routledge.

Breed, Allen G. 2004. "England Called to Explain Her 'Bit of Fun' on Her Abu Ghraib Night Shift." *The Independent* 4 August: 6.

Brooks, David. 2003. "What Whitman Knew." *Atlantic Monthly* 291.4: 32–33. Available: http://www.theatlantic.com/issues/2003/05/brooks.htm (Accessed: April 2009).

Bush, George. 2001. "9/11 Address to the Nation" in *American Rhetoric*. September 11. Available: www.americanrhetoric.com/speeches /gwbush911addresstothenation.htm (Accessed: December 19, 2014)

Bush, George W. 2001. Cited in "Bush Says It Is Time for Action" *CNN.com/U.S.*, November 6, 2001. Available: http://edition.cnn.com/2001/US/11/06/ret.bush. coalition/

Bush, George. 2002. "State of the Union Address" (January 29, 2002) in *Miller Centre* Available: http://millercenter.org/president/speeches/detail/4540 (Accessed: November 26, 2013).

Butler, Judith. 2004. *Precarious Lives*. London: Verso: 19–49.

Cain, Caleb. 2005. "Fine Specimen." *New York Magazine*, June 5. Available: http://nymag.com/nymetro/arts/books/reviews/11940/ (Accessed: April 2009).

Carter, Chelsea J. and Ashley Fantz. 2014. "ISIS Video Shows Beheading of American Journalist Steven Sotloff," *CNN: International Edition*, September 9. Available: http://edition.cnn.com/2014/09/02/world/meast/isis-american-journalist-sotloff/

Chase, Richard. 1955. *Walt Whitman Reconsidered*. New York: William Sloane.

Cochran, Joel Surnow and Robert. 2001. *24*. Image Entertainment/Fox.

Coetzee, J. M. 1985. "Confession and Double Thoughts: Tolstoy, Rousseau, Dostoevsky." *Comparative Literature* 37.3, Summer, 193–232.

Coetzee, J. M. 1992. "Into the Dark Chamber: The Writer and the South African State (1986)." In *Doubling the Point: Essays and Interviews*. Edited by David X. Atwell. Cambridge, MA: Harvard University Press, 361–368.

Coetzee, J. M. 2007. *Diary of a Bad Year*. London: Vintage Books, 2007.

Conte, Joseph M. 2011. "Don DeLillo's Falling Man on the Age of Terror." *MFS Modern Fiction Studies*, 57.3, Fall: 580–581

Corrigan, Maureen. 2008. "'Netherland' Flirts with Greatness of 'Gatsby.'" *National Public Radio*, July 2. Available: http://www.npr.org/templates/story/story .php?storyId=92133294 (Accessed: March 30, 2012).

Cowley, 2005. "From here to Kashmir." *The Observer*, Sunday, September 11. Available: http://www.guardian.co.uk/books/2005/sep/11/fiction.salmanrushdie

Crownshaw, Richard. 2011. "Deterritorializing the 'Homeland' in American Studies and American Fiction after 9/11." *Journal of American Studies* 45: Special Issue 04. Nov., 757–776.

Cunningham, Michael. 2005a. *Specimen Days*. London: Harper Perennial.

Cunningham, Michael. 2005b. "America's Bard." In *Specimen Days*. London: Harper Perennial: 2–4. [Section with separate pagination.]

Cunningham, Michael. 2005c. "P.S. Ideas, Interviews and Features." In *Specimen Days*. London: Harper Perennial: 5–16 [Section with separate pagination].

De Certeau, Michel. 1984. *The Practice of Everyday Life*. Translated by Steven Randall. Berkeley: University of California Press: 91–105.

Delillo, Don 2007. *The Falling Man*. New York: Scribner.

Demos, John. 1994. *The Unredeemed Captive: A Family Story from Early America*. New York: Alfred A. Knopf.

Denlinger, Elizabeth. 2002. "Caught Between Worlds: British Captivity Narratives in Fact and Fiction." *Biography* 25.2, Spring: 391–394.

Dhume, Sadanand. 2008. "Terror in Mumbai: Two Faces of Globalization." Available: Http://yaleglobal.yale.edu/. Yale Center for the Study of Globalization, December 1, 2008. Available: http://yaleglobal.yale.edu/content/terror-mumbai-two-faces-globalization (Accessed: July 10, 2014).

DHS. 2008. "TOPOFF: Exercising National Preparedness." Available: http://www.dhs (October 6).

Dionísio, Mário. 1982[1945]. *As Solicitações e Emboscadas*, 2ed. Mem Martins: Publicações Europa-América.

Dionísio, Mário. 1987. *Autobiografia*. Col. Autobiografias 3. Lisboa: O Jornal. Available: http://www.centromariodionisio.org/autobiografia_mariodionisio.php

Dovey, Teresa. 1998. "J.M. Coetzee: Writing in the Middle Voice." In *Critical Essays on J.M. Coetzee*. Edited by S. Kossew. New York: G.K. Hall & Co.: 18–28.

Erkkila, Betsy. 1989. *Whitman the Political Poet*. New York: Oxford University Press.

European Commission - Economic and Social Research Institute. 1997. *The Cases of Greece, Spain, Ireland and Portugal*. The Single Market Review Series Subseries VI Aggregate and Regional Impact, 2, Luxembourg.

Extremely Loud and Incredibly Close. 2011. Dir. Stephan Daldry. Warner Brothers and Paramount Pictures. Released: December 25. Film.

Faludi, Susan. 2007. *The Terror Dream: Fear and Fantasy in Post-9/11 America*. New York: Metropolitan Books.

Foer, Jonathan Safran. 2005. *Extremely Loud and Incredibly Close*. London & New York: Hamish Hamilton.

Folsom, Ed. 2005. "'What a Filthy Presidentiad:' Clinton's Whitman, Bush's Whitman, and Whitman's America." *Virginia Quarterly Review* 81. Spring: 96–113.

Folsom, Ed and Kenneth M. Price (eds.). "Image 003." In *The Walt Whitman Archive*. Available: http://www.whitmanarchive.org/multimedia/image003.html?sort=year &order=ascending&page=1 (Accessed: May 2009).

Folsom, Ed and Kenneth M. Price (eds.). "Pictures & Sound." In *The Walt Whitman Archive*. Available: http://whitmanarchive.org/multimedia/image003.html?sort=ye ar&order=ascending&page=1 (Accessed: April 21, 2015).

Folsom, Ed and Ted Genoways. 2005. "This Heart's Geography's Map: The Photographs of Walt Whitman." *Virginia Quarterly Review* 81.2. Available: http:// www.vqronline.org/articles/2005/spring/genoways-this-hearts-geographys/ (Accessed: May 2009).

Foucault, Michel. 1986 [1967] "Of Other Spaces." *Diacritics* 16. Spring: 22–27.

Freire, André and Marina Costa Lobo. 2006. "The Portuguese 2005 Legislative Election: Return to the Left" in *West European Politics*, 29.3, 581–588. Available: http://cde.usal.es/master_bibliografia/practicas/sistemas_comparados/portugal .pdf (Accessed: November 21, 2013).

Freud, Sigmund. 1936. *Inhibitions, Symptoms and Anxiety*. London: Hogarth Press.

Freud, Sigmund. 1957 [1917]. *Mourning and Melancholia*. London: Hogarth Press. Standard Edition 14: 243–58.

Freud, Sigmund. 1961 [1923]. *The Ego and the Id*. London: Hogarth Press. Standard Edition 19: 12–66.

Freud, Sigmund. 1966. "Introductory Lectures on Psychoanalysis." In *The Standard Edition of the Complete Psychological Works of Sigmund Freud*. Volume XV–XVI. Edited by James Strachey in collaboration with Anna Freud and translated by James Strachey. New York: Norton.

Furedi, Frank. 2002. *The Culture of Fear*. London: Continuum Books.

Furedi, Frank. 2006. *Politics of Fear. Beyond Left and Right*. London: Continuum.

García Ortega, Adolfo. 2009. *El Mapa de la Vida* by Adolfo García Ortega. Barcelona: Seix Barral.

Giddens, Anthony. 1991. *Modernity and Self-Identity. Self and Society in the Late Modern Age*. Cambridge: Polity.

Giddens, Anthony. 1999. "Risk and Responsibility." *Modern Law Review* 62.1: 1–10.

Godden, Richard. 1990. *Fictions of Capital: The American Novel from James to Mailer*. Cambridge: Cambridge University Press: 83.

Gray, Richard. 2011. *After the Fall: American Literature Since 9/11*. Chichester: Wiley & Sons.

Gutiérrez Aragon, Manuel. 2009. *La Vida Antes de Marzo*. Barcelona: Editorial Anagrama.

Hamid, Mohsin. 2007. "My Reluctant Fundamentalist." *Powells's Books*. Available:
http://www.powells.com/essays/mohsin.html. (Accessed: March 30, 2012).

Hamid, Mohsin. 2008 [2007]. *The Reluctant Fundamentalist*. London: Penguin Books.

Hastert, Dennis. 2006. Interviewed by BBC News. See "Final Approval for US
Patriot Act," *BBC News*, March 8, 2006. Available: http://news.bbc.co.uk/2/hi
/americas/4784694.stm.

Hill, Barry. 2007. "A Masochistic Scalpel: JM Coetzee's 'Diary of a Bad Year'" The
Monthly, September. Available: http://www.themonthly.com.au/books-barry-hill-
masochistic-scalpel-jm-coetzee-s-diary-bad-year-619 (Accessed: June 2, 2013).

Hodgkin, Katherine and Susannah Radstone (eds.). 2006. *Memory, History, Nation:
Contested Pasts*. New Brunswick, NJ: Routledge

Hume, Mike. 2004. *Is Abu Ghraib the Military Version of Reality TV*. May 28.
Available: http://www.spiked-online.com/Articles/0000000CA551.htm

Jalabi, Raya. 2014. "David Haines Video Has Marked Similarities to Sotloff and
Foley Killings." *The Guardian*, September, 14. Available: http://edition.cnn
.com/2014/09/02/world/meast/isis-american-journalist-sotloff/

Junod, Tom. 2003. "The Falling Man." *Esquire*, September 1: 177–199.

Kakutani, Michiko. 2005. "A Poet as Guest at a Party of Misfits." *The New York Times*,
June 14. Available: http://www.nytimes.com/2005/06/14/books/14kaku.html
(Accessed: April 2009).

Kakutani, Michiko. 2008. "Post 9/11, a New York of Gatsby-Size Dreams and Loss,"
May 16. Available: http://www.nytimes.com/2008/05/16/books/16book.html
(Accessed: March 30, 2012).

Kakutani, Michiko. 2011. "The Right Architect With the Wrong Name." *The New
York Times*, August 15. Available: http://www.nytimes.com/2011/08/16/books/
the-submission-by-amy-waldman-review.html (Accessed: July 10, 2014).

Kaplan, Amy. 2003. "Homeland Insecurities: Some Reflections on Language and
Space." *Radical History Review* 85. Winter: 82–93.

Keniston, Ann and Jeanne Follansbee Quinn (eds.). 2008. *Literature after 9/11*.
Abingdon, Oxon: Routledge.

King, Michael Patrick. 1998–2004. *Sex and the City*. Darren Starr/HBO.

Kirsch, Adam. 2008. "Demons Inner and Outer" in *The New York Sun*, August 6.
Available: http://www.nysun.com/arts/demons-inner-and-outer/83262/ (Accessed:
December 12, 2014).

Knapp, Kathy. 2011. "Richard Ford's Frank Bascombe Trilogy and the Post-9/11
Suburban Novel." *American Literary History* 23.3, Fall: 500–528.

Knelman, Martin. 2007. "Even non-TIFF Movies Got Deals," *Toronto Star*, August 17.
Available: http://www.thestar.com/opinion/columnists/2007/09/17/even_nontiff
_movies_got_deals.html (Accessed: December 12, 2014).

Kumar, Avita. 2005. "Amitava Kumar on Salman Rushdie's 'Shalimar the Clown'" Amitava Kumar's site. August 6, 2005. Available: http://www.amitavakumar .com/?page_id=35 (Accessed: June 1, 2013).

Lacan, Jacques. 1966. *Écrits*. Paris: Seuil.

Lamothe, Dan. 2014. "Once again, Militants Use Guantanamo-Inspired Orange Suit in an Execution." *Washington Post*, August 28, Available: http://www. washingtonpost.com/news/checkpoint/wp/2014/08/28/once-again-militants -use-guantanamos-orange-jumpsuit-in-an-execution/

Lang, Luc. 2006. *11 Septembre, Mon Amour*. Paris: Stock.

Laplanche and Pontalis. 2004 [1973]. *Dictionary of Psychoanalysis*. London: Karnac: 466.

Lasdun, James. 2007. "The Empire Strikes Back." *The Guardian*, March 3. Available: http://www.guardian.co.uk/books/2007/mar/03/featuresreviews.guardianreview20 (Accessed: March 30, 2012).

Le Guin, Ursula K. 2006. "The Plague of Blank Ballots." *The Guardian*, Saturday, April 15. Available: http://www.theguardian.com/books/2006/apr/15 /featuresreviews.guardianreview16 (Accessed: December 18, 2014).

Lefebvre, Henri.1991. *The Production of Space*. Oxford and Malden: Blackwell,.

Lévy, Bernard-Henry. 2006. *American Vertigo: Travelling America in the Footsteps of Toqueville*. Translated by Charlotte Mandell. New York: Random House.

Luckhurst, Roger. 2010. "Beyond Trauma: Torturous Times." *European Journal of English Studies* 14.1: 11–21.

Malik, Kenan. 2001. "Beyond a Boundary. His Writings on Race, Cricket and Colonial Rebellion Turned C. L. R. James into an Icon of Black Radicalism. So Why Today Is He so Misunderstood?" *New Statesman*. July 30. Available: http:// www.newstatesman.com/200107300035 (Accessed: March 30, 2012).

Marr, David. 1988. *American Worlds since Emerson*. Amherst, MA: University of Massachusetts Press.

Mascaro, Lisa. "Congress Votes in Time to Extend Key Patriot Act Provisions." *Los Angeles Times*. May 27, 2011. Available: http://articles.latimes.com/2011/ may/27/nation/la-na-patriot-act-20110527 (Accessed: May 30, 2001).

Mateo Díez, Luis. 2006. *La Piedra en el Corazón*. Barcelona: Galaxia Guttenberg.

McEwan, Ian. 2005. *Saturday*. London: Jonathan Cape.

McInerney, Jay 2001. "Brightness Falls." *The Guardian*, September 15, sec. Saturday Review: 1–2.

McInerney, Jay. 2001. "Brightness Falls." *The Guardian*, September 15, 2001: 1.

McInerney, Jay. 2005. "The Uses of Invention ." *The Guardian*, September 17, 2005.

Mendes, Sam. 1999. *American Beauty*. Los Angeles: Dreamworks Pictures.

Menéndez Salmón, Ricardo. 2009. *El corrector*. Barcelona: Seix Barral, 52–53.

Messud, Claire. 2011. "A Novel of Grief, Memorials and a Muslim Architect in Post-9/11 America." *The New York Times*, August 19. Available: http://www.nytimes.com/2011/08/21/books/review/the-submission-by-amy-waldman-book-review.html?_r=0 (Accessed: 17 July 2014).

Messud, Salmon. 2013. Cited in Coutinho. "O mal é um tema inesgotável." *Público-Ípsilon*. Available: http://ipsilon.publico.pt/livros/entrevista.aspx?id=232759 (Accessed: November 21, 2013).

Metcalf, Stephen. 2005. "French Twist." *New York Times Book Review*, April 17: 9.

Miller, Laura. 1998. "The Salon Interview: Ian McEwan." March 31.

Miller, Laura. 2005. *Windows on the World by Frédéric Beigbeder*. Available: http://dir.salon.com/story/books/review/2005/03/20/beigbeder/index.html.

Miller, Laura. 2006. "A Disorder Peculiar to the Country: Ken Kalfus' Ingenious New Book about an Explosive Divorce Might Be the Best Novel yet about 9/11." *Salon*. July 25. Available: http://www.salon.com/2006/07/25/kalfus_3/ (Accessed: April 26).

Mishra, Pankaj. 2005. "Massacre in Arcadia" *The New York Review of Books* 52, no. 15, October 6. Available: http://javous308.blogspot.pt/2011/05/massacre-in-arcadia.html (Accessed: February 8, 2012).

Mortimer, Barbara. 2000. *Hollywood's Frontier Captives: Cultural Anxiety and the Captivity Plot in American Film*. New York: Garland Publishing, Inc.

Namias, June. 1993. *White Captives: Gender and Ethnicity on the American Frontier*. Chapel Hill & London: The University of North Carolina Press.

Nichols, John. 2003. "Poetic Protests against War, Censorship." *The Nation*, February 4. Available: http://www.alternet.org/waroniraq/15100/ (Accessed: April 2009).

O'Hagan, Sean, 2008. "He's Got Something to Declare,." *The Observer*, June 1. Available: http://www.guardian.co.uk/books/2008/jun/01/fiction1/print (Accessed: March 30, 2012).

Ónega, Sonseloes. 2007. *Donde Dios No Estuvo*. Madrid: Grand Guignol Ediciones.

O'Neill, Joseph. 2009 [2008]. *Netherland*. New York: Harper Perennial.

Obama, Barak. 2006. *The Audacity of Hope: Thoughts on Reclaiming the American Dream*. New York: Random House.

Oliveira, Maria José. 2008. *Público - Ípsilon*, November 26 Available: http://ipsilon.publico.pt/livros/texto.aspx?id=218810 (Accessed: November 21, 2013).

Orlebeke, Andrew. 2010. "'Netherland' Presents Modern Take on 'Gatsby.'" *Chimes*, March 5. Available: http://www-stu.calvin.edu/chimes/article.php?id=4697 (Accessed: March 30, 2012).

Otterman, Sharon. 2014. "Developer Scales Back Plans for Muslim Center near Ground Zero." *The New York Times*, April 29. Available: http://www.nytimes

.com/2014/04/30/nyregion/developer-scales-back-plans-for-muslim-center-near
-ground-zero.html.

Pankaj, Mishra. 2011. "After 9/11: Our Own Low, Dishonest Decade." *The Guardian*,
Guardian News and Media, September 3. Available: http://www.theguardian.com
/books/2011/sep/02/after-september-11-pankaj-mishra (Accessed: May 3, 2015).

Pape, Robert A., Michael Rowley, and Sarah Morell. 2014. "Why ISIL Beheads Its
Victims. The Islamic State's Brutality Has a Strategic Logic." October 7. Available:
http://www.politico.com/magazine/story/2014/10/why-isil-beheads-its
-victims-111684.html#ixzz3GJVTig1a (Accessed: May 3, 2015).

Pease, Donald E. 2003. "The Global Homeland State: Bush's Biopolitical Settlement."
Boundary 2 30.3: 1–18.

Pease, Donald E. 2004. "The Extraterritoriality of the Literature for Our Planet." *ESQ*
50.1–3: 177–221.

Pease, Donald E. 2013. "Barack Obama's Orphic Mysteries." In *The Imaginary and Its
Worlds: American Studies After the Transnational Turn*. Edited by Laura Bieger,
Ramon X. Saldivar, Johannes Voelz. Lebanon, NH: Dartmouth College Press

Probyn, Fiona. 2002. "J.M. Coetzee: Writing with/out Authority." *Jouvert: Journal of
Postcolonial Studies*: 7.1. Autumn. Available: http://english.chass.ncsu.edu/jouvert
/v7is1/probyn.htm

Raban, Jonathan. 2006. *Surveillance*. London: Picador.

Rafferty, Terrence. 2005. "'Specimen Days': Manahatta My City." *The New York
Times*, June 26. Available: http://www.nytimes.com/2005/06/26/books
/review/26RAFFERT.html?pagewanted=prin (Accessed: April 2009).

Ramalho Santos, Irene. 2003. *Atlantic Poets: Fernando Pessoa's Turn in Anglo-
American Modernism*. Hanover, NH: University Press of New England.

Rancière, Jacques 2006. "De la peur à la terreur." In *Les aventures de la raison
politique*. Edited by Adauto Novaes. Paris: Éditions Métailié: 275–291.

Randall, Martin. 2011. *9/11 and the Literature of Terror*. Edinburgh: Edinburgh
University Press.

Riemer, Andrew. 2007. "Diary of a Bad Year," *The Sydney Morning Herald*,
August 25. Available: http://www.smh.com.au/news/book-reviews/diary-of-a-bad-
year/2007/08/24/1187462503346.html?page=fullpage

Riestra, Blanca. 2008. *Madrid Blues*. Madrid: Alianza Editorial, 2008.

Rose, Jacqueline. 2005. "Entryism." *London Review of Books*, September 22. Available:
http://www.lrb.co.uk/v27/n18/rose01_.html (Accessed: April 2009).

Rothberg, Michael. 2008. "Seeing Terror, Feeling Art: Public and Private in Post-9/11
Literature." In *Literature after 9/11*. Edited by Ann Keniston and Jean Follansbee
Quinn. New York: Routledge: 123–142.

Rothberg, Michael. 2009. "A Failure of the Imagination: Diagnosing the Post–9/11 Novel: A Response to Richard Gray." *American Literary History* 21.1: 152–58.

Rothberg, Michael. 2010. "Seeing Terror, Feeling Art: Public and Private in Post-9/11 Literature." In *Literature After 9/11*. Edited by Ann Keniston and Jean Follansbee Quinn. London: Routledge: 123–142.

Rumsfeld, Donald. 2002. "DoD News Briefing—Secretary Rumsfeld and Gen. Myers U.S." *Department of Defence. News transcript*, February 12. Available: http://www .defense.gov/transcripts/transcript.aspx?transcriptid=2636

Rushdie, Salman. 1992. *Imaginary Homelands: Essays and Criticism 1981–1991*. London: Penguin.

Rushdie, Salman. 2005a. Interview with Jack Livings. "Salman Rushdie, The Art of Fiction No. 186." *The Paris Review* 174. Summer 2005. Available: http://www .theparisreview.org/interviews/5531/the-art-of-fiction-no-186-salman-rushdie

Rushdie, Salman. 2005b. "India and Pakistan's Code of Dishonor,." *The New York Times*, July 10. Available: http://www.nytimes.com/2005/07/10/opinion/10rushdie. html (Accessed: December 27, 2012).

Rushdie, Salman. 2005c. "Muslims Unite! A New Reformation Will Bring Your Faith into the Modern Era." *The Times*, 11 August; Available: http://yaleglobal.yale .edu/content/muslims-unite-new-reformation-will-bring-your-faith-modern-era (Accessed: June 3, 2013).

Rushdie, Salman. 2006 [2005]. *Shalimar the Clown*. London: Vintage Books.

Rushdie, Salman. 2012, Interviewed by NPR staff. "Becoming 'Anton,' Or, How Rushdie Survived A Fatwa," September 18. Available: http://www.npr.org/2012/09/18/161172489 /becoming-anton-or-how-rushdie-survived-a-fatwa (Accessed: May 21, 2013).

Russell, Frederick. 1989. "Children's Crusade." In *Dictionary of the Middle Ages*. Edited by J. R. Strayer. New York: Scribner: 14–15.

Said, Edward W. 2004. *Humanism and Democratic Criticism*. New York: Columbia University Press, 10.2013–09–20 17:38:42.

Sampaio, Jorge. 2013. Cited in Catarina Falcão, "Cimeira das Lajes. Iraque era a menor das preocupações para Portugal e Espanha," *Jornal i*, March 18. Available: http://www.ionline.pt/artigos/portugal/cimeira-das-lajes-iraque-era-menor-das -preocupacoes-portugal-espanha (Accessed: April 14, 2014).

Saramago, José. 2004. Cited in "Saramago apela ao voto em branco." *TSF Radio Notícias*, March 30. Available: http://www.tsf.pt/paginainicial/interior .aspx?content_id=768164 (Accessed: May 2015).

Saramago, José. 2007 [2004]. *Seeing*. London: Vintage.

Saramago, José. 2008 [1995]. *Blindness*. Translated by Giovanni Pontiero. New York: Harvest.

Saramago, José. 2013. Nobel Lecture: "De como a personagem foi mestre e o autor seu aprendiz." *Nobelprize.org*. Nobel Media AB 2013. Web. November 14. Available: http://www.nobelprize.org/nobel_prizes/literature/laureates/1998 /saramago-lecture-p.html (Accessed: November 21, 2013).

Schmid, Alex P. 2011. "The Definition of Terrorism." In *The Routledge Handbook of Terrorism Research*. Edited by Alex P. Schmid. London and New York: Routledge.

Simpson, David. 2006. *9/11: The Culture of Commemoration*. Chicago: The University of Chicago Press.

Smith, Zadie. 2008. "Two Paths for the Novel." *The New York Review of Books*, 55.18: November 20. Available: http://www.nybooks.com/articles/22083 (Accessed: March 30, 2012).

Sontag, Susan. 2004. "Regarding the Torture of Others." *New York Times*, May 23: 25.

Sontag, Susan. 2004. "Regarding the Torture of Others," *New York Times Magazine*, May 23. http://www.nytimes.com/2004/05/23/magazine/regarding-the-torture-of -others.html (Accessed: May 9 2015).

Stein, Leon. 1962. *The Triangle Fire*. New York: Caroll & Graf/Quicksilver Book.

Stiffel, Timothy. 1996. "Whitman's Daguerreotypes: Objects of Democratic Union." In *Emory MOO, Conference in Romanticism*. Available: http://prometheus.cc.emory .edu/panels/4B/T.Stifel.html (Accessed: May 2008).

Tait, Theo. 2005. "Flame-Broiled Whopper," *London Review of Books* 27. no. 19, October 6, 2005. Available: http://www.lrb.co.uk/v27/n19/theo-tait/flame-broiled -whopper (Accessed: June 1, 2013).

Teverson, Andrew. 2008. "Rushdie's Last Lost Homeland: Kashmir in *Shalimar the Clown*," *The Literary Magazine*, 1(1). Available: http://litencyc.com /theliterarymagazine/shalimar.php (Accessed: June 1, 2013).

Thomas, M. Wynn. 1982. "Walt Whitman and Mannahatta-New York." *American Quarterly* 34.4: 362–378.

Thomson, David. 2005. "Rushdie Returns to Form—But His Epic Falls Short." *New York Observer*, December 9. Available: http://observer.com/2005/09/rushdie -returns-to-form-but-his-epic-falls-short/ (Accessed: June 1, 2013).

Trachtenberg, Alan. 1989. "Mirror in the Marketplace: American Responses to the Daguerreotype." In *The Daguerreotype: A Sesquicentennial Celebration*. Edited by J. Wood. Iowa City: University of Iowa Press: 60–73.

Traubel, Horace. 1906. "*With Walt Whitman in Camden*," vol. 1. The Walt Whitman Archive. Edited by Ed Folsom and Kenneth M. Price. Available: http://www.whitmanarchive.org/criticism/disciples/traubel/WWWiC/1/whole .html (Accessed: April 2009).

Traubel, Horace. 1914. *With Walt Whitman in Camden*, vol. 3. The Walt Whitman Archive. Edited by Ed Folsom and Kenneth M. Price. Available: http://www.

whitmanarchive.org/criticism/disciples/traubel/WWWiC/3/whole.html
(Accessed: April 2009).

Updike, John. 2005. "Paradise Lost: Rushdie's 'Shalimar the Clown,'" *The New Yorker*. September 5. Available: http://www.newyorker.com /archive/2005/09/05/050905crbo_book (Accessed: June 1, 2013).

Versluys, Kristiaan. 2007. "9/11 as a European Event: The Novels." *European Review* 15.1: 65–79.

Versluys, Kristiaan. 2009. *Out of the Blue: September 11 and the Novel*. New York: Columbia University Press.

Vieira, Patricia I. 2009. "The Reason of Vision: Variations on Subjectivity in José Saramago's Ensaio sobre a Cegueira." *Luso-Brazilian Review* 46.2: 1–21.

Voigt, Lisa. 2009. *Writing Captivity in the Early Modern Atlantic: Circulations of Knowledge and Authority in the Iberian and English Imperial Worlds*. Williamsburg, NC: University of North Carolina Press.

Waldman, Amy. 2012 [2011]. *The Submission*. London: Windmill Books.

Webb, Justin. 2009. "Obama Interview: The Transcript." *BBC World Service*, June 2. Available: http://www.bbc.co.uk/worldservice/news/2009/06/090602_obama _transcript.shtml (Accessed: March 30, 2012).

White, Duncan. 2014. "Discontent and Its Civilisations: Dispatches from Lahore, New York and London by Mohsin Hamid, review: 'a humane and rational voice.'" *The Telegraph*, December 15 2014 (Accessed: 25 May, 2015).

White, Michael and Patrick Wintour. 2001. "Blair Calls for World Fight against Terror." *The Guardian*, Wednesday, September 12, 2001. Available: http://www. guardian. co.uk/politics/2001/sep/12/uk.september11~

Whitman, Walt. 1984. *Notebooks and Unpublished Prose Manuscripts*. Vol. 1. Edited by E. F. Grier, New York: New York University Press.

Whitman, Walt. 2004. "From *Specimen Days*." In *The Portable Whitman*. Edited by M. Warner. London: Penguin.

Whitman, Walt. 2007. "Death of Abraham Lincoln." In *Prose Works 1892. Volume II: Collect and Other Prose*. Edited by Floyd Stovall New York: New York University Press.

Wood, James. 2008. "Beyond a Boundary." *The New Yorker*, May 26. Available: http:// www.newyorker.com/magazine/2008/05/26/beyond-a-boundary (Accessed: May 4, 2015).

Zarobila, C. 1979. "Walt Whitman and the Panorama." *Walt Whitman Review* 25: 51–59.

Žižek, Slavoj. 2002. *Welcome to the Desert of the Real*. London: Verso.

Index

Note: locators with an "n" denote note numbers

CPSIA information can be obtained
at www.ICGtesting.com
Printed in the USA
LVOW04*1708180516

488851LV00017B/209/P